Dr. Elizabeth H. Rowell, a professor of elementary education, teaches reading at Rhode Island College and has extensive teaching experience at all grade levels, K–12, in both the United States and abroad. She has written widely for professional publications and has served both as an editor and editorial board member for several professional journals, including six years as editor of the *New England Reading Journal*. She contributes frequently as a reading consultant, speaker, and workshop leader at numerous professional conferences throughout the nation, sharing creative ideas to stimulate reading growth in young people.

Dr. Thomas B. Goodkind, a professor of curriculum and instruction, teaches social studies and environmental/energy education at the University of Connecticut and has a wide range of teaching experience throughout the United States and abroad, in the public schools, in classroom, school camping, and other environmental education settings. He is a frequent contributor on social studies, environmental, and energy education topics as a consultant, speaker, and workshop leader throughout the nation. He writes extensively for professional publications and has served both as editor and as an editorial board member of several professional journals.

Dr. Rowell and Dr. Goodkind, who are married to each other, collaborate on many joint educational ventures.

To our parents, Willie Mae and Robert Rowell, and Mabel and Herbert Goodkind, who first taught us the pleasures of reading.

ELIZABETH H. ROWELL
THOMAS B. GOODKIND

Illustrations by Beverly Armstrong

Teaching the Pleasures of Reading

A SPECTRUM BOOK

Prentice-Hall, Inc., Englewood Cliffs, NJ 07632

Library of Congress Cataloging in Publication Data

Rowell, Elizabeth H.

  Teaching the pleasures of reading.

  "A Spectrum book."
  Includes bibliographies and index.

  1. Reading. I. Goodkind, Thomas B.
II. Title.
LB1050.R64   1982   372.4'1   82-9781
                                AACR2

ISBN 0-13-895029-6
ISBN 0-13-895011-3 (pbk.)

This Spectrum Book is available to businesses and organizations
at a special discount when ordered in large quantities. For
information, contact Prentice-Hall, Inc., General Publishing
Division, Special Sales, Englewood Cliffs, N.J. 07632.

ISBN 0-13-895029-6

ISBN 0-13-895011-3 {PBK}

Cover design by Jeannette Jacobs
Manufacturing buyer: Cathie Lenard
Editorial, design, and production supervision by June Wolfberg

Cover illustrations by Beverly Armstrong published with permission
from Girl Scouts of the U.S.A.

Prentice-Hall International, Inc., *London*
Prentice-Hall of Australia Pty. Limited, *Sydney*
Prentice-Hall Canada, Inc., *Toronto*
Prentice-Hall of India Private Limited, *New Delhi*
Prentice-Hall of Japan, Inc., *Tokyo*
Prentice-Hall of Southeast Asia Pte. Ltd., *Singapore*
Whitehall Books Limited, *Wellington, New Zealand*

Contents

Foreword

Teaching the Pleasures of Reading is an important addition to the professional field of education. Elizabeth H. Rowell and Thomas B. Goodkind demonstrate their comprehensive knowledge of theory and practical ideas about the effective use of humor, television, music, art, and the outdoors in language arts programs.

This book is valuable because the authors understand the needs and interests of both teachers and students. Its pages are crammed with hundreds of ideas which can turn the teaching experience into a meaningful, long-lasting learning experience. The drudgery of drill has been replaced by imaginative, sensitive, appealing activities which involve the students in the learning process.

Each section reinforces every other section of the book. Activities suggested in the chapter on humor can easily be correlated with cartooning in art and musical comedy in music and the varieties of comedy as presented on television.

This is not a book of mere "enrichment." To laugh is human. To develop the aesthetic senses, stimulate curiosity, and provide a variety of outlets through which students can demonstrate learning are all basic humanistic goals in teaching; and in our technological world these goals are particularly essential. Reading, writing, speaking, listening, and feelings are key elements in the communications process. This book shows many ways to reach more students through joyful pursuits in learning.

M. Jerry Weiss
Distinguished Service Professor
of Communications
Jersey City State College

Acknowledgments

Grateful acknowledgment is given to the following authors and publishers:

Harry N. Abrams, Inc., for quotations on pp. 41, 52, and 72 from *Television: The First 50 Years*, by Jeff Greenfield. Copyright © 1977 by Harry N. Abrams, BV. Used by permission.

Wayne Bloomingdale and *American Music Teacher*, for quotation on p. 168 from "Creston's Songs: The Art of Communication," by Wayne Bloomingdale, in *American Music Teacher*, 28 (Jan. 1979). Used by permission.

Harper & Row, Publishers, Inc., for the origins of the terms "cobweb," "daisy," and "dandelion," used on pp. 208–209, from *Horsefeathers and Other Curious Words* by Charles Earl Funk, Litt. D. and Charles Earle Funk, Jr. Copyright © 1958 by Charles Earl Funk, Jr. Reprinted by permission of Harper & Row, Publishers, Inc.

National Council of Teachers of English, for quotations on pp. 46 and 48 from *Television and the Teaching of English*, by Neil Postman (New York: Appleton-Century-Crofts, 1961).

Oasis Water Coolers, EBCO Manufacturing Company, Columbus, Ohio, for permission to reproduce an advertisement for Oasis Water Coolers on p. 116.

Pergamon Press, Inc., for permission to quote on p. 45 from the foreword by Alberta Engvall Siegel, and on p. 65 from the text by Robert M. Liebert, John Neale, and Emily S. Davidson, of *The Early Window: The Effects of Television on Children and Youth*. Copyright © 1975 by Pergamon Press, Inc. Used by permission.

Prentice-Hall, Inc., for permission to reproduce material on pp. 207–210 from *Secrets in Animal Names*, by Gladys R. Saxon. Copyright © 1964 by Prentice-Hall, Inc. Used by permission.

Sherwin-Williams Paint Company, for permission to quote on pp. 104–105 their names for colors.

Frederick Ungar Publishing Co., Inc., for the quotation on p. 68 from *The Age of Television*, by Leo Bogart. Copyright © 1956, 1958, 1972 by Frederick Ungar Publishing Co., Inc. Used by permission.

Women on Words and Images, for quotation on p. 57 from *Channeling Children—Sex Stereotyping in Prime-Time TV*, by Betty Miles (Princeton, NJ: Women on Words and Images, 1975). Used by permission.

The authors would like to express their gratitude to the many students, classroom teachers, reading consultants, art and music specialists, and outdoor educators who so generously contributed to this project through their support and encouragement.

Introduction

*It has been said that he (she) that loves reading
has everything within his (her) grasp.*[1]

There is no doubt that the ability to read is a basic necessity in today's world. But teaching the pleasures of reading can be an elusive and frustrating task. Today many school systems are requiring teachers to devote more time to the basics of reading. It is however no secret that students and teachers alike can become bored with simply spending increased time on the same types of activities; and it becomes self-defeating if, in the process of learning to read, students also learn to dislike reading.

Teaching basic reading skills can be fun. In a comprehensive, well-balanced reading program, enjoyable experiences can easily be incorporated, not only as interest-arousing and motivational devices, but also to teach basic reading skills. To ensure that students gain as much as possible from reading instruction throughout their school years, the structure, content, and activities of the reading program should be varied. When planning for reading experiences, students' natural interests should be utilized as motivational factors. When reading activities are based upon their interests, students often become so engrossed that they forget that they are actually working on their basic reading skills. (Teachers have found this to be the case when field-testing the activities in this book.)

The goal of this book, then, is to help children build reading skills at the same time as they learn truly to enjoy reading. The book will serve as a

[1]William Godwin, *Enquirer: Early Taste for Reading.*

resource for novel, motivational activities that can be easily and effectively incorporated into any existing skills program. These experiences can be used with any basal reading series or can be correlated with a criterion-referenced or individualized reading program. The activities can be used by reading teachers and those in other curriculum areas, such as art, music, science, social studies, and outdoor/environmental education.

The activities in this book can also help students to see that reading is related to all aspects of life. Although they are primarily aimed at developing basic reading and language arts skills in the elementary school years, most of them can be easily and effectively utilized in junior high and high school, particularly as motivating devices for students with weak reading skills and interest. The activities can also be used by parents and others in out-of-school settings to improve basic reading skills.

This book is divided into five chapters that reflect areas of interest to most young people: humor, television, art, music, and the outdoors. Each chapter contains background information and a brief rationale, a description of supportive research findings, and a wide range of activities related to the basic components of a reading program.

To provide motivating experiences for students while reinforcing basic reading skills, one topic, such as humor or art, could be the theme for additional reading activities for several weeks, a month, or for one day each week for a school year. Two possible arrangements are suggested:

Monthly Thematic Activity Schedule		Daily Thematic Activity Schedule	
September–October	Outdoors	Monday	Art
November–December	Art	Tuesday	TV
January–February	TV	Wednesday	Music
March–April	Music	Thursday	Humor
May–June	Humor	Friday	Outdoors

The background information and research studies included in each chapter support this type of thematic approach. Also included in each chapter are a list of suggested materials and a questionnaire or other device to determine students' specific interests related to the theme. The activities related to each topic are sequenced according to level of difficulty into the following areas of reading skill development:

- Reading Readiness
- Language Experience
- Decoding
- Vocabulary Building

- Comprehension
- Reading Study Techniques
- Language Arts
- Reading Interest Building

If students' interests are carefully considered when providing reading skill practice, the process of learning to read can be made more meaningful and more enjoyable. Whether using Miss Piggy, a painting of the Old West by Frederic Remington, John Denver's "Sunshine on My Shoulders," or animal tracks in the woods, the thematic activities in this book are designed to teach children the many pleasures of reading.

chapter one
using **HUMOR**
to stimulate reading growth

Introduction

Without love and laughter, there is no joy.[1]

Everybody loves to laugh, children perhaps most of all. In fact, humor is the reason most often given by students for valuing a particular book. But the sound of laughter is not often heard during reading time. This is unfortunate, for the use of humorous materials and techniques provides an easy and delightful way of making the process of learning to read more fun.

Yet even the sounds of learning can appear to be "just noise" to the parent or school administrator walking by. It is therefore important that teachers utilizing humor in the classroom understand some of the relevant theories and research so that, if asked how students can be learning to read amid so much hilarity, the rationale for these activities can be supported by a sound theoretical base.

In most studies of humor, laughter is assumed to show an individual's genuine appreciation of something humorous (McGhee 1976a).[2] However, in order to appreciate humor, one must understand the joke or funny element, and this involves a cognitive, creative problem-solving process (Beecher 1978). It has also been found that the humor response is strongest when there is some challenge to understanding the joke or funny element (McGhee 1976b). Therefore, when students are enjoying humorous reading activities, they can also be improving their thinking-reasoning skills.

Although laughter is usually spontaneous, it can be developed or changed. Studies with young mothers show that babies laugh and cry with almost equal ease and that they can be taught to laugh instead of cry on

[1]Quintus H. F. Horace, *Epistles.*
[2]Chapter readings and references appear on page 38.

many occasions (Cross 1977). Students who seldom laugh or smile in the classroom can also be encouraged to develop a sense of humor through carefully selected humorous reading activities.

Studies indicate that there are many different kinds of laughter and a teacher should be aware of the following types when planning for humorous reading activities:

- **Soundless laughter.** This is the inner enjoyment experienced when people are alone, perhaps reading an amusing book.

- **Audible chuckle.** Enjoyment of humor is heightened and changed when another person is nearby, though not communicating. When students are silently reading a humorous story in a small reading group, they will often chuckle in a subconscious desire to share a humorous incident.

- **Soliciting laughter.** This stage is reached when a student cannot refrain from quoting a humorous passage aloud, and in turn is rewarded by laughter from others. This mutual sharing of an experience is a social phenomenon that should be encouraged.

- **Socially appropriate laughter.** Students of all ages sometimes laugh simply because it seems like the socially appropriate response for the situation even if they do not think the joke is funny or do not get the humorous intent. (Cross 1977)

Medical evidence indicates that a good hearty laugh can cure a number of ailments. Laughter can clear the respiratory system, benefit the lungs, stabilize blood pressure, stimulate circulation, facilitate digestion, provide a healthful emotional outlet, combat boredom, provide an opportunity to discharge extra energy, and help to eliminate shyness, tension, and worry (Cross 1977). People who enjoy humor are also generally found to be in sound mental health (Keith-Spiegel 1972). In short, people often feel better and are more relaxed after laughing. Through participation in humorous reading activities, students can experience the psychological and physiological benefits of humor even as they increase their reading proficiency.

Laughter is an important ingredient in presenting a favorable appearance. Children who laugh easily and often are more likely to be considered beautiful, handsome, or attractive than those who seldom laugh or smile (Cross 1977). Laughter, along with a sense of humor, is also a sign of intelligence. The sharper a person's intellect, the more likely he/she will be to appreciate humor. A study by *Instructor* magazine even showed that outstanding teachers were more humorous and had more fun (Tschudin 1978).

Laughter leaves a feeling of well-being, personal satisfaction, and contentment. It can eliminate nervous tension and rid the air of annoyance and resentment. Laughter can also initiate social interaction and create and reinforce a sense of solidarity and intimacy within groups (Martineau 1972). When students are working on humorous reading activities, laughter can encourage cooperation and create a common bond among students, although they may be in different reading groups and working on different reading levels. Laughter can also relieve the dullness or boredom that some students associate with learning to read. So it is very important that students be given opportunities to laugh and enjoy humor during reading, for their physical and mental health as well as for viewing reading and learning as pleasurable and enjoyable.

SOURCES OF HUMOROUS MATERIALS

Humorous materials are readily available and can be used for a variety of reading activities. The same material can often be used with students at different reading levels. A beginning reader will enjoy the nonverbal humor depicted by a cartoon, while a more advanced reader may get more meaning from the dialogue. The following materials can be used for a number of humorous reading activities:

Riddles	Bumper stickers
Nursery Rhymes	T-Shirts
Books	Comics
Short Stories	Greeting Cards
Poems	Posters
Folktales	Children's folklore
Advertisements	(cheers, riddles, jokes, jump-rope
Graffiti	and counting rhymes,
Newspapers	superstitions)
(comics, cartoons, Dear Abby,	
Erma Bombeck, Art Buchwald	
political cartoons, riddle pages)	

KNOWING WHAT WILL MAKE THEM LAUGH

When selecting humorous materials and activities, it is important to know what kinds of things will be funny to students. Because each class situation is different, specific prescriptions cannot be given for types of humor to use in every classroom (Aho 1979). It is nonetheless known that children of all ages usually respond with laughter to the following:

• Amusing use of words, including misuse of big words, puns, nonsense words and double meanings

• Funny characters

• Surprising ideas that are incompatible with the reader's expectations

• Chaotic and ridiculous situations (Monson 1977)

However, to identify the types of things a specific group of children finds humorous, the following suggestions can be used:

Observe students' reactions to stories in their reading materials. What makes them laugh?

Observe students' reactions to humorous materials that are read aloud to them.

Ask students what was the funniest book they ever read.

Consult with the school librarian about the types of humorous materials that are checked out or requested.

Observe students at free time, before school, at recess, and during lunch. What types of jokes do they tell? What do they laugh at?

Arrange a variety of humorous books and materials on a special shelf or table. Ask students to sample them and give their reactions.

Rollicking Their Way to Readiness

The most utterly lost of all days
is that on which one has not laughed once.[1]

Many kinds of early experiences are necessary for students to develop the requisite skills for learning to read. Visual skills such as visual discrimination, memory, and imagery are vital. Students need to be able to see differences in letters and words, remember what they have read, and be able to see or visualize in their minds' eyes what they are reading.

Another important aspect of reading is relating printed symbols to oral sounds. If a child does not correctly perceive aural impressions, confusion in auditory discrimination can result. Without the ability to discern likenesses and differences in sounds, a child may be unable to distinguish between words such as *pat* and *bat,* or *cut* and *cot.* Training in auditory discrimination is the foundation upon which instruction in phonics is based. Some children's inability to discriminate auditorially may be so great that they need work with gross sound discrimination of objects before they can tackle discrimination between speech sounds.

This section contains activities for developing students' visual and auditory skills which are essential for reading through humorous activities. Other activities for the readiness stages can be adapted from activities in the vocabulary, comprehension, and reading interest sections of this chapter.

[1] Sebastian R. N. Chamfort, *Maximes.*

VISUAL SKILL DEVELOPMENT

1. Finding What Doesn't Belong

Make a paste-up or a collage picture with one unusual humorous element. Ask students to find the part that doesn't belong, such as a deer in a bathtub, a glass of milk upside down on a table, or a hat on a car. Students could make their own "mixed-up" pictures and ask others to find the items that don't belong.

2. Locating What Is Out of Sequence

Show students a series of sequence pictures with one picture that is silly and does not pertain to the series. Have them point out the picture that doesn't belong.
example:

3. Following the Leader

Have students watch and then mimic silly actions performed by a leader, such as making funny faces or patting their heads while hopping on one foot. Students could take turns being the leader.

AUDITORY SKILL DEVELOPMENT

1. Following Oral Directions

Give students a series of funny oral directions for them to listen to and then follow. Gradually increase the number of directions in the series.
example:
> Pat your head.
> Wiggle your nose.
> Pull your ear.
> Stamp your feet.

2. Playing "Simon Says"

Improve students' listening skills by playing "Simon Says" giving them oral directions to listen to and then to follow. Remind the students that they must only do the activities when they are preceded by the expression "Simon Says." If they follow other directions, they must sit out for the rest of the game. The number of directions to follow can be increased throughout the game.

example:

"Simon says to pat your foot." (Students must follow the direction.)

"Hop on one foot." (Students should not follow the direction as it was not preceded by "Simon Says.")

"Simon says to hop on one foot and then pat your head." (Students must follow the direction.)

3. Drawing a Funny Picture

Give students oral directions for drawing a funny picture. Tell them to listen carefully as you will say the direction only once.

example:

Draw a purple cat with a green nose.

4. Saying Nonsense Words and Silly Sentences

Tell students to listen carefully while you tell them a series of funny words. Then have them repeat what was said. Start with one-syllable words, such as *flib, flum, slom,* or *glab* and then gradually add longer nonsense words, such as *flingledrote* or *dimity-dram,* and then proceed to silly sentences, such as "The flingledrote flibbed a glab."

5. Listening to Humorous Rhymes

Poems, nursery rhymes, jingles, limericks, and amusing rhyming stories such as those in the Dr. Seuss books, can be used to teach students the concept of rhyme. After reading a selection aloud to the students, have them review the rhyming words. Tell them a word and ask them for the one that rhymes, such as horner–corner, muffet–tuffet, cat–hat.

6. Making a Funny Jingle

Help students to make up their own funny rhyming jingles. Say a first line and let them supply the rest.

example:

First Line	**Student Answers**
I saw a clown. . .	Laugh and frown.
	In my town.
	Jump up and down.

Humorous Language Experiences

Beware of him (her) who hates the laugh of a child.[1]

When young children, or students of any age, are just beginning to read, it is very important that they see and understand the magic, thrill, and pleasure of the speech–print connection—that those funny little black squiggles are speech words that can be written down and read back exactly again and again and again. One of the best ways to do this is to have the students dictate their own stories and have someone write down exactly what they say.

Stories that the students dictate can then become the basis for a variety of meaningful reading-related activities, such as identifying known words, matching words that look alike or start with a given sound, learning left-to-right progression while following a line of print, and listening to the teacher read with good oral expression.

Using humorous topics for student-dictated stories can make the language experience activities even more enjoyable to the beginning reader.

1. Laughable Language Experience Stories

Give students a funny object, such as a picture of a clown doing a trick, an amusing stuffed animal, or a clever puppet. Let them discuss what they think is funny about it. Then have the students dictate funny sentences that make a story about the object. Students could also locate words they know in the story and match word cards to words in the story.

example:

RAGTAG THE CLOWN

"Ragtag is a funny clown," said Janice.

"His ears are big and his nose is like a shiny red ball," said Bob.

"He has a funny hat on and his clothes are made of patches," said Beth.

"He makes us laugh," said Ann.

Find these words in the story:

    clown   laugh   ball   are   hat

Find two words you already know in the story.

2. Language Experience Jokes

Have students dictate jokes or silly sentences.

[1]Johann Kaspar Lavater, *source unknown.*

3. Our Funny Book

Help students to make a class "Funny Book" composed of things they think are funny. The book could contain the following types of items that have been dictated and illustrated by the students:

Some Funny Stories	Books That Make Us Laugh
Our Favorite Jokes	Funny Songs We Like to Sing
Funny TV Programs	Our Favorite Cartoons

Delirious Decoding Activities

A good laugh is sunshine in a house.[1]

When a reader encounters too many unknown words in a selection, the author's meaning can be lost. Students need a large number of words they identify at sight as well as an assortment of skills and techniques that will help them to gain meaning from unfamiliar printed words. The development of word-identification skills is of major importance in learning to read, and mastery of these skills requires much practice; a touch of humor will make the practice more interesting. The following activities can be used to further develop students' recognition of sight-words and their skills in phonics, structural and contextual analysis, and dictionary usage in ways that are fun.

SIGHT-WORD RECOGNITION

1. Creating a Laugh or Smile

Put words students need to review into a humorously decorated container. As each child draws out a word, ask him or her to make up a funny sentence with that word.

2. Silly-Word Pictures

Provide necessary sight-word review by giving students silly pictures to draw. Words chosen for review can consist of words with which students are experiencing difficulty from their reading or content area books or frequently used words from the list on page 11.
example:
Draw a picture for each of these sentences.

[1]William Makepeace Thackeray, *Sketches: Love, Marriage.*

FREQUENTLY USED WORDS

a	don't	jump	out	them
about	down	just	over	then
after			own	there
again	each	keep		these
all	eat	kind	pick	they
almost	enough	knew	play	thing
along	every	know	please	think
always	fall		pretty	this
am	far	laugh	pull	those
an	fast	left	put	through
and	find	let		time
another	fly	light	ran	today
any	found	like	read	together
anything	from	little	ready	told
are	full	live	ride	tomorrow
as	fun	long	right	too
at	funny	look	road	took
ate		lost	round	try
away	gave		run	
	get	made		under
bad	give	make	said	up
be	go	many	same	upon
because	goes	may	saw	us
been	gone	maybe	say	use
before	good	me	see	
began	got	met	shall	very
behind	grow	might	she	
best		more	should	walk
better	had	much	show	want
big	has	must	sing	was
both	have	my	sit	we
bring	he	myself	sleep	well
brought	help		small	went
but	her	never	so	when
buy	here	new	some	where
by	him	next	something	which
	his	no	sometimes	who
call	hold	not	soon	why
came	hot	nothing	start	will
can	how	now	stop	with
cold		of		won't
come	I	off	take	work
could	if	old	talk	would
	I'll	on	tell	write
did	in	once	than	
do	is	only	thank	yes
does	it	open	that	you
doesn't	it's	other	the	your
done	its	or	their	yours

COMMON PREFIXES AND SUFFIXES

Prefix	Meaning	Example
ante	before	antedate
anti	against	antifreeze
auto	self	autobiography
be	complete covering, excessive, by	becloud, bewilder, beside
bi	two	biannual
com, co	together, with	compact, coauthor
contra, counter	against	contraband, counteract
de	away, from	depart
dis	not, remove	disobey, disarm
en, em	in	enjoy, embrace
ex	out	export
fore	before	forewarn
hemi	half	hemisphere
hyper	too much	hyperactive
hypo	too little, below	hypoactive, hypodermic
in, im	into	input, impound
il, in, im, ir	not	illegal, incorrect, imperfect, irreplaceable
inter	between	interstate
mid	middle	midtown
mis	wrongly	misspell
mono	one	monologue
multi	many	multicolored
non	not	nonliving
over	too much, on top of	overcome, overcoat
poly	many	polysyllable
post	after	postwar
pre	before	prewar
pseudo	false	pseudonym
quasi	almost	quasi-victory
re	again	rewrite
semi	half, partly	semicircle, semitropical
sub	under	subway
super	better	superman
trans	across	transcontinental
tri	three	triangle
un	not	unnatural
uni	one	unicycle

Suffix	Meaning	Example
able, ible	capable of being	likeable, forcible
ance, ence, hood, ment, ness, ship, sion, tion	state of	tolerance, persistence, childhood, amazement, loudness, friendship, decision, sanitation
age	act of	bondage
en	made of or as	sweeten
er, or	doer of action	hunter, actor
ful, ous, y	full of	beautiful, dangerous, windy
ic	pertaining to	comic
ish, like, ly	similar to or characteristic of	foolish, lifelike, friendly
ist	one who performs	violinist
less	without	wingless
port	to carry	transport
ward	in the direction of	foreward

Cow *in* a can.

Horse *on* a house.

A box *of* tigers.

Students could also make up their own silly things to draw using sentences from their individual review wor packets or from a list of designated words.

example:

> Write silly sentences for someone to draw pictures about using these words: *was, out, over.*

3. Riddle-Making Words

Most riddles begin with *why, what, when, where, who, how* or *if.* Students could review these often troublesome words in the following ways:

a. Work on one riddle-making word during a session. Discuss the word with the students and ask them to read just that word while you read the rest of the riddle.

> **examples:** Word for the day: *Why*
>
> *Why* do elephants wear green sneakers?
> *Answer:* Their red ones are dirty.
>
> *Why* do chickens cross the road?
> *Answer:* To get to the other side.

b. Give the students riddles with the question-making word omitted. Then ask them to supply the correct word.

> **examples:**
>
> (What) bites but has no teeth?
> *Answer:* Frost.
>
> (When) the rain comes down, what goes up?
> *Answer:* Umbrellas.

c. Give the students several question-making words to use to compose their own riddles.

> **example:**
>
> Write two riddles using the word *who.*

4. Creating Jokes with Review Words

Write riddles, jokes and funny sentences for the students to read aloud using primarily those words that they need to review. Pictures could be used to represent difficult words.

PHONICS REVIEW

1. Phonic Riddles

Children enjoy riddles of all kinds and phonic riddles can be a delightful

vay to review phonemes. Riddles can be made up by the teacher or by the
hildren and shared aloud.
mple:

> I am thinking of something that starts with an *r*, like *rabbit*. This is what you
> like to do with a book. What is it? (*Answer:* Read.)

2. Tongue-Twisters

It is difficult for students to keep from laughing when their tongues are
tangled up in a tongue-twister. Tongue-twisters can be carefully selected
or created to give students necessary review of a specific phonic element,
such as *b*, as in Betty Botter. These tongue-twisters can be presented
orally for review of a specific sound or can be written on the chalkboard,
an overhead transparency, or a ditto, to enable the students to get more
practice associating the letter/sound correspondence. Students could
work first on short tongue-twisters.
examples:

> Silly Sally sips soup.
> Baby Bobby Burns blows beautiful big bubbles.

They could then build up to longer, more complex ones.
example:

> Betty Botter bought a bit of butter.
> But, she said, the butter's bitter.
> If I put the bitter butter in my batter,
>
> It will make my batter bitter.
> But a bit of better butter
> Would make my batter better.
> So she bought a bit of better butter,
> Better than her bitter butter.
> And put the better butter in her batter.
> And the batter was not bitter.
> Thus, 'twas better that
> Betty Botter bought a bit of better butter
> For her batter.

3. Funny Phonic Stories

Students can create and illustrate funny phonic stories stressing words
that begin with a specified element. Ask students for all the words they can
think of that start with a specific sound, such as *r*. Make sure that common
and proper nouns, verbs, adjectives, and adverbs have been included.
Then ask them to think up a humorous sentence or story in which most of
the words start with the same sound. These student-created tongue
twisters could be compiled into a class book and enjoyed by all.
example:

Common Nouns	Proper Nouns	Adjectives	Verbs	Adverbs
rat	Rachel	red	ran	rudely
rhinoceros	Robert	round	ranted	
		rude	raved	

Robert, the rude rhinoceros, ran rudely around Rachel, the red rat.

4. Pronouncing Nonsense-Words

When students are asked to pronounce nonsense-words, they are given an excellent opportunity to practice their phonic skills. However, to avoid confusion, they must be told that the words are pretend or nonsense words. Younger students could be told that they are going to be asked to sound out or pronounce some "funny" or "pretend" words. Older students could be advised that the words they will be working with are nonsense words. Supply words such as *lup, plit, crad, limflit,* and *floopdubber*; or students could even make up their own nonsense words for others to pronounce.

STRUCTURAL ANALYSIS

1. Dividing Silly Words

Review basic syllabication principles by having students divide into syllables a list of nonsense words, such as *pralif, trimple,* and *atram.* Then ask them to pronounce the funny words.

2. Suffix and Prefix Creations

Give students a number of root words, suffixes, and prefixes. Ask them to make up a "new" word and give its meaning.
examples:
    nonfeedable (not able to be fed)
    repracticing (practicing again)

Humorous sentences could also be made with the "new" words. Use the lists of common prefixes and suffixes on page 12 for this activity.

3. Confounding Compound Riddles

Riddles that are based on compound words can be used to call students' attention to the two distinct parts of a compound word and also to its intended meaning.
examples:
    What kind of house is full of feathers?
    Answer: A birdhouse.

    What kind of dream don't you have at night?
    Answer: A daydream.

Students could then create their own riddles using compound words such as the following:

armchair	bedroom	bookend	cowhand
bagpipes	bedspread	broomstick	cupboard
baseball	beehive	bulldog	daylight
battleship	bookcase	cardboard	daytime

doghouse	flashlight	mousetrap	softball
doughnut	foghorn	necktie	springtime
dragonfly	football	pancake	streetcar
driveway	handbag	raincoat	suitcase
eggplant	headlight	scarecrow	tablespoon
evergreen	houseboat	schoolhouse	teaspoon
farmhouse	jaywalk	schoolroom	toothbrush
farmyard	leapfrog	shoelace	wallpaper
			wishbone

CONTEXT-CLUE USAGE

1. Topsy-Turvy Context Clues

"Topsy-Turvies" are delightful additions to a school day. In a Topsy-Turvy, each second sentence ends with a word whose meaning is deliberately opposite to the content of the two sentences. The students must use context clues to determine the incorrect word and supply the correct one.

Ask the students to do two things to each Topsy-Turvy:

- Underline the incorrect word.

- Supply the correct word by writing it above the incorrect word.

examples:

A great big dog ran up behind me and pushed me down.

sad
That makes me so *happy*.

big
My dog weighs 150 pounds. He is *little*.

Students could write their own Topsy Turvies to share with others. These could be based on stories they have read.

2. Nursery Rhyme Cloze

Delete some words from a nursery rhyme or jingle. Have students supply the missing words. Discuss their choices.
examples:

Little Miss Muffet _____ on a tuffet
Eating her curds _____ whey.
Along came a spider and _____ down beside her
And _____ Miss Muffet away.

3. Silly Syntax

Have students correctly order the words in the answers for riddles.
example:

What is red and green and dangerous?
Answer: of olives gallon a stampeding stuffed.

(*Answer in correct order:* A gallon of stampeding stuffed olives)

4. Scrambled Context

Give students a ditto with a humorous story that has some scrambled words. Direct them to use the context to help them unscramble the words so that the story will make sense. Have the students write the correct word above the scrambled word.
example:

(clowns)
Danny and Amy went to the circus to see the *ncolws*. The first one had big

(feet)   (wagon)
shoes on his *tefe.* He pulled a red *nwoag* with a pig in it. He did funny

(laugh)
tricks and made the children *galuh.*

5. The Missing Plurals

Give students a funny story that does not sound right because some of the words are missing an *s, es,* or *ies* to make them plural. Have students read the story and supply the plural endings.
example:

MY THREE PINK DRAGON

My three pink dragon were so much fun. Two dragon had strong tail. The other one had polka dot on her front leg. They liked to eat apple and worm. Sometime they would sing song and tell funny story to each other. They liked to catch fly and worm. My friend all enjoyed my three pink dragon.

DICTIONARY PRACTICE

1. Alphabetizing Nonsense-Words

Give students a list of nonsense words, such as *amd, cag, bem,* and *dod,* to put into alphabetical order.

2. Dictionary Fun

Have students write riddles or jokes using the dictionary pronunciations of words.

example:

> wi du kawz go o-ver hilz?
> (Why do cows go over hills?)
> *Answer:* Because they can't go under them.

3. Humorous Definitions

Ask students to write their own definitions of words such as *laugh, smile, humor* and *giggle.* Then have them compare their definitions with those in the dictionaries. Discuss the differences.

4. Looking Up Unusual Words

Give students questions to answer using unusual, funny-sounding words that they need to look up in the dictionary.
examples:

1. What would you do if you were in a palanquin?
   a. swim for an hour   b. sit quietly   c. play baseball
2. What would you do if someone gave you a saiga?
   a. wear it to school   b. hang it on the wall   c. give it to the zoo

5. Understanding Slang

Write on the board informal and slang words that are often used by students, such as *okay, nope, yep,* and *gab.* If the dictionary does not contain the words, have the students make up their own dictionaries of slang, including pronunciations, definitions, and examples of the words used in appropriate sentences.

Blues-Vanishing Vocabulary Activities

Laugh and the whole world laughs with you. . . .[1]

Children are confronted from birth with a bewildering variety of words and soon become aware that people close to them respond in different ways to different words. Unfortunately, the process of learning new words at school sometimes becomes so mechanistic that students lose interest in increasing their vocabularies. Since accurate understanding of the meanings of words is a necessary prerequisite for reading with understanding, successful vocabulary enrichment experiences must be planned for and included in the reading program. It should not be assumed that students will automatically learn new words as a byproduct of other instruction.

Learning new words should be an exciting part of the school day.

[1] Ella Wheeler Wilcox, *Solitude.*

The activities in this section can be used to show students that vocabulary acquisition can be fun.

1. Understanding Tongue-Twisters and Nursery Rhymes

Ask students the meanings of some of the words that they encounter in familiar tongue-twisters and nursery rhymes.
examples:
> What do pickled peppers taste like?
> How many peppers would be in a peck?
> What is a dish of curds and whey?

2. Funny Definitions

Let students read funny definitions that others have created:
examples:
> Thermos bottle—thirst-aid kit
> Outdoor grill—sauna for hot dogs
> A pond—waterbed for ducks

Then have them create their own to share with others. Make sure students are aware of the real definitions of the words.

3. Creating Word-Pictures

Combine art and reading by studying *Wordplays* or words that speak for themselves that often appear in daily newspapers.
example:

WORDPLAY

Then have students show that they know the meanings of words by depicting them in their own word pictures. Start with relatively easy words to picture, such as the following:

TALL small WIDE CURLY NAILS

Other words that are *easy* to use to create word-pictures are as follows:

fire	drip	hot
ice	rain	cold
round	triangle	skinny
square	cloud	fat

4. Puns in Jokes and Riddles

Riddles that are based on words that have more than one meaning can be used to enlarge students' vocabularies. The unusual use of a familiar word in these riddles could be discussed; then ask students to write their own riddles based on an unfamiliar use of a common word, such as *eyes, ears, cub, club, teeth,* or *foot.*

examples:

What has ears but cannot hear?
Answer: Corn.

What has teeth but cannot eat?
Answer: Comb

5. Homophone Riddles

Riddles that involve the use of homophones can be written out on small cards and given to individual students to read out loud to others.

example:

What is black and white and *read* all over?
Answer: Newspaper.

After sharing the answer to the riddle and discussing other homophones, students could create their own riddles using words such as:

aisle/isle	fir/fur
ant/aunt	flea/flee
ball/bawl	flower/flour
bare/bear	hair/hare
be/bee	knew/new/gnu
beet/beat	knight/night
berry/bury	pair/pare/pear
blue/blew	pane/pain
buy/by	rain/reign
cent/scent/sent	right/write
cereal/serial	rose/rows
cheap/cheep	sea/see
chili/chilly	soar/sore
close/clothes	stake/steak
creak/creek	sun/son
dear/deer	toad/towed
doe/dough	vane/vein/vain
eight/ate	would/wood
eye/I	

6. Humorous Synonyms and Antonyms

Students can stretch their vocabularies by listing all the synonyms (words that mean the same or nearly the same) and antonyms (words that mean the opposite) of humorous words such as *laugh, smile,* and *giggle.* This is a good group activity.

examples using the word *laughter:*

Synonyms	Antonyms
1. giggle	1. groan
2. snicker	2. wail
3. cackle	3. weep
4. chuckle	4. cry
5.	5.
6.	6.

Then have the students search for synonyms and antonyms in the dictionary or in reference books of synonyms and antonyms. Students could discuss their meanings and see if they agree that they are appropriate synonyms or antonyms for a given word. They could then write sentences or stories using the new words they have encountered.

7. Creating a New Title or Phrase

Have students create a different title for a nursery rhyme, story, or common phrase. Older students could use a dictionary or thesaurus.

example:

"The Three Little Pigs" could be changed to "A Trio of Diminutive Swine"

"The cow jumped over the moon" could be changed to "The bovine leaped over the natural satellite of the earth."

8. Paraphrasing

Have students rewrite a Mother Goose rhyme using a dictionary or thesaurus as a source of synonyms.

examples:

Petite Mistress Muffet occupied a seat on a hassock partaking of her morning meal that consisted of hot cereal. Suddenly an arachnid approached and occupied a position in the approximate vicinity. This startled the lass and caused her to flee.

9. Cartoons

Some cartoons deal with vocabulary meaning. Keep a collection of these to show students that the study of vocabulary meaning can be fun. Have students make their own cartoons showing they know the meanings of certain terms.

example:
>Make a cartoon to show that you know the meaning of bookworm.

10. Stretching Vocabularies via Humorous Couplets

A couplet is a humorous rhyming definition. Students must know the meaning of the words as well as how to make rhymes before they can make their own couplets. First give them opportunities to enjoy couplets others have created. Then ask them to create their own.

examples:
>What is a library? A book nook.
>What is an overweight feline? A fat cat.
>What is a tuna salad? A fish dish.

11. Word-Symbol Riddles

Some riddles are based on the symbolic use of words. This type of riddle can be used to encourage older students to remember that words are just symbols of actual things.

examples:
>What is the longest word?
>*Answer:* Smiles, because there is a mile between the s's.
>
>What is at the end of everything?
>*Answer:* The letter g.
>
>Where can you always find money?
>*Answer:* In the dictionary.

Comical Comprehension Builders

Laugh if you are wise.[1]

The most important goal in reading instruction is to equip the students to understand what they have read. The development of reading comprehension is a long process and students need work in this area at *every* grade level. The benefits of using humor in the reading program are perhaps the greatest in the area of comprehension. Students of all ages enjoy humorous materials and will usually be motivated to try to understand them. The activities in this section can be used to help students improve basic comprehension skills through activities that they will find enjoyable.

[1]Marcus V. M. Martial, *Epigrams.*

FOLLOWING DIRECTIONS

1. Read and Draw

Give students written directions for drawing a ridiculous picture.
example:
> Make a large purple flower with orange leaves.
> Draw a tiny blue house under the flower.
> Put a green dog near the house.
> Draw a pink frog on the dog's head.

2. Read and Do

Pass out a dittoed sheet similar to the one in the example below. Ask students to read it and follow the directions. Afterwards, discuss what they should have done to correctly follow the directions.
example:

FOLLOWING DIRECTIONS

Read the whole paper first. Then follow the directions.

1. Make three small boxes. _____
2. Write the word "happy." _____
3. Cross out the word "sentence" in this sentence.
4. Tell what 4 × 4 is. Write the answer. _____
5. Write down how many windows we have in this room. _____
6. Draw a flower here.
7. Write down the name of the President of the United States. _____
8. Write down the name of this month. _____
9. Just do numbers 2, 3, 6, and 8.

Did you follow the first direction? It said, "Read the *whole* paper first!"

GETTING THE MAIN IDEA

1. Appreciating Humorous Material

Give students an opportunity to read or listen to humorous ballads, poems, or stories and discuss the main ideas of the selections as well as their amusing aspects. This will help students to realize and understand the types of things they find amusing.

2. Posting a Joke of the Day

Post a new joke each day on a designated space on a chalkboard or bulletin board so that students can start off each day with a smile. Have them explain the joke to those that don't "get it." Eventually students could each be given an opportunity to select a day's joke with teacher approval.

3. Understanding Political Cartoons

Students often ignore political cartoons from which much can be learned. Explain to the students that a political cartoon is the cartoonist's view of politics. Bring in relevant political cartoons from the newspaper and ask students to interpret them. Then give them a situation and ask them to create their own political cartoons.

UNDERSTANDING IDIOMS

1. Idioms a la *Amelia Bedelia*

Students of any age will derive more enjoyment out of the study of idioms if they are first read the humorous story of Amelia Bedelia, the house-maid, who follows all instructions literally. For instance, Amelia runs away with home base when told to steal home plate during a baseball game. She also puts dried prunes on branches when told to prune the hedges. Illustrations from the book *Amelia Bedelia* could be projected on a screen using an opaque projector for viewing and discussion by the class. Students should discuss the intended meanings of the idioms and the confusion Amelia encountered when she understood only the literal meanings.

2. Intended Meanings of Idioms

Have students illustrate the literal meaning of an idiom or figurative expression, explain the idiomatic or intended meaning, and then use the expression correctly in a sentence.

examples:

Some figurative and idiomatic expressions are written below. Choose one and draw a picture to illustrate its literal meaning. Underneath your illustration, write the expression and its intended meaning. Then write a sentence using the expression correctly.

FIGURATIVE AND IDIOMATIC EXPRESSIONS

Took the words right out of my mouth	Keep an ear to the ground
An idea hit me (struck by an idea)	In hot water
Yelling their heads off	Fingers in the pie
Name was mud	Look a gift horse in the mouth
Finding a needle in a haystack	Chip off the old block
Afraid of one's own shadow	Shake a leg

Barking up the wrong tree
Raining cats and dogs
Won by a nose
Beating around the bush
Hold your horses
Too many cooks spoil the broth
Bite off more than you can chew
Burn the candle at both ends
Cry over spilled milk
The early bird catches the worm
Apple of your eye
Every cloud has a silver lining
Face the music
Hold your tongue
Frog in your throat
Hair stands on end
Horse of a different color
Irons in the fire
Jump out of your skin
Hit the nail on the head
In a nutshell

Handle with kid gloves
I'm all wound up
We must stick together
It curled my hair
A chip on your shoulder
Saved by a hair
I'm in a spot
My lips are sealed
I am all ears
Your eyes are bigger than
   your stomach
Change horses in midstream
Butterflies in your stomach
Cart before the horse
Cat's got your tongue
Can't see the forest for the trees
Put your foot down
Great oaks from little acorns grow
Head in the clouds
Grass is always greener on the
   other side of the fence

Expression: "Yelling their heads off"

Intended meaning: _____

Sentence using the idiom:

Expression: _____

Intended meaning: _____

Sentence using the idiom:

3. Comic Strip Idioms

Idioms are often the subject of newspaper cartoons. Bring some to class and discuss their literal and intended meanings. Students could then be asked to create their own cartoons to illustrate the literal meanings of expressions often used. Then ask them to define the intended meaning of each expression.

example:
> Make up your own cartoon to illustrate the literal meaning of one of the following expressions:
>
> - walking on air
> - laughing up one's sleeve
> - lost in a good book
> - in the doghouse
> - play it by ear
>
> What does the expression really mean? _____
>
> Use the expression in a sentence. _____

4. Acting Out Idioms

Give students individual envelopes or boxes containing idioms and the materials needed to act them out. For example, supply a large card with the word *air* written on it and directions for the student to place the word on the floor and walk on it (to act out "walking on air"). Another envelope could contain a small paper basket with some paper eggs and directions for the student to place some but not all of the eggs in the basket ("Don't put all your eggs in one basket"). Other students could guess the idioms and their intended meanings (Lorenz 1977).

5. Riddles and Idioms

Riddles that are based on idioms can be used to expose students to both the literal and inferential meanings of idioms. Most idiomatic riddles are based on the literal and incorrect meaning of these terms.
example:
> Why did Rachel throw the clock out the window?
> *Answer:* She wanted to see time fly.

Students could be asked to compare the literal and the inferential or intended meaning of each idiom they encounter in riddles. They could also write their own idiomatic riddles.

6. Understanding Idioms About Laughter

26   Have students discuss the meanings of commonly used English preposi-

tional idioms that deal with laughter. Then have students compose their own sentences using selected idioms.
examples:

- Laugh *at* (person, joke, story)—when the person or thing directly provokes the laughter: "We often laugh at a funny story."

- Laugh *about* (person or thing)—when something in or about a person or thing provokes laughter: "We were laughing about your brother telling about the burglary."

- Laugh *over* something—when one discusses or thinks of something: "We have often laughed over that story."

- Laugh *off*—shrug off, brush aside with laughter: "It's best to laugh off an insult."

- Laugh *on* the other side of the face—exchange amusement for disappointment, sorrow or regret: "She may laugh at our problem now, but before long she'll be laughing on the other side of her face."

- Laugh *up* one's sleeve—laugh secretly, being amused without openly expressing it: "We had a feeling that she was laughing up her sleeve at her brother." (Wood 1967)

RECOGNIZING DETAILS

1. Eliminating Extraneous Details

Some riddles are tricky because the clues are misleading even though the answers are realistic.
example:
Why do firemen wear red suspenders?
Answer: To hold up their pants.

Students must read this type of riddle in a literal, factual way and eliminate extraneous details, in order to determine the answer.

2. Analyzing a Cartoon Picture

Analyze a cartoon picture for details: How large are the characters? How old are they? What kinds of clothing do they wear?

SEQUENCING

1. Cartoon Sequencing

Cut out a cartoon strip from the newspaper, separate the individual frames, and have students put the frames in their correct order by numbering them *1, 2,* and *3.*

2. Nursery-Rhyme or Funny-Story Sequencing

Have students put into correct order the events of a humorous rhyme, jingle, or story.

example:
List these events in correct order by numbering the sentences *1, 2, 3,* and *4.*
_____A spider sat down beside her.
_____He frightened Miss Muffet away.
_____Little Miss Muffet sat on a tuffet.
_____She was eating her curds and whey.

CHARACTERIZATION

1. Describing a Favorite Humorous Character

Have students write a description of a favorite humorous character in a cartoon, TV program, basal-reader story, or well known trade book. Have other students (1) try to guess the identity, or (2) match descriptions of humorous characters:

example:
Match the character to the proper description:

Pecos Bill	A small town boy from Missouri
Paul Bunyan	An adventurous Texas cowboy
Tom Sawyer	A giant lumberjack from Minnesota

2. Developing Empathy

Discuss some humorous reading material and ask the students how the various characters probably felt. Help them to see that always being the target of a joke, as are Charlie Brown in *Peanuts* and Ira in *Miss Peach,* can be uncomfortable.

3. Illustrating Personal Characteristics

Often students do not get the full meaning of a picture. Help them to get more meaning by studying commonly used comic strip symbols as shown on the facing page.

4. Creating Dialogue for Cartoon Characters

Cover up the dialogue in a cartoon and ask students to write their own. Then compare students' work with the original.

COMIC STRIP SYMBOLS

confused

unprintable

gloomy or sad

thinking

sleeping

words are coming from telephone, radio, or TV

shivering from fright or cold

an idea

in love

hot or relieved

in a hurry

shiny or bright

in a daze or something has been hit

COMIC STRIP FACIAL EXPRESSIONS

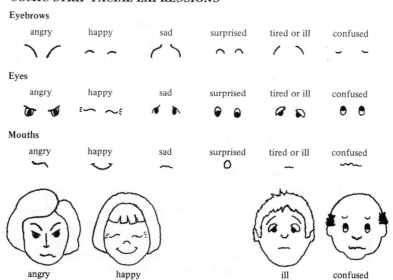

Eyebrows

| angry | happy | sad | surprised | tired or ill | confused |

Eyes

| angry | happy | sad | surprised | tired or ill | confused |

Mouths

| angry | happy | sad | surprised | tired or ill | confused |

angry

happy

ill

confused

From **The Teacher's Book of Lists** © 1979, Goodyear Publishing Company, Inc.

RECOGNIZING POINT OF VIEW

1. Dealing with Opinions

Give students selected quotations about humor to read and discuss. This will involve a study of unfamiliar words and also some reference to the originator of the quotation. Ask the students to explain the quotation in their own words and see if they are in agreement. Give students opportunities to look through books of quotations to find sayings about humor with which they agree or disagree.

WHAT OTHERS THOUGHT ABOUT LAUGHTER AND HUMOR: STUDYING "FAMOUS" QUOTATIONS

"Laughing is the sensation of feeling good all over, and showing it principally in one spot."

Billings, *Laffing*

"Nothing shows a man's (woman's) character more than what he (she) laughs at."

Goethe, *Maxims*

"A jest loses its point when he (she) who makes it is the first to laugh."
Schiller, *Fiesco*

"He (she) laughs best that laughs last."
Vanbrugh, *The Country House*

"I hate scarce smiles: I love laughing."

Blake, Gilchrist, *Life*

"Joking and humor are pleasant, and often of extreme utility."
Cicero, *De Oratore*

2. Analyzing Humorous Advertisements

Bring in examples of humorous advertisements from magazines and newspapers. Have students discuss why some advertisements are so humorous and appealing. What is the purpose of each advertisement? How is humor being used to sell a product?

MAKING PREDICTIONS

1. Developing Predictive Skills

Develop students' appreciation of humorous reading materials through the following teacher-directed activity that encourages students to make predictions:

    a. *Teacher expectation.* Tell the students that they are going to read or listen to a funny story, and that they will enjoy it and laugh. (Caution them not to laugh too loudly or they might disturb the class in the next room.)

b. *Student prediction.* After reading the title of the story or studying some of the pictures, ask the students what they think will be amusing about the story or what will be the funniest part. Then ask them to read or listen to the story to see if they were correct.

c. *Follow-up.* Discuss the story to see if the students were correct in their predictions. What could have made the story even more humorous?

2. Predicting the Conclusion

Give the students a comic strip with the last frame missing. Ask them to predict what will happen, draw the missing picture, and complete the dialogue.

MAKING COMPARISONS

1. Classification

Have students list their favorite humorous cartoon strips, TV programs, magazines, and books, and then categorize them as to those that feature such things as children, animals, sports, outer space, hobbies, or olden times. Discuss the similarities and differences in the various types of humorous materials and their contents.

2. Realistic or Fantasy

Many humorous stories could actually happen, such as *To Think That I Saw It on Mulberry Street* (Seuss 1937) and the *Amelia Bedelia* episodes (Parish 1963, 1964). Other stories, such as *Mary Poppins* (Travers 1972), are pure fantasy. Discuss the differences between realistic and fanciful stories and have the students classify their favorites by story type.

CRITICAL/CREATIVE THINKING

1. Determining Cause and Effect

Have students identify the cause of humorous events in a story:
examples:
> Why did Amelia Bedelia bake a cake out of rubber? (Effect)
> She was told to bake a sponge cake. (Cause) (Parish, *Amelia Bedelia*)

> Why was Horton the elephant sitting on a nest in a tree? (Effect)
> The Mazie bird took advantage of his kind nature. (Cause) (Seuss, *Horton Hatches the Egg*)

2. Creative Problem-Solving

Many humorous tales involve a character's inappropriate solution to a problem. Have students suggest alternative, more feasible means to resolving the problems.

examples:

> What would you do if a bird asked you to sit on its nest of eggs? (Seuss, *Horton Hatches the Egg*)

> What would you do if your dog, Clifford, grew to be as big as a house? (Birdwell, *Clifford, The Big Red Dog*)

3. Analyzing the Reason for Laughter

Have students discuss some jokes or stories that have made them laugh. Then have them try to analyze why they laughed. Reasons given might include confusion, mistaken identity, put-down, slapstick, satire, or timing.

4. Creative Riddle-Solving

Absurd jokes call for very creative reading and thinking because the answers aren't realistic. This type of riddle can be used to encourage creative thinking.

example:

> How can you fit six elephants into a VW?
> *Answer:* Put three in the front and three in the back.

Humor and the Study Skills

*Every time a man (woman) smiles,
but much more when he (she) laughs, it adds something
to this fragment of life."*[1]

Work on reading study skills should be an essential part of an elementary reading program. Not only can these skills help to make students' informational reading more efficient, they can also help students to study more successfully and independently. The activities in this section are designed to provide instruction and practice in basic reading/study skills through the use of humorous activities so that students will be able to enjoy the process of acquiring these essential tools.

1. Making a Date-Line

After students have read or listened to a humorous tale, have them make a date-line of the chronological order of events.

2. Constructing a Map

Have the students use a map to locate places mentioned in a humorous story, such as places in Paul Bunyan tales.

[1]Laurence Sterne, *source unknown.*

3. Locating Information About Humorists

Have students do some research about their favorite comedian, cartoonist, or humorous author. They could use a variety of up-to-date reference tools and/or write to the humorist, if living, for information.

4. Researching Humor in Other Lands

Each country pokes fun at something uniquely its own. Expose students to the humor of other countries. The United Nations book, *Laughing Together* (Walker 1977), is a good source of this type of material. In addition to making comparisons with American humor, sources of similarities and differences in humor among many nations could be explored. Have students find on the map the locations of the countries whose humor they are studying.

5. Recording Local Folklore

Children's own folklore, such as jump rope and counting rhymes, cheers, riddles, and jokes, can be used to improve students' reading, writing, and research skills and also to help them make the vital connection between their own personal worlds and the world of reading. Have students write down their own individual "folklores," or have them work in teams of two, one dictating and one writing. Then have them interview older people, such as their grandparents, and write down their folklore. The results of their research could be compiled into a class booklet of folklore favorites.

Laughter and the Language Arts

*Better to write of laughter than of tears, because to
laugh is proper to the man (woman).*[1]

The four language skills—reading, writing, speaking, and listening—are closely related. Practice and development of one skill can increase the potential for development in the others, and unless students have facility in all the communication skills, they may not realize the true value of reading as a communicative process.

Students will also better appreciate the literary efforts of others after they have attempted to be creative themselves. The activities in this section foster reading growth and creativity through a variety of language arts activities that revolve around humor.

[1] Francois Rabelais, *Works: To the Reader.*

1. "Dear Cartoonist"

Review letter-writing techniques by having students write letters to their favorite cartoonists or comedians. Among other questions, they could ask their favorites about the importance of reading, both in their careers and personal lives. Before students compose their letters, review elements such as heading, date, salutation, closure, the proper style to use in the body of the letter, the importance of careful proofreading, and the information to be included on the envelope.

2. Cartoon Story-Writing

Show students a complete cartoon strip (not from a serial that is continued the next day) and have them each write a story about it. Put the stories on a bulletin board with the cartoon strip.

3. Writing Their Own Tall Tales

After students have listened to or read stories about Paul Bunyan, Pecos Bill, or others, have them write their own tall tales. They could write about these characters or create their own.

4. Creating Humorous Limericks

Read to students or have them read humorous limericks. Then ask them to write their own to share with others. Remind them that the first, second, and fifth lines must rhyme and that the third and fourth lines must rhyme.
example:
> There was a young fielder named Kit,
> Who at baseball would show her true grit;
> For while chasing a ball
> She took a bad fall
> But still caught the ball in her mitt!

5. Writing Humorous Poetry

Give students opportunities to individually or collectively create a humorous poem. Provide them with the first line of a poem and ask them to complete it. The class could generate a list of rhyming words and then look in a book of rhyming words for others. Make sure they know the meaning of each word.
examples:
> Finish these poems:

> The little man had a jolly laugh.

_____

_____

_____

> Virginia had a lovely smile.

_____

_____

_____

Children, books, and laughter

_____

_____

_____

Need help? Look in a book of rhyming words. Or use the following:

laugh		**laughter**	**smile**	
chaff	paragraph	after	while	compile
draff	phonograph	rafter	style	crocodile
epitaph	photograph	hereafter	tile	defile
epigraph	riff-raff		pile	domicile
autograph	staff		versatile	erstwhile
flagstaff	stenograph		vile	file
giraffe	telegraph		while	guile
graph	behalf		wile	infantile
lithograph	calf		aisle	juvenile
monograph	half		awhile	meanwhile
			beguile	mercantile
			bile	mile

6. Improving Oral Reading with Riddles

Riddles are excellent for oral-reading activities. They are short and usually contain two parts. If riddles are selected that have easy and more difficult parts, students of different reading abilities can enjoy them together. Put students in groups of two to practice their oral-reading skills using riddles. Care must be taken to make questions sound like questions and statements sound like statements. Oral reading could be tape-recorded and played to other students to elicit their reactions.
example:
>(*More capable reader*) What has arms and legs but no head?
>(*Less capable reader*) A chair.

7. Dramatizing Humorous Materials

Have students act out a nursery rhyme or humorous scene from a book using mime or speaking parts.

8. Punctuating Humor

Differences in punctuation of sentences often provide humorous changes in meaning. Through an activity using a variety of sentences and possible variations in punctuation, students can see the importance of proper punctuation in communicating the intended meaning of their ideas.

example:

Let's eat, Grandma, I'm hungry! Let's eat Grandma, I'm hungry!

Have students make up their own sentences using different punctuation to alter the meanings. Have them read the sentences aloud to convey the proper expression.

9. Punctuating Cartoon Strips

Give students a cartoon strip and ask them to circle all the punctuation marks. Then have them read the cartoon strips aloud and pay careful attention to the punctuation. Then give students another cartoon strip in which all of the punctuation marks have been covered or eradicated. Ask the students to supply the appropriate punctuation and then read the cartoon strip aloud correctly. Discuss how punctuation or lack of it can alter the intended meaning.

Building Lifelong Readers Through Laughter and Humor

*Happy is he (she) who has laid up in his (her) youth
a genuine and passionate love for reading.*[1]

Teaching students to value reading, be interested in reading, and want to read on their own for information or pleasure is an important goal of the reading program. If children know how to read but never read for their own enjoyment, they will miss invaluable opportunities to strengthen their reading skills and enrich their lives through independent reading. Giving students an opportunity to respond freely in class to humorous materials will help them to discover that reading can be pleasurable and fun. The activities in this section can be utilized to expose students to a variety of humorous reading materials in a relaxed manner.

36 [1]Rufus Choate, *source unknown.*

1. Come Read and Laugh Center

Fill this corner or shelf with humorous materials, including joke books, comic books, cartoons, amusing items from the newspaper, books of political cartoons, humorous trade books, handouts of humorous sayings, and student jokebooks. Encourage students to spend some time each week at this center selecting humorous materials to read.

2. Humorous Show and Tell

Have a short session periodically during which students can read aloud their favorite jokes, puns, poems, or excerpts from funny stories. Encourage expressive reading.

3. Joke-of-the-Week or Humorous-Story-of-the-Month Contest

Encourage students to contribute jokes anonymously to a contest box. Then have students each draw a joke from the box and read it to the class while a panel of impartial judges rates the audience's response.

4. Exploring American Humor

Have a reading unit devoted to the special humor that developed with the growth of our country. Include folktales, almanacs, short stories, newspaper columns, fables, poems, essays and novels. Explain to students that much American humor began as oral jokes and anecdotes exchanged around campfires, cowboy trails, and riverboats. These were then expanded and developed into tall tales such as those of Paul Bunyan and Pecos Bill. Throughout American history, writers such as Benjamin Franklin, O. Henry, Oliver Wendell Holmes, Mark Twain, Art Buchwald, Mary Kerr, and Erma Bombeck have used their special understanding of our nation and its people to help us learn to laugh at ourselves.

Read to students or have them read selected samples of American humor. An excellent source for background information for teachers is *The American Way of Laughing* (Weiss 1977). Each student could then research a favorite author or type of humorous material, such as the tall tale or political cartoon; or students could write their own modern folk tales, fables, tall tales, or humorous editorials.

5. Humorous Book Reports

Require students to each read at least one humorous book during the year and then report on it in an amusing way. Students could make a cartoon strip booklet of major events, write a humorous poem, illustrate the most amusing incident, or dress as the funniest character. Students who are more avid readers could be encouraged to read several different types of humorous books, such as tall tales, amusing novels, or joke books.

6. Humorous Sustained Silent Reading

Give students a fifteen- or twenty-minute period once a week in which each one picks out some humorous reading material and silently reads just for pleasure.

7. Developing Humorous Reading Appreciation

Students will often appreciate listening to humorous materials that they are not yet capable of reading themselves. It is important for the person reading aloud to show an appreciation of the humorous materials so that the listeners will have a good model to copy. Give the students an opportunity to discuss the material so that they can begin to realize why they laugh at some things more than others.

8. Poetry Memorization

Give students an opportunity to select favorite humorous poems to memorize and share with the class. They may be creating a happy memory bank that will give them a lift on a difficult day.

Humor is everywhere. It can be found in print in many forms. It lightens our lives and produces a happy feeling that helps us maintain balance and perspective on our world. Humor is a natural resource and stimulus to utilize in improving reading skills in students of all ages.

Readings and References

AHO, MARY LOUISE. "Laughing with Children." *Childhood Education,* Vol. 56 (October 1979), pp. 12–15.

BEECHER, EUGENE L. "Notes On: What is Humor? What Are Some

Functions of Humor Within the Classroom Setting." *Inservice Insights.* Vol. V, No. 1, January 1978. Rhode Island College: Providence, Rhode Island.

BIRDWELL, NORMAN. *Clifford—The Big Red Dog.* New York: Scholastic, 1966.

CROSS, FARRELL and WILBUR. "Cheers: A Belly Laugh Can Help You Stay Well." *Science Digest,* November 1977, pp. 15–18.

KEITH-SPIEGEL, PATRICIA. "Early Conceptions of Humor: Varieties and Issues." *Psychology of Humor: Theoretical Perspectives and Empirical Issues.* Eds. Goldstein and McGhee. New York: Academic Press, 1972.

LORENZ, ESTELLE. "Excuse Me but Your Idiom Is Showing." *Reading Teacher* (October, 1977), pp. 24–27.

MARTINEAU, WILLIAM H. "A Model of the Social Functions of Humor." *Psychology of Humor: Theoretical Perspectives and Empirical Issues.* Eds. Goldstein and McGhee. New York: Academic Press, 1972.

MCGHEE, PAUL E. "Children's Appreciation of Humor: A Test of the Cognitive Congruency Principle." *Child Development,* 47 (1976), pp. 420–426.

MCGHEE, PAUL E. "Sex Differences in Children's Humor." *Journal of Communication* (Summer 1976), pp. 176–189.

MONSON, DIANNE. "What's So Funny?" *Early Years,* Vol. 7 (February 1977) pp. 26–29.

PARISH, PEGGY. *Amelia Bedelia.* New York: Harper & Row, Pub., 1963.

PARISH, PEGGY. *Thank You Amelia Bedelia.* New York: Harper & Row, Pub., 1964.

SEUSS, DR. [Theodore S. Geisel] *And to Think that I Saw It on Mulberry Street.* New York: Vanguard, 1937.

SEUSS, DR. [Theodore S. Geisel] *Horton Hatches the Egg.* New York: Random House, 1946.

TRAVERS, PAMELA L. *Mary Poppins.* New York: Harcourt Brace Jovanovich, Inc., 1972.

TSCHUDIN, RUTH. "Secrets of A+ Teaching." *Instructor,* Vol. 88 (September 1978), p. 74.

WALKER, BARBARA K. *Laughing Together.* New York: Four Winds Press, 1977.

WEISS, HELEN S. and M. JERRY WEISS. *The American Way of Laughing.* New York: Bantam, 1977.

WOOD, E. T. *English Prepositional Idioms.* New York: Macmillan, 1967.

chapter two

turning **TV** watchers into readers

Introduction

Television is the pervasive American pastime,
cutting through ethnic, class and cultural diversity.
It is the single binding thread of this country,
the one experience that touches all of us.[1]

Since the 1950's commercial television has been an important aspect of almost every American child's life. Virtually all American homes (98%) have working television sets (R. Liebert 1977).[2]

Most children are conscious of TV from the time they begin to talk, and by the age of three they are regular viewers (Garry 1967). The Gallup education poll (1977) showed that, on the average and regardless of age, children in the United States spend more time each weekday looking at TV than they spend on homework and recreational reading combined; they either watch several shows each day deliberately, or are subjected to a turned-on set for several hours, or both (Gallup 1977).

Television is the single most important source of news, entertainment, and leisure time activity in the U.S. Once a set is purchased, it permits adults and children alike to be entertained inexpensively and informally at home. Children love TV and watch it for several reasons: to be entertained, to get information, and to be with other people (Schramm 1961).

Commercial TV is a continual source of fascination for children. They talk about their favorite programs, play-act or mimic scenes and

[1]Jeff Greenfield, *Television: The First 50 Years.*
[2]Chapter readings and references appear on page 82.

characters, and spend time carefully planning their viewing schedules. Their thoughts are often with what they have seen, are seeing, or will see on TV.

In our schools, it does little good to teach as if TV did not exist. As John Dewey said in 1897, "The subject matter of education cannot be separated from the actual everyday experiences of the persons being taught" (Dewey 1966). Instead of considering TV to be an anti-education monster, it should be accepted as an integral part of a child's life and its drawing power used to help teach reading. Since most students are going to watch TV anyway, why not use it in a positive way and relate it directly to reading?

Many teachers have found that when interest in TV-viewing is used, children not only learn better but teacher-student relationships also improve. Better rapport often develops when students feel that a teacher recognizes the importance of TV in their lives. Many teachers find that even reluctant readers show increased interest when school lessons are linked with television (Potter 1979; Steinberg 1976).

Studies have shown that students have improved in their reading ability while using TV-related reading activities. A program using commercial songs heard on TV to teach reading skills showed appreciable gains in reading achievement. The students had more confidence in themselves, read more fluently, and substantially increased their sight vocabularies. Their increased store of sight words enabled them to approach their regular reading lessons with better word recognition and more motivation for reading. The pupils already knew the language of the familiar TV tunes and there was little need to develop their background for the songs. The pupils were learning to read what they could already sing. The material could also be worked on again without the students' losing interest (Soloman 1975).

Students participating in a TV reading program using scripts in the Philadelphia schools gained at least a year and a half in achievement for every year in the program (Dalzell 1976). Another study using TV scripts showed that even students who were struggling with reading and were unmotivated began interacting, reading, writing, and developing creative skills as they worked with both commercial TV scripts and wrote their own (Waters 1974).

Research has also shown that children can learn critical thinking skills, such as how to recognize propaganda techniques on TV, and can then transfer this learning to recognizing propaganda in print (Cook 1973). Another study indicated that children do learn sight words and pick up vocabulary from TV and that teachers' knowledge of TV viewing habits could be converted to reading lessons that could make use of what students know of televised words (Mason 1965). It is possible to transform TV from a kind of sedative that often dulls the senses into a stimulant that can help students improve their reading and thinking skills.

Many TV programs stimulate reading. Following the TV productions of *Peter Pan* and *The Borrowers,* for example, there was a resurgence of interest in those books. A strong linkage has developed between books based on TV programs and promotions of books on TV. Children often prefer these books because they can already relate to them before they are opened and find them easier to read as a result. One study found that 89 percent of the students surveyed had watched at least one program on TV that had caused them to read a book (Busch 1978). Some teachers have also used students' TV interests to make book selections that students enjoyed reading (Spiegler 1956). Thus, television not only has the power to motivate interest in reading, but can be used effectively as an important link to reading. Books connected to television-viewing can be used specifically to help improve students' basic reading and thinking skills.

While working on reading-related TV activities, students can also be helped to make better use of TV to expand and enrich their lives. One study found that when students read *TV Guide* in class and discussed the selections, less time was spent in viewing TV and students did other things instead, such as play with companions, school work, read, go to clubs, and work with hobbies (Folger 1953).

This chapter gives suggestions for ways to improve basic reading skills through children's interest in commercial and public TV programs. Each activity contains either work with print or suggestions for a reading-related activity. The ultimate goal of most of these activities is to show students that many of the things they are viewing or similar things can also be found in written form. They can apply the same skills and thought processes. But care must be taken to transfer these skills to apply them to reading. Many of these activities will not only help students to improve in basic reading skills and attitudes, but will also help them to develop the skills and attitudes necessary to become thoughtful, discriminating viewers.

The activities suggested in this chapter can be accomplished with a variety of programs, not just the ones given as examples. Also, since television favorites change from season to season, the activities can be modified to fit current favorites. Most of these TV-related activities are also easily adaptable to any age group.

However, some caution is needed when requiring students to watch a certain TV program. Television viewing is often a family activity and students may not have exclusive access to the TV set when the assigned program is being broadcast. It is best to suggest team viewing in someone's home, if possible, or give an alternate but related assignment to those that aren't able to watch a particular program.

Most teachers find it exciting to work with TV in a positive manner to help students acquire new reading skills and practice the ones they already possess. The potential for the constructive use of commercial and public TV to teach reading is limited only by the imagination of the teacher.

SOURCES OF TV-RELATED MATERIALS

Reading materials related to television programs are readily available and each can be used for a variety of reading activities. The same material can often be used with students at different reading levels. The following sources can be used for TV-related reading activities:

TV guides
TV reviews
Posters of TV characters or programs
TV magazines
Books and stories about TV stars and programs
Books and stories about subjects mentioned on TV
Books and stories based on TV programs
TV programs based on books and stories
Video or audio-taped recordings of TV programs based on books and stories
Scripts of TV programs
TV star coloring books
TV-related comic books
TV-related cartoons
TV-related advertisements
TV-related greeting cards
TV-related film strips
TV-related bumper stickers
TV-related toys and games

DISCOVERING STUDENTS' TV INTERESTS

It is helpful to be aware of the favorite TV programs of students since TV offerings and students' preferences change rapidly. Programs popular in one part of the country may not be popular in another due to time differences or geographical preferences. Differences in socio-economic levels, intelligence, maturity, and general background are also related to variations in TV preferences (Becker 1973). A knowledge of students' favorites can serve as a basis of reference to TV programs and their characters when planning a variety of reading activities.

To get an idea of the kinds of programs students enjoy, it is helpful to ask them some questions either orally or through a written questionnaire about the programs they watch. Much information can also be gleaned through listening to their conversations at informal times, such as at lunch, before and after school, and at recess.

The following brief questionnaire may prove helpful:

TV-Interest Questionnaire

1. What kinds of TV programs do you like to watch best? Put checks beside your two favorites.

_____ cartoons   _____ mystery   _____ sports

_____ comedy   _____ news   _____ western

_____ doctor   _____ space   _____ other (list type)

_____ game shows   _____ soap operas   _____

2. What are your two favorite TV programs?

3. What do you like about each of your two favorites?

4. Who is your favorite person on TV? Why?

5. How many hours do you usually watch TV after school each day?

6. How many hours do you usually watch TV on weekends?

7. What kinds of programs do you wish were on TV? Why?

8. What kinds of programs do you wish were not on TV? Why?

Using TV to Get Students Ready to Read

For the very young child, television is the "early window onto the world."[1]

Young children are usually fascinated by television and spend many hours watching it. They can often repeat numerous details from their favorite programs and describe and mimic their favorite characters. Some of the first songs they sing are jingles they have heard on TV.

The use of familiar TV programs and characters as the basis for reading readiness activities can help students to relate their home experiences with their school activities and thus help bridge the gap between home and school. The activities in this section can be used to develop students' reading readiness skills while other activities for the readiness period can be adapted from those in the vocabulary, comprehension, and reading interest portions of this chapter.

1. Directed Watching and TV

Direct children to look for something specific when they are watching TV at home, such as different animals, types of jobs people have, or the program settings. Then, the next day in school, discuss the things they saw. This type of activity will help them to develop visual discrimination and memory skills.

2. Directed Listening and TV

Ask children to listen for and remember certain types of sounds they hear on TV and the next day discuss what they heard. They could listen for animal sounds, machine sounds, or indoor and outdoor sounds, for

[1] Alberta Engvall Siegel, *The Early Window: Effect of Television on Children and Youth.*

example. This type of activity will help them to develop their auditory discrimination and memory skills.

3. Remember and Draw

Have students draw a picture about a TV program they have watched. Then have them talk about their picture and the program.

4. Real or Make-Believe

Ask students to decide whether the programs they watch are real or make-believe, and why. For instance, they could compare Miss Piggy of The Muppets with a real pig.

5. Matching a TV Program with a Picture Book

Place a number of picture books in a prominent place in the room. Ask students to find a book that reminds them in some way of a TV program, through its characters, events, or settings. Then have students explain why.

6. Naming the TV Character

Place pictures representing students' favorite television programs on small cards. Put the cards in a box. Have students each draw a card and tell the name of the character and the program.

7. TV-Puppet Talk

Help students to make simple sock or paper bag puppets of their favorite TV characters. Then have them talk about their puppets or act out a scene from a program.

TV Techniques to Make the Speech–Print Connection

Long before they have learned to read . . . children may accumulate, through television, a fund of knowledge that was simply inaccessible to pretelevision children.[1]

Language-experience lessons in which the students dictate a story that someone writes down for them are educationally sound, but it is sometimes difficult to find a topic that will stimulate the students to verbalize. However, most students respond eagerly to opportunities to talk about TV, and a TV-related topic will often encourage them to open up and discuss things at great length.

[1]Neil Postman, *Television and the Teaching of English.*

The activities in this section are designed to stimulate students to use their interest in TV to dictate materials that can be used to create their own early reading stories.

1. TV Talk-Producers

The following are TV-related topics that can be used as topics for student-dictated stories.

- My favorite TV program
- My favorite TV character
- My favorite TV animal
- My favorite TV thriller
- My favorite TV comedian
- My favorite TV commercial
- My least favorite TV program
- The TV person I would most like to be
- Programs I would like to see on TV
- The program I would like to be on

2. Class TV-Booklet

A class booklet of student-dictated stories about their favorite TV characters and programs can be made and used frequently. Because these booklets can be kept and reread exactly as they were first stated, they will demonstrate the permanence of print.

3. Recycling for Reading

Make a classroom television set from an old TV set with the insides removed or from a cardboard box with two dowels for winding strips of paper (see illustration). Have students draw pictures to illustrate the sequences in their experience stories, attach the pictures to a long strip of paper, and have a good reader or the teacher read the stories while the illustrations are being shown.

box

roll of paper behind
opening in box

4. A New TV Program

Have students create their own TV show. Let them dictate the script and then either draw illustrations to show the appropriate actions or pantomime the parts.

Decoding via the TV Tube

*Teachers should not overlook the fact that television
is in itself a constant and interesting source of
linguistic information.*[1]

Children need to be taught ways in which to transfer the unknown printed form of a word to the oral form they already know so that they can increase their reading vocabularies. This section includes ways to use students' interest in television as the basis for developing their skills in sight-word recognition, phonics, structural analysis, context-clue usage, and dictionary practice.

SIGHT-WORD RECOGNITION

1. TV Sight-Word Treasure Hunt

To review words students are trying to learn to recognize at sight, have them categorize the words that they need to review according to a TV theme. After they have located the appropriate words, they should read them aloud for extra review.

examples:

- Find all the words that begin like a TV character's name, such as Mork or Laura.

- Find all the words that end like a TV character's name, such as Kermit or Mindy.

- Find all the words that name things that Miss Piggy can do.

- Find all the words that name things that Kermit can't do.

- Find all the words that tell about the Fonz.

2. Singing Commercials and Sight Vocabulary

Record some of the more popular singing commercials on audio tapes. Play the tapes and have the students sing along with them. Then write the

[1]Neil Postman, *Television and the Teaching of English.*

words to the commercials on the chalkboard and have students follow the words as they sing. Eventually, have them read the words without singing. Ask students to match isolated words and phrases, identify words they know, and put mixed-up lyrics into the proper order.

3. TV Sight-Word Review

Have students make up sentences about their favorite TV programs or stars using words they need to review.

4. TV Guide Sight-Word Search

Give students a copy of a TV guide and ask them to circle designated review words, such as *and, the, is, very, that, put,* or *when.* Suggest that students say each word as they circle it.

PHONICS REVIEW

1. TV Key-Words

Use TV characters as examples for beginning sounds. Post large pictures of these on the bulletin board with the beginning letters underneath. Have students make their own TV character sound booklets and draw pictures of the characters to help them remember the sounds.
examples:

F   Fonzie
K   Kermit
L   Laura
M   Mork
P   (Miss) Piggy

2. TV Beginning-Sounds

Have students think up TV-related words for each beginning sound. List these on chart paper with appropriate illustrations and add to them as students think of more.
examples:
   M   Mork, Mindy, Mighty Mouse, Maude, Munchkin

3. TV Tongue-Twisters

Have students dictate TV-related sound stories in which most of the words start with the same sound.

examples:
> Kermit kissed a kitty.
> The Fonz fought five fights.
> Mork made many mistakes on Monday.
> Miss Piggy poured purple punch from a pink pitcher at a party for poor pigs.

4. Combined Response TV Name Game

Say a TV character's name and, instead of calling on just one person, encourage all students to respond at the same time. Have each student select and hold up the letter that begins the name.

5. TV-Listings Sound-Hunt

Give students copies of the TV-listings page in the newspaper and ask them to pick out all the letters that sound like the first sound in Mork's or Benson's name, or ask them to list all the words that end like Piggy, or circle all the words with short vowels.

6. Blends, Digraphs, Vowels and TV

Use TV characters and program titles to review more advanced phonic skills.
examples:
- What blends do you hear in *Brady Bunch, Flintstones?*
- What digraphs in *Sha Na Na, Chips?*
- What vowel sounds in *MASH, Muppets?*

STRUCTURAL ANALYSIS

1. TV-Star Syllabication

Have students clap their hands for each syllable they hear as someone calls out the names of some favorite TV Stars.

2. Practicing Syllabication Skills

Have students practice their syllabication skills by dividing the names of their favorite stars or programs in the appropriate places.
examples:
> Shir/ley   *Hap/py Days*   Pig/gy

3. Structural-Analysis TV-Hunt

Give students a TV-listings page and ask them to list all the compound words, plurals, and contractions.
examples:

Compounds	Plurals	Contractions
Woodpecker	*The Dukes of Hazzard*	*Three's Company*
Flintstones	*Diff'rent Strokes*	*The Joker's Wild*
Battlestar	*The Jeffersons*	*I'm a Big Girl Now*

4. TV-Commercial Contractions

Copy phrases from TV commercials containing contractions on the chalk-board or on ditto paper. Have the students locate the contractions and then write out the two words that were joined together to make the contraction.

examples:

"*It's* the real thing." (it is)
"*You've* got a lot to live." (you have)

CONTEXT-CLUE USAGE

1. Finding the Missing Word

Give students dittoed exercises in which they must use the other words in the sentence to decipher the missing word.

examples:

There are eight _____ in the large family on *Eight is Enough.*

Mork has trouble understanding Earth's ways because he is from another

_____ named Ork.

2. Replacing the Incorrect Word

Give students dittoed exercises in which they must find the word that does not fit.

examples:

                                       strong
The Incredible Hulk has power because he is so *weak.*

               eight
There are *two* children on the program, *Eight Is Enough.*

3. Words from Outer Space

Some TV programs feature characters who use special languages or expressions. Ask students to explain what Mork means, for instance, when he says "na-noo-na-noo," "shazbut," "nimnul," or "bleem."

4. TV Noun–Pronoun Match

Give students some TV-related paragraphs into which they must insert appropriate pronouns.

example:

Miss Piggy and Kermit were going to the swamp for a picnic. _____

decided to ask John Denver to go. _____ went to the swamp with

_____ .

DICTIONARY PRACTICE

1. TV-Guide Alphabetical Order

Have students look through a TV guide and list a series of programs in alphabetical order.
example:
- **A** *Archie Bunker's Place*
- **B** *Brady Bunch*
- **C** *Carol Burnett and Friends*
- **D** *Dukes of Hazzard*

2. TV Dictionary-Keys

Have students make up their own TV dictionary-keys using TV words as key words.
examples:

short *a* (ă): *Dukes of Hăzzard*
long *a* (ā): *Dating Gāme*

3. TV Words of Multiple Meanings

Some words have different meanings when used in connection with TV. Have students look up such words in the dictionary, pick out the definitions which most relate to TV, and use the TV-related terms in oral or written sentences.
examples:

cast, channel, crew, pilot, screen, set, show, stage, star, tube, tune, spin-off.

Video Viewing to Build a Reading Vocabulary

The medium, by its very reach, can alter the American idiom overnight.[1]

Children have several vocabularies—listening, reading, speaking and writing—which change in importance and use with age. The reading vocabulary is built upon the listening and speaking vocabularies. Since

[1]Jeff Greenfield, *Television: The First 50 Years.*

getting the meaning is the most important part of reading, children cannot really read a word until they have had listening and speaking experiences with it. And because many phrases and statements frequently heard on TV are not fully understood by students, their vocabularies can be increased while reviewing the meanings of "TV words."

1. Meanings of TV Expressions

Write familiar TV expressions on the board and ask the students to explain what they mean.
examples:

"When donkeys fly"
"Cool it"
"It's ouchless and helps booboos heal faster"
"It's the real thing"
"Tired blood"

2. Making Sense of TV's Technical Terms

Give students a list of technical words or phrases often heard on TV. Ask them what they think is meant and then review the intended TV-related meanings. Ask them to collect other terms or phrases that they think are confusing. Keep a class dictionary of these terms in which the students write the meanings in their own words and give examples with the words or phrases used in context. A list of the terms and simplified definitions can be posted in the room and added to by the students.

adapted for TV
air waves
audio difficulty
based on
broadcast
cameo appearance
closed circuit
coming up next
credit
cue cards
film footage
flashback

live audience
live studio audience
live TV
made for TV
message from the sponsor
mini series
network
newsbreak
preempted
premiere performance
prerecorded
prime time

public service announcement
rebroadcast
rejoin
replay
rerun
schedule
series host
sign off
situation comedy

special edition
spin-off
sponsor
supporting characters
technical difficulties
telecast
teleprompter
video difficulty
will air from _____ to _____

The story that you have seen was true. Only the names have been changed to protect the innocent.

Any resemblance between these characters and any persons living or dead is purely coincidental.

Portions of this program were prerecorded before a live studio audience.

This program was filmed on location in _____.

Parental discretion is advised.

This program has been preempted so that we may bring you the following special.

We interrupt this broadcast for the following report.

We rejoin the network for the program already in progress.

3. Origins of TV Terms

Explain to students that the word *television* comes from *tele,* a Greek word meaning "far away," and *videre,* a Latin word meaning "to see." Then discuss with the students the fact that most TV-related words were adapted from words already in use when TV came into existence. Have them look up the origins of some TV-related words, such as *antenna, channel, series, star,* or *tube.*

4. TV Workers

Have students make a list of the jobs of people who are employed by the television industry. Discuss what each person does.
examples:

actress
actor
anchorperson
announcer
cameraperson
cinematographer
costumer
director
editor
engineer
lighting director
make-up artist
master of ceremonies
meteorologist

music director
narrator
newscaster
producer
production director
program director
prop person
public relations
director
set designer
scriptwriter
sportscaster
station director
writer

5. Alternative TV Titles

Stretch students' use of words by asking them to rename some of their favorite programs. Older students could use a thesaurus.
examples:

Think up a different name for these TV Programs:

The Muppets	Kermit's Club
Battle Star Galactica	Space Adventures
Little House on the Prairie	Life with the Ingalls
Mork and Mindy	Opposites Attract
Happy Days	The Great '50's

6. Supernatural Words

Many students are fascinated by supernatural or science fiction programs. Have them identify some of the types of beings on the programs, such as demons, devils, animal-type creatures, ghosts, genies, warlocks, were-wolves, witches, vampires, monsters, and space creatures. Have them look up the definition of each term and, if possible, its origin. Some students might be encouraged to read about one or more types of characters in an encyclopedia to gain additional information.

7. TV Crossword Puzzles

The TV crossword puzzles that appear in a variety of TV guides are an interesting way to stretch students' vocabulary. Duplicate the puzzles or laminate the originals and encourage students to try to solve them.

TV VOCABULARY HOMEWORK

Many words are seen on television; but just as students often avoid pictures when reading textbooks, they often avoid looking at printed words when watching TV. Homework assignments that call for students to notice the printed words on TV will not only prove to be more enjoyable for the students, but will also cause them to notice and read more of the words they are exposed to on TV. The following are TV related home-work activities that can stimulate students' vocabulary growth.

1. Listen and Remember

Encourage students to listen carefully to the spoken words on television; much new vocabulary can be learned in this way. Occasionally have a "New TV-Word Time" when students share words they have learned from TV. List the words, have the students explain their meanings, use them in sentences, and encourage them to incorporate the words into their writing and speaking.

2. See It, Write It, Study It

Ask students to write down four or five words they see on TV. Some words will be from lists of frequently used words; others will be proper nouns used in advertising, and some will be special TV-related terms. These words can then be classified by parts of speech and divided into the following categories:

names of people	names of products
names of places	television terms

3. TV Abbreviations

Have students make a list of all abbreviations and symbols used on TV and discuss their meanings.

examples:

lb.	N.B.C.
m.p.h.	F.O.B
yr.	D.O.A.

4. TV Descriptive Adjectives

Have students choose a commercial and list all the adjectives used to sell the product.

examples:

crispy, crunchy, delicious, healthy, nutritious

5. Antonyms and TV Ads

Have students rewrite a TV ad using antonyms of the adjectives and adverbs used and notice the effects. It might be helpful to make an audio recording of the commercial first and transcribe it from the recording.

examples:

"This delicious tasting crunchy breakfast cereal will delight your family."

"This horrible tasting soggy breakfast cereal will horrify your family."

Building Comprehension Skills Through Television

Every television program does make some impression on a child, as it does on every viewer.[1]

Whether televised, broadcasted on radio, printed, or simply spoken, for communication to be understood requires relating to and integrating someone else's ideas. Hence before working on students' reading comprehension skills, it can be helpful to introduce or review the necessary thinking skills. These can be studied first in reference to favorite TV programs, and then later applied to printed material.

The comprehension skills in this chapter can be developed by using TV-related situations. However, to make sure the transfer to reading is complete, these skills must also be reinforced in print. Some of the activities directly involve print. Others use TV to work on the necessary thinking skills; these can then be further developed through related reading activities.

GETTING THE MAIN IDEA

1. Main-Idea Match

Give students a short paragraph with a theme related to a TV character and have them select the correct main idea.

example:

> Miss Piggy was upset because she was not allowed to sing, on *The Muppets*. The guest star, Dolly Parton, was given all the songs. Miss Piggy told Dolly why she was upset and Dolly asked Miss Piggy to sing a song with her.

> Underline the main idea.

> a. All pigs can talk.
> b. Share your problems with a friend.
> c. Dolly Parton had a sore throat.

2. Main-Idea Debate

Have students who have watched the same program each write a one-sentence summary of the main idea. List all the main ideas on the chalkboard and have students select the best one or rewrite another. Then have them each write a one sentence summary of a story recently read and pick the best one.

RECOGNIZING DETAILS

1. Describing TV Characters

Ask students to each write a description of one of their favorite TV

[1]Betty Miles, *Channeling Children: Sex Stereotyping in Prime-Time TV.*

characters using as many details as possible. Have others read their descriptions and try to identify the proper characters.

example:

> This character is young, has brown hair, wears suspenders, is from another planet, doesn't understand all American ways. (Mork.)

2. TV Trivia or Awareness of Details

Have students think up questions concerning details of some of their favorite programs to ask others. The students who make up the questions must have the answers available. Follow up this activity with one in which students ask questions concerning details of stories they have read.

examples:

> What are the names of all members of the family in *Eight is Enough*? How many are males, females? What are their ages?

3. Identifying the TV Program

Have students list details about a TV program and let other students try to guess the name of the program.

examples:

1. two main characters	1. puppets that talk
2. Boulder, Colorado	2. guest stars
3. another planet	3. frog announcer
(Mork and Mindy)	*(The Muppets)*

This same type of activity can be done with a group of stories or books the students have read.

examples:

> 1. family story
> 2. shipwreck
> 3. island
> 4. resourceful
> (Wyss, *The Swiss Family Robinson*)

4. Analyzing TV Settings

Many students do not place proper emphasis on the setting in which a story they are reading takes place. The setting involves time as well as place. To help them give greater emphasis to the setting, ask them to watch a favorite TV show with a story line and then list all the different locations in which the story took place and also the different times of the day or the week. Repeat this type of activity with something they are reading.

SEQUENCING

1. Remembering the Sequence

Ask students to describe in order three different things that happened in their favorite TV show the last time they watched it. Then have them do the same type of activity in reference to a story they have just read.

2. Following the Usual Order of Events

Ask students to tell the usual order of events in a show frequently watched, such as *Laverne and Shirley, Little House on the Prairie,* or *The Incredible Hulk.* Explain to students that many programs follow a set order, such as:

- introduction of characters and setting
- introduction of problem
- search for solution to the problem
- solution of problem
- ending

Have students watch two of their favorite programs to see if they follow this order. Then have them analyze two stories they have read to see whether the stories follow this order of events or another sequence.

3. TV Scheduling

Have students study a TV schedule. Ask them if they see a time pattern in the types of programs offered. Are certain types of programs usually offered at 6 P.M. (news), 3–5 P.M. (children's programs), 1–4 P.M. (soap operas)? Have them discuss reasons for this type of scheduling.

CHARACTERIZATION

1. TV Characters and Descriptive Parts of Speech

Pick one well-known TV character and ask students to "brainstorm" about what he or she is like, using parts of speech. This same type of activity can be done based on a character in some material the students have read.
example:

Adjectives	Nouns		Verbs	Adverbs
beady-eyed	outlaw		rob	sneakily
rat-faced	cowboy		rustle	terribly
sneaky	villain		ride	grumpily
surly	man		sneer	slyly
evil-minded	coward		growl	loudly
rotten	thief		spit	lazily
low-down	crook		kick	dangerously
no-good	bum		stomp	menacingly
brainless	weasel		slouch	stupidly

ROTTEN RUFUS

2. Characteristics of TV Personalities

Have students carefully watch a character on a TV show and describe his/her personality. Then have them list examples of actions that support these descriptions and then explain why the TV personality might have these characteristics. Repeat this type of activity with a character in material the students have read.

example:

MORK

Characteristic	Example of Action by Character
dependable	Mork reports each week to Orson about America.
helpful	Mork helped a boy who ran away from home.
confused	When he could not open a can with the can opener, Mork peeled the label off the can because he thought he could get to the food that way.

Why do you think Mork has these characteristics?

Mork is trying to be helpful to everyone and dependable because he is from another planet and does not want to be sent back. He is confused because he does not understand everything that happens on Earth.

3. Likenesses and Differences in TV Characters

Ask the students how the characters in programs they enjoy are alike and different. If characters on programs such as *Benson* and *Diff'rent Strokes* were to go on a picnic, whom would they invite? If Laura, from *Little House on the Prairie,* could have a best friend from another program, whom would she pick? Then have them compare characters in materials they are reading.

4. Determining Accurate Characterizations

List different types of people or professions often seen in programs and commercials. Ask students to watch and discuss how they are portrayed. Help them to see how different programs often show common characteristics of these people. Then have them compare what they see on TV with what they have observed about these people in real life and also with what they have read. Are the TV characterizations accurate or stereotypes? Then have them look through their readers to see if different types of people are always shown in the same way.

examples to consider:
> cowboys, police and detectives, doctors, the elderly, homemakers, teenagers, men, women

5. Distinguishing Speech Patterns and Dialects

Ask students to describe the special speech patterns of characters such as Miss Piggy, The Fonz, Laverne, Boss Hogg, and Arnold. How is the conversational style of each one unique? Discussing the different kinds of speech used on TV can help students to better appreciate speech patterns when they read. Then have them read aloud selections with special types of speech and dialects, such as those found in the Pecos Bill stories (Bowman 1964).

6. Emotions and Moods of TV Characters

Have students list the types of emotions they observe in characters in TV programs. What kinds of feelings did the characters exhibit on *Mork and Mindy, Dukes of Hazzard, Little House on the Prairie, Eight Is Enough* or *The Muppets*? How were these emotions or moods expressed? Then have them do a search for different types of emotions or moods in a story they are reading.

example:

TV MOOD AND EMOTION SHEET

Program: *The Muppets*

Mood or Emotion	Ways Expressed
Anger	Miss Piggy slammed the door in Kermit's face
Embarrassment	Kermit hid behind the curtain when he lost his collar

7. Costuming and Characterization

When students read, they must usually imagine the types of clothing worn by the characters; but on TV, costuming plays a very important role. Have students discuss the style and appropriateness of the clothing worn by some of the characters on TV. Then ask them to imagine the kinds of clothing being worn by the characters in the selections they are reading.

example:

Analyze the clothing worn by these TV characters:
Miss Piggy, Mork, the Fonz, Laverne, The Incredible Hulk, The Ingalls family

RECOGNIZING POINT OF VIEW

1. Determining Point of View

Have students discuss how different characters on a TV program would regard the same thing. For example, how would Kermit feel about visiting the swamp where he was born? Would Miss Piggy feel the same way? How would Laura on *Little House on the Prairie* feel if she cut her hair? Would her father or husband feel the same way? This same type of activity can then be done in reference to some material the students are reading.

2. Empathy and Perspective

To get more out of what they read, students need to be able to put themselves "into another's shoes." Ask them how they would feel if they were Mork and trying to make sense of Earth, or if they were Mary, the blind daughter on *Little House on the Prairie*? Then have them try to empathize with characters in the materials they are reading.

MAKING COMPARISONS

1. TV Program Categorization

Have students list and then categorize their favorite TV programs. This type of activity can also then be done with the various types of stories they have read.

examples of categories:

adventure shows	movies
animal shows	musical programs
cartoons	news
comedies	panel shows
crime shows	police stories
debates	science fiction
documentaries	soap operas
drama other than crime	specials
educational programs	sports
family dramas	talk shows
game shows	variety shows
interviews	young adult comedies
medical dramas	

2. Comparing News on TV and in Newspapers

Discuss with students the types of items covered on TV news programs. Guide the students to recognize that a TV news program is not able to describe a full day's worth of world and local events, or to provide the detailed background information that a newspaper or newsmagazine can offer. However, a TV news program's coverage is much more current, often including videotape or film highlights of fast-breaking stories, and live reports, sometimes transmitted from far away by satellite. Have students watch a local TV news program and then compare it to the news in a local newspaper or news magazine. What is missing from the TV news? What is missing from the newspaper or news magazine report?

3. Determining Fact or Opinion

Help students to become more critical when they read or watch the news. Explain to them how bias can be present in the presentation of news. Have students watch the news several nights in a row and try to detect bias. Examples of what they might look for include:

Which candidate for election does the newscaster seem to favor?

Which athlete or team does the sportscaster appear to favor?

Documentaries could be critiqued in the same way. Are only facts being presented or is the program trying to influence the viewer? Encourage critical thinking and skepticism. These same types of activities can then be done with newspapers and factual books.

4. Critiquing the Critic

Have students watch a TV program and give their opinion of it. Then have them read a published review and compare it with their own. How are they similar, how are they different, and why?

DETERMINING CAUSE AND EFFECT

1. Relating Cause and Effect

Help the students to see the relationship between cause and effect by asking them questions such as:

> When Arnold and Willis on *Diff'rent Strokes* went to live with Mr. Drummond, what effect did this have on their lives? What effect did it have on Mr. Drummond's life?
>
> When Mary on *Little House on the Prairie* lost her sight, how did this affect her life? her parents' lives?

Then have them do this same type of activity based on events in materials they have read.

2. Determining Cause and Effect in Commercials

Have students find examples of how TV advertisements are used to show cause and effect. Then have them do this type of activity using advertisements from newspapers or magazines.
example:
> "Ring around the collar" is caused by _____ and cured by _____.
>
> Headache is caused by _____ and cured by _____.

Continue the discussion by asking students if these are the only solutions.

CRITICAL/CREATIVE THINKING

1. Reality or Fantasy

Some students think everything they see on TV is real. Help them to recognize that some programs, such as *The Incredible Hulk*, are fantasy. List students' favorite programs on the board and have them consider whether they represent real or fantasy situations. Similar activities can be done with stories they have read.

example:

State whether each of these programs could be real or is fantasy.

_____ *The Muppets*   _____ *The Incredible Hulk*

_____ *Laverne and Shirley*   _____ *Mork and Mindy*

_____ *Happy Days*   _____ *Little House on the Prairie*

2. TV Believability, Consistency, and Originality

Discuss the terms believability, consistency and originality in terms of popular TV shows such as *Happy Days* and *Mork and Mindy*. How believable is the story, how consistent is the format of each different program, and how original is the plot or theme? Then have the students do the same type of activity with series books they have read, such as *The Hardy Boys, Nancy Drew* Series and the Laura Ingalls Wilder books.

3. Effects of Special Effects

Discuss the roles that special-effects experts play in making things seem to happen which really can't, like Peter Pan flying, vampires turning into monsters, chairs and bottles being broken over people's heads without leaving a cut, David Banner turning into the Incredible Hulk, or dinosaurs walking in New York City. Then have the students discuss some problems they might encounter if they were trying to make a story they were reading into a TV production. What special effects might they need? How would they do them?

4. Analyzing Story Elements

Use commonly watched TV programs to begin an analysis of story elements. Assign students who are planning to watch the same program to look for and take notes on different program characteristics, such as plot, setting, dress, dialogue, and characterization. Students who cannot watch the program could be given a similar play or story to read or some background literature about plot, setting, or other story elements so that they could contribute to the class discussion. The following day discuss the program, letting each student comment on his/her assigned aspect. The same type of activity can be done with a story that is read. Assign different students a different aspect of the story on which to concentrate. Then have a group discussion on the different elements of the story.

Protecting the Young Consumer

And a little child shall lead them to your product.[1]

Television commercials occupy about 20 percent of TV time (Summers 1966). During the seven hours that the average TV set is on each day, about 100 commercials are shown. In a year's time, about 36,000 commercials are broadcast on the average TV set (Claro 1974). Companies pay to have their products advertised and this money pays for the production and broadcast of the programs shown on commercial TV.

Children are sometimes confused about the purpose of commercials. Preschool to five- and six-year-olds sometimes think that their purpose is educational—that is, to tell how to do things like wash clothes with the right kind of soap or what kinds of cereals are the best to buy. By fourth grade, most children have a clearer indication of the profit-seeking motives of advertisers (Liebert 1977). Talk to students about their reactions to commercials. Do they think these advertisements always tell the complete truth?

Discuss the TV commercials aimed at children. Help the students to see that some ads try to persuade them to buy things that they don't need—or to urge them to persuade their parents to buy these things for them. Ask them to analyze which ads make them most eager to buy things and why. Have students compare ads on TV with ads on the radio and in newspapers and magazines. Help them to see that most ads on TV use the same kinds of appeals as ads in other media, but that the versatility of television can often make TV ads the most effective.

The activities in this section can help students to take a more realistic look at advertisements both on TV and in magazines and newspapers. In the process, they can be motivated to improve their basic reading skills and in particular their critical thinking and decision-making skills. To encourage student interest in studying advertising techniques, it might be best to first approach the subject from TV-related advertisements and then do similar activities with advertisements in newspapers, magazines, and on billboards.

1. Tabulating TV Advertisements

Have students keep a chart showing how many commercials they see during their daily TV viewing and the approximate amount of time allotted for commercials. They can then tabulate the number of advertisements seen in a magazine they like to read and the approximate amounts of space used for the ads. By calculating how many TV commercials they see in one hour or dividing the number of magazine advertisements into the number of pages of the magazine, they can get a

[1]Robert M. Liebert, John Neale, and Emily S. Davidson, *The Early Window: Effects of Television on Children and Youth.*

rough idea of the extent of advertising. Comparisons can be made between the amount of advertisements on TV and in magazines.

example:

Keep track of each commercial seen while watching TV. List the program, time period, the product being advertised, and length of the commercial.

Program: *The Muppets*
Time Slot: 7:30–8:00 P.M.

Advertisement	Length of Commercial
1. Frisky Corn Flakes	1. 30 seconds
2.	2.
3.	3.

2. Studying TV Advertising Techniques

Ask students to list several TV commercials, slogans, or jingles. Discuss why they remembered these and if they have ever made a purchase that was influenced by advertising. Help students to understand that ads are persuasive techniques and that they must learn to evaluate them on the basis of the real information given and their own personal experiences and knowledge. Discuss various advertising techniques used, including the following:

comparison approach
glittering generalities
emotional appeal
bad names or scare approach
glad names
testimonials of experts
testimonials of well-known people
testimonials of ordinary people
close-up shots of a product
music or songs or jingles
making the volume louder
repetition
nostalgia or "good-old-days" approach
patriotic appeal

back-to-nature approach
humor, cartooning
bandwagon approach ("everybody is doing it")
stacking the cards (telling only part of the truth)
showing experiments using the product
citing statistics ("four out of five doctors surveyed")

Have students suggest other techniques they have observed. Which techniques seem to be more persuasive? Have students each choose one commercial and analyze the ways it attempts to persuade the viewer. In some cases, they might find that more than one technique has been used. This same type of activity can then be done with magazine or billboard advertisements.
example:

ADVERTISING TECHNIQUES OBSERVED

PRODUCT ADVERTISED	Glad Names	Famous Person	Common Person	Band-wagon	Humor	Repetition
Oscar Mayer Bologna	___	___	X	___	X	X

3. TV Advertisements and Personal Needs

Ask students to watch a TV advertisement and relate it to themselves.
example:

COMMERCIAL VIEWING FORM

1. What is the commercial asking me to do?

2. Do I need what is being advertised? If so, why?

3. Does the advertisement tempt me to buy the product? If so, how?

4. Does it state or hint that anything will happen to me if I don't purchase the product?

4. Relevance of TV Advertisements to TV Programs

After the students have listed the commercials shown during a TV program, ask them to decide whether the commercials go with the type of program and the audience. Ask them if a certain commercial would be more appropriate if shown with a different program. Then have them look at advertisements in different types of magazines, such as home, comics, sports, and hobby magazines. Discuss how the advertisements are different in each type of magazine. Students could also look at the different types of ads in newspapers and discuss what kinds of advertisements are found in the sports section, home section, and other parts of the paper.

5. Making Their Own Commercials

Have different groups of students create a TV commercial for a fictional product using one or more of the advertising techniques listed in Activity

2. Remind them that they must keep within the fifteen-, thirty-, or sixty-second time frame. Then have them modify the same advertisement for use in a magazine or newspaper. TV advertisements could be drawn on transparencies or posters with the audio portion recorded on tape and presented to the class. The other students could then try to determine which type of advertising technique has been used.

Using Television to Teach Reading Study Skills

Television—like motion pictures and radio before it—
stimulates curiosity in a diverse range of subjects.[1]

Students need to utilize reading study skills when they are gathering information on their own. These skills can help them to locate, understand, and remember information they read. The level of mastery of these skills helps to determine how efficiently students will be able to learn in the different subject areas of the curriculum. Students' interest in learning and utilizing these necessary study skills can be enhanced when taught in reference to favorite television programs. The TV-related activities in this section can be used to develop some of the important study skills.

1. Summarizing

Have students study TV summaries or reviews and then write their own summaries or reviews of a program. Compare their efforts wth those in a TV guide.

2. Reporting and Note-taking

Ask students to watch a factual program, such as a *Jacques Cousteau Special* or *Wild Kingdom,* and take notes on the information given. Then have them write summaries of the programs from their notes and present them to the class. Students who have watched the same programs could compare their reports and synthesize the information to present to the class.

3. Using Typographical Aids

Discuss with students the different sizes of print used in TV ads either as seen on television or in TV guides. Discuss the reasons for using different sizes of print. Then let them examine their own textbooks to see how different sizes of type are used in their own textbooks.

[1]Leo Bogart, *The Age of Television.*

4. Understanding TV Symbols

Obtain copies of weather maps from local TV stations and discuss the symbols used. Students could keep a daily weather chart and give a weather announcement each day. Have them study the presentation styles of TV weather people and model their own announcements on them.

5. See the Show, Skim the Book

After students have seen a TV program that was adapted from a story or book, have them skim the book to find specific scenes remembered from TV. If several copies of the book or story are available, have students see who can locate the scene first.

6. Analyzing TV "Research"

After discussing the value of research, ask students to note if and how research is mentioned in TV ads. Is the actual data given or is it just mentioned that "research says"? Is the data given in possibly misleading or vague terms, such as "four out of five of the people surveyed" or "your results will vary"?

7. Conducting TV Program Research

Have students make up an interview form and question other students to try to determine which TV programs are most popular in their school. Put the results on the board summarized in graph form and use this to develop skills in reading and interpreting graphs and charts.

8. Logging TV Commercials

Have students learn how to make and read a daily log by making logs of the commercials they see each day. After making the logs, they could tabulate the number of commercials seen for each type of product advertised. They could also compare the different types of commercials shown at different hours of the day.
example:

TV-COMMERCIAL LOG

Commercial	Product	Time	Mon.	Tues.	Wed.	Thurs.	Fri.	Sat.	Sun.
Dunkin' Doughnuts	snack food	7:00 A.M.						X	
Meow Mix	cat food	7:30 P.M.		X		X			X

9. My TV-Viewing Log

The make-up and use of daily logs can also be studied by having students keep track of their own TV viewing. They could then tabulate the total hours they watched TV and the total hours they watched different types of programs, such as game shows or cartoons.

example:

MY TV-VIEWING LOG

Time Watched Week of _____ to _____

Program	Type	Mon.	Tues.	Wed.	Thurs.	Fri.	Sat.	Sun.
3–2–1 Contact	educational	6:00–6:30 P.M.						
The Muppets	comedy	7:30–8:00 P.M.					7:30–8:00 P.M.	
The Dukes of Hazzard	comedy					9:00–9:30 P.M.		

Total Hours
Watched Per Day   ____   ____   ____   ____   ____   ____   ____

Total Per Week
____

TOTAL HOURS WATCHED

_____ cartoons	_____ game shows	_____ soap operas
_____ comedy	_____ mystery	_____ sports
_____ doctor	_____ news	_____ western
_____ educational	_____ space	_____ other (list type)

10. Interviewing Techniques

Invite a TV station employee, such as a camera operator, set designer, lighting specialist, make-up person, director, actor, graphic artist, or weather reporter, to visit the class. Before the guest arrives have students discuss the types of things they would like to learn from the guest. Review techniques commonly used by interviewers on TV. Following the visit, list the things learned about TV, write "thank you" notes, and guide students to books and pamphlets that deal with TV careers.

11. Making TV-Program Time-Lines

Have students make a time-line to show the time settings of their favorite programs.
example:

1870–80s	1950s	1960s	Present	Future
Little House on the Prairie	*Sha Na Na* *MASH*	*Laverne & Shirley*	*Diff'rent Strokes* *Jeffersons* *Mork & Mindy* *Dukes of Hazzard*	*Star Trek* *Space 1999* *Battlestar Galactica*

12. Locating Program Settings

Have students locate the setting of some of the programs that mention real locations, such as *Mork and Mindy* (Boulder, Colorado), *WKRP* (Cincinnati, Ohio), *MASH* (Korea). Have students do research about the areas in encyclopedias or atlases. They could also write to local chambers of commerce for information and city maps of places in the United States; they could write to the Departments of Tourism or Embassies of foreign countries. Then have them note visual aspects of the programs that give clues to the geographical setting. For example, in *MASH*, notice the type of clothing worn and the pictures of the terrain. They could also make notes about verbal clues that give information about the geographical setting. On a large outline map, have them put markers showing the locations of their favorite programs.

13. Mapping Fictitious Settings

Have students list all the information they know about the geographical setting for a program that has a fictitious setting, such as *Gilligan's Island*. Then have them make up maps giving this information. The map that is judged the most accurate could be enlarged and posted in the room with additions or corrections made as more information is obtained from watching the program.

14. Using the TV Listings as a Reference Tool

Have a class discussion about the value and use of a TV guide. Encourage students to see that a TV guide is a reference tool that can aid them in making better program selections. Point out that guides to TV programs are found in daily and Sunday newspapers, shopping center newspapers, and in the magazine called *TV Guide.* Have them compare different types of TV guides and note that most of these guides give the dates, times, channels, and summaries of selected programs. Duplicate the TV section of a daily newspaper or project it using an opaque projector and ask specific questions that can help students to better understand and use it.

examples:

1. What kind of information is given in this part of the paper?
2. How could this part of the paper be of use to you?
3. What are the meanings of these terms: *rerun, repeat, special, paid advertisement, Part I, vs., premiere, (P), (HBO), (R), feature film, to be announced.*
4. How can you tell the difference between the name of the program and the description? (Different style of type is usually the answer.)
5. Where is the time of day listed, the date, the channel?
6. What two programs might give you the same information?
7. What two programs would you like to see that are on at the same time? Which would you select and why?

15. Using a TV Guide for Program Selection

Have students read a TV guide and plan two hours of viewing each day of the week for different types of people. Have them discuss the reasons for their selections. Students may enjoy planning selections for the following:

- a new immigrant to America
- a four-year-old child
- an elderly person
- a teenager in bed with the flu
- a student with a good sense of humor

16. Verifying Factual Knowledge from TV

Ask students to list any interesting facts they have learned from watching educational TV shows, such as *Wild Wild World of Animals, 60 Minutes, 20/20, 3–2–1 Contact,* or *National Geographic Specials.* Guide the students to realize that they can learn a lot about people, places and problems they might never encounter by watching these types of programs. Have them verify the information they get from TV with sources such as encyclopedias and maps.

Reading, Television, and the Language Arts

It is called a medium of communication, but it only reaches one way.[1]

Students need to realize that reading is related to listening, oral expression, and writing. Their interest in TV can be a great stimulus for a variety of activities that involve reading, writing, and speaking.

Many different languge arts skills are used to create the programs students enjoy. Help them understand the relationship between TV programming and the printed word. For example, a typical TV show "begins life" with a verbal description and a script. Activities can easily be employed to emphasize that both oral and written form of communication are vital to TV. The activities in this section are designed to use students' interest in commercial TV to develop their language arts skills.

[1]Jeff Greenfield, *Television: The First 50 Years.*

1. TV, Reading, and Writing

Have students practice using their new reading words by writing them in sentences that tell something about TV.

example:

> Use each of the following review words in a sentence about TV: *through, done, money, happy.*
>
> The Incredible Hulk walked *through* the door.
> When my homework is *done,* I can watch TV.
> A TV set costs a lot of *money.*
> Mindy usually looks *happy* when she is with Mork.

2. "Dear Mork"

For practice with letter-writing skills, encourage students to write letters to their favorite TV personalities asking them about what they like to read. It is usually best to write to actors in care of the production company listed in the program's credits; or contact the local or national TV station for information.

3. Talking Back to TV

Have students write to newspapers, TV stations, networks, the F.C.C., F.T.C., the National Association for Better Broadcasting, Action for Children's Television, and advertisers, about what they like or don't like on TV. Encourage them to be specific in their comments and to give examples. As most of the entertainment programs are supplied by independent production companies, it is best to write the networks for the addresses of the production companies involved.

> American Broadcasting Co., Inc. (ABC)
> 1330 Avenue of the Americas
> New York, New York 10019
>
> Columbia Broadcasting System, Inc. (CBS)
> 51 West 52 Street
> New York, N.Y. 10019
>
> National Broadcasting Co. (NBC)
> 30 Rockefeller Plaza
> New York, N.Y. 10020

National Association for Better Broadcasting
373 Northwestern Ave.
Los Angeles, California 90004

Federal Communication Commission (FCC)
1919 M St., N.W.
Washington, D.C. 20554

Federal Trade Commission (FTC)
Bureau of Consumer Protection
Washington, D.C. 20580

Public Broadcasting System (PBS)
485 L'Enfant Plaza S.W.
Washington, D.C. 20024

Action for Children's Television (ACT)
46 Austin St.
Newtonville, Mass. 02160

4. Script-Writing and TV Producing

Have students write and produce their own TV script and describe scenes, characters, settings, plot and sound effects. The play could be produced with a student cast and videotaped, if at all possible, so that students could see the results of their efforts.

5. Writing TV Takeoffs

Have students try writing a takeoff, or parody, of a show they watch frequently. Read some examples of takeoffs first, such as those in *TV: Behind the Tube* (Scholastic 1974) or in *Mad* Magazine. Have the students pick a favorite show and think about its interesting features. How is this show different from other shows? How can they exaggerate these features so that they will be humorous? Or can they reverse some feature, such as making the Incredible Hulk into the Incredible Bit.

6. TV-Inspired Creative Writing

Use TV shows as a source for creative writing topics.
examples:
>   What TV Means to Me
>   My Favorite TV Show and Why
>   My Favorite TV Character and Why
>   The Person on TV I'd Most Like to Be and Why
>   A Program I Wish Were on TV and Why
>   A Martian's View of America via TV Programs

7. Writing a TV News Story

Have students select a news story from the front page of a local newspaper and plan a TV news report on the same topic. The news report should be limited to one minute or less. Have students write the story and plan the types of pictures that will accompany the report.

8. Inventing a TV Show

Have students create a show that they think would be successful with their age group, write a description of the characters, the format, and an outline for the content of one episode.

Using TV to Hook Students on Reading

*Librarians report that children frequently ask for books
on subjects in which their interest has been aroused
through watching a television program.*[1]

One of the major goals of a reading program is to motivate students to want to read, to generate excitement about and enthusiasm for the printed word, and to help students develop a lifelong habit of reading for pleasure. Publishers for school book clubs and librarians alike have found that books related to TV programs are much in demand by children of all ages. And although the literary value of some of these materials may sometimes be questionable, the fact is that students are nonetheless reading, practicing their reading skills, and finding pleasure in print. With encouragement and direction, it is likely that they will go on to more traditional types of reading for pleasure.

If students want to read about TV topics, a variety of reading materials on different reading levels should be made availble to them. The activities in this section can be employed to use young people's interest in TV as a stimulus to getting them excited about reading, as a pleasurable, lifelong habit.

1. Hooking Them on Reading via Scripts

Most students enjoy reading a script, supplying appropriate sound effects, and pausing for commercials. Reading a TV script is more complex than watching TV, but it is an interesting and motivating activity. Sometimes even the most reluctant readers can be turned on to reading through TV scripts from popular shows. Students with reading problems could read the easiest parts or produce the appropriate sound effects. Contact a local TV station or the following for information about obtaining scripts:

> Prime Time School Television
> 120 South LaSalle
> Chicago, Illinois 60613

> Teachers' Guide to Television
> Box 564
> Lenox Hall Station
> New York, New York 10021

[1]Leo Bogart, *The Age of Television.*

2. TV-Events Table

Have an ongoing display that features books, magazines, articles, and newspaper clippings about TV events, such as the World Series, Super Bowl, Olympics, or National Geographic Society specials.

3. TV and Reading Interest-Center

Display TV-related books, magazines, articles, posters, and newspaper clippings in a TV and Reading Interest-Center on a shelf, table, or bulletin board in the room.

4. TV-News Period

Much is written about TV in the newspapers and magazines. Have a short TV-News Period each week and ask students to bring in items about TV from newspapers and magazines. This can often get them interested in reading more of the newspaper and a wider variety of magazines.

5. TV Recommendations

Put announcements of important programs in a special place or on a special bulletin board. If possible, include pictures from a TV guide or those obtained from local TV stations to advertise the program, as well as hints on what might be interesting to read before or after viewing the program. Information about authors, actors, directors, and settings could also be included. However, be careful not to give too much preparation, or "overkill," as it might dull students' anticipation. These announcements can alert students to programs of merit and also help them to begin a critical appraisal of TV programs. Change announcements regularly; don't leave them posted once the program has been on the air.

6. TV-Related Reading

Students might see a special on TV, such as *The Primates* with Jane Goodall or *Ocean Wonders* with Jacques Cousteau, and not only be interested in reading more about these things, but also gain some background information that will make the materials they select easier to read.

TV shows can often help develop the informational background needed to understand the content of a book as well as bring familiarity with some of the vocabulary used by the characters. Help students to become aware of programs that originate from books and have these books available for them to read and compare with TV versions. Encourage them to read other stories by the same authors or books on similar topics. The following are examples of TV programs or movies shown on TV that are book spinoffs:

> *Mary Poppins,* Pamela Travers
> *Little House on the Prairie,* Laura Ingalls Wilder
> *The Wizard of Oz,* Frank Baum
> *The Borrowers,* Mary Norton
> *The Story of Dr. Dolittle,* Hugh Lofting
> *The Grinch That Stole Christmas,* Dr. Seuss
> *Peanuts,* cartoons and books by Charles Schulz

7. The Program Versus the Book

After seeing a TV show that is related to a book the students have read, encourage them to discuss the differences, if any, between the TV show and the book. Have the students read aloud their favorite part of the TV story as it was written in the book. Encourage students to dramatize their oral reading as if they were the TV characters. What scenes were not in the book or TV production? What scenes should have been dramatized on TV?

8. Encouraging TV-Related Reading

If students seem to enjoy a certain type of program, encourage them to read similar things by recommending or reading aloud to them portions of similar types of books. Students could look up topics in the school library and make a bibliography of related books for their classroom. Programs and topics to use as points of departure: *Battlestar Galactica* (science fiction); *Little House on the Prairie* (historical fiction); also sports stories connected with athletic events on TV.

9. Keeping TV and Reading Logs

Help students to realize how much time they spend watching TV by having them keep personal TV logs, listing and evaluating the programs they watch. Maintaining the log will involve writing, reading, and critical thinking skills and will make them more aware of the amount of time they spend watching TV and the types of programs they watch. Students could compare their logs with each other during a brief viewer-sampling or survey. Then have them make logs of their recreational reading time, noting what they read, how long they send reading, and how they rate the materials read.

example:

Monday

Time Watching TV	Program(s)	Rating (great, good, fair, poor)
_____	_____	_____

Time Reading	Material(s)	Rating (great, good, fair, poor)
_____	_____	_____

10. The Day the TV Broke

Have students imagine what it would be like without TV. Have them interview older people who could tell them what they did for enjoyment before TV came into their lives. Have students "brainstorm" for a list of things they could do instead of watching TV. Post the list on the board and encourage students to add to it.

THINGS TO DO INSTEAD OF WATCHING TV:

read	ride a bike
visit a friend	write a letter
play a sport or game	listen to records
go for a walk	listen to the radio
take a hike	bake a cake

11. Comparing Reading and TV

Help students to see the differences between reading and TV viewing through an informal discussion. Guide students to see that there are some unique and special characteristics of reading such as:

- The reader is the boss:

    You can read what you want to, when you want to, and at your own pace. You can put down a book and pick it up at the same place, and reread difficult or especially interesting parts. A TV viewer is not really in control. You can turn the TV set on and off, but you can't slow it down, speed it up, or put it aside for a few hours. You have to watch the program when it is being offered regardless of other things you might want to do (unless you have a video recorder).

- You can take reading material anywhere:

  You can take a book to read on the bus. You can take it to the beach, in a backpack while camping, or carry it in your pocket. Although it is really difficult to carry a TV while floating on a rubber raft on a lake, a book or magazine can easily come along.

- You can dream while reading:

  Help students to realize how wonderful it is to use their imaginations—their "mind's eyes"—when reading. While reading, you can make each character look exactly the way you want him/her to look. Once you have seen a character on TV, he/she will always look like that in your memory.

- Books are inexpensive and easily available:

  Many students cannot afford to own their own personal TV sets, but it is very easy to borrow books from a public library.

- Books offer more variety:

  When selecting a TV program to view, you must choose one from a rather limited selection. However, when choosing a book from a library, there is a vast, almost unlimited choice.

12. Making TV-Book Commercials

Discuss TV commercials. Talk about the devices advertisers use to get people to buy the product. Then have students plan a TV commercial to "sell" a book they have read. Remind them that they must keep within the fifteen-, thirty-, or sixty-second time limit.

Television has been an important part of the lives of most Americans for many years and its impact upon the thinking and activity of young people is well documented. TV can thus provide an attractive resource for teachers interested in stimulating growth in basic reading skills. Since national studies indicate that young people spend more hours watching TV than they do attending school, TV is a force of tremendous influence that cannot be denied. Rather than fighting TV or trying to compete with it, teachers can easily and effectively utilize TV to help students develop basic skills in reading and learn to see reading, whether related to TV

81

experience or not, as a pleasurable and rewarding activity throughout their lives.

Readings and References

BAUM, L. FRANK. *The Wizard of Oz.* New York: Dover, 1960.

BECKER, GEORGE J. *Television and the Classroom Reading Program.* Newark, Delaware, 1973.

BOWMAN, JAMES. *Pecos Bill.* Racine, Wisconsin: Whitman, 1964.

BUSCH, JACKIE S. "Television's Effects on Reading: A Case Study." *Phi Delta Kappan,* Vol. 59, No. 10 (June 1978), pp. 668–671.

CLARO, JOSEPH. *TV: Behind the Tube.* New York: Scholastic Book Services, 1974.

COOK, JIMMIE ELLIS. "A Study of Critical Listening Using Eight to Ten Year Olds in an Analysis of Commercial Propaganda Emanating from Television." Unpublished doctoral dissertation, West Virginia University, 1973.

DALZELL, BONNIE. "Exit Dick and Jane." *American Education,* 12, 6 (July 1976), pp. 9–13.

DEWEY, JOHN. *Lectures in the Philosophy of Education—1899.* Edited by Reginald Archambault. New York: Random House, 1966.

DIXON, FRANKLIN W. *The Hardy Boys Mysteries.* New York: Grosset & Dunlap, Publishers, 1928–69.

FOLGER, SIGMUND. "Programs Report on TV." *Elementary School Journal, Vol. 53 (May 1953), pp. 513–516.*

GALLUP, GEORGE H. "Ninth Annual Gallup Poll of the Public's Attitudes toward the Public Schools." *Phi Delta Kappan,* Vol. 59, No. 1 (September, 1977), pp. 33–48.

GARRY, RALPH. "Television's Impact on the Child." *Children and TV.* Washington, D.C.: Association for Childhood Education International, 1967, pp. 7–13.

KEENE, CAROLYN. *Nancy Drew Series.* New York: Wanderer, 1980.

LIEBERT, DIANE. "Television Advertising and Values." *Television Awareness Training.* Edited by Ben Logan. New York: Media Action Research Center Publication, 1977, pp. 69–74.

LIEBERT, ROBERT M. "Television: An Overview." *Television Awareness Training.* Edited by Ben Logan. New York: Media Action Research Center Publication, 1977, pp. 69–74.

LOFTING, HUGH. *The Story of Doctor Dolittle.* Philadelphia: Lippincott, 1932.

MASON, GEORGE E. "Children Learn Words from Commercial TV." *Elementary School Journal.* Vol. 1965 (March 1965), pp. 318–320.

NORTON, MARY. *Adventures of the Borrowers.* New York: Harcourt Brace Jovanovich, 1953.

POTTER, ROSEMARY LEE. "TV-Based Q & A," *Teacher,* February 1979, pp. 32–36.

SCHRAMM, W. L.; J. LYLE, and E. B. PARKER. *Television in the Lives of Our Children.* Stanford, California: Stanford University Press, 1961.

SCHULZ, CHARLES. *Peanuts Treasury.* New York: Holt, Rinehart & Winston, 1967.

SEUSS, DR. [Theodore Geisel]. *How the Grinch Stole Christmas.* New York: Random House, 1957.

SOLOMAN, BERNARD. "To Achieve—Not to Please." *Learning Today,* 8 (Winter 1975), pp. 48–51.

SPIEGLER, CHARLES G. "Johnny Will Read If He Wants to Read." *Developing Permanent Interest in Reading.* Supplementary Ed. Monograph No. 81. Compiled by Helen M. Robinson. Chicago: University of Chicago Press, 1956, p. 185.

STEINBERG, ZINA. "Batman Books: Homemade First Readers." *Reading Teacher,* April 1976.

SUMMERS, ROBERT E. and HARRISON B. SUMMERS. *Broadcasting and the Public.* Belmont, California: Wadsworth Publishing Co., Inc. 1966.

TRAVERS, PAMELA L. *Mary Poppins.* New York: Harcourt Brace Jovanovich, 1934.

WATERS C. R. "Thank God Something Has Finally Reached Him." *TV Guide,* 22 (January 19, 1974), pp. 6–9.

WILDER, LAURA INGALLS. *Little House on the Prairie.* New York: Harper & Row, Pub., 1953.

WYSS, J. R. *The Swiss Family Robinson.* West Haven, Connecticut: Pendulum Press, 1978.

chapter three

motivating reading growth
through the joys of **ART**

Introduction

As the sun colors flowers, so does art color life.[1]

Throughout the ages, the creation and appreciation of visual arts have been among the most pleasurable and meaningful experiences in life. From earliest times, people have expressed themselves and learned through art and have turned to art for relief from the monotony of everyday activities.

Since art is the visual expression—just as words are the verbal expressions—of ideas and feelings, there is a strong relationship between the visual arts and reading. To learn to see anything really well is a basic skill that demands interaction of the whole personality with the things around it, whether one is looking at a picture or reading. Thus both the creation and appreciation of art can play significant roles in stimulating growth in basic reading skills.

Children enjoy art, whether they are viewing it or creating it. The National Assessment of Educational Progress for art has shown that students of all ages and background can become interested and active in such pursuits as drawing, crafts, and designing, both in and outside of school (NAEP 1977). Research studies have shown that reading skills can be improved through activities based upon art. From the late 1960's through the summer of 1978, twenty-one special programs incorporating art into the curriculum were studied. The programs were based in inner-city and suburban schools as well as in small, rural communities. Their goal was to improve the quality of education by including the arts in the school program. Results from the programs showed that the arts appeared to humanize the curriculum and the school environment, the

87

[1] Sir John Lubbock, *Pleasures of Life.*

students showed better self-concepts and increased reading scores, and there was reduced vandalism in the schools (Hall 1979).[1]

The Title I Children's Program, *Learning to Read Through the Arts,* sponsored by the Board of Education of New York in conjunction with the Guggenheim Museum, was designated as one of twelve exemplary programs endorsed as effective by the U.S. Office of Education. This program, which has been in operation since 1971, with one winter and one summer program each year, has utilized the arts in forms interesting to children and related to their needs. The basic goal is to improve the reading ability of those who are reading two or more years below grade level. The program focuses on the improvement of reading skills through motivating pupil interest in the arts. Activities revolve around painting, sculpture, mixed media, drawing, print-making, puppetry, crafts, film-making, cartoon animation, photography, cultural field-trips, student journals, and vocabulary introduction and reinforcement. According to test results, students involved in this program have made significant gains in reading (Seiferth 1975).

Combining art and reading can help students begin at an early age to be more sensitive to the visual aspects of their world. Art can make the learning environment look and feel more attractive and alive. Set aside one part of the room as an ever-changing art gallery in which to exhibit reproductions of great art, students' art work, and correlated art and reading activities. Attractive displays in the halls, cafeteria or gym will encourage casual inspection and informal learning during off moments and non-class periods. It is never too early to begin exposing students to beauty and to the works of recognized artists. If students become more aware of their school environment because it is interesting and attractive, perhaps they will feel the need to beautify their home and community environments as well.

MATERIALS FOR ART AND READING ACTIVITIES

Any teacher can use art in the classroom to motivate growth in reading; formal training or expertise in art is not necessary. Rather, a teacher needs to be enthusiastic and resourceful and recognize the value of teaching reading through art. Accumulate a supply of art materials, some colorful art reproductions, and a selection of art books at different reading levels (Rowell p.p.).

1. Art Materials

Suitable art materials must exhibit several qualities. They must be well adapted to pupils' levels of muscular development so that the students can handle and work with them quickly and spontaneously. Materials must also not be too expensive. Art materials available in the school that can be used for art and reading activities might include:

[1]Chapter readings and references appear on page 133.

chalk	clay	paint	paste
charcoal	crayons	paper	photography equipment

In addition, "found" or "scrounged" materials might be available in students' homes:

artifacts from different countries	greeting cards
blunt carving materials	magazines
boxes	newspapers
containers of all types	paper bags
dried flowers	wallpaper
egg cartons	wrapping paper
fabric and thread	yarn

2. Sources of Art Reproductions

When selecting art reproductions, it is important to get clear, colorful pictures. Black and white or poor-quality reproductions can limit the beauty and effectiveness of a painting. Large colorful prints are best for display in the classroom, but slides are often preferable when discussing art with a large group. When a slide is shown on a large screen, all the students can direct their attention to it (Rowell p.p.). Colored slides can easily be made from pictures in books and post cards using a regular camera or an *Ectographic* kit.

Inexpensive art reproductions are readily available from the following sources:

museums

art galleries (some galleries, including the National Gallery in Washington D.C., offer educator discounts)

art materials suppliers

educational publishers often have selections of inexpensive prints, slides, postcards, and multimedia kits

newsmagazines, such as *Time* and *Newsweek*, often contain art reproductions

educational magazines, such as *Instructor*, often have an art reproduction on the cover with a discussion of the art work within the magazine

department stores

bookstores

3. Books About Art

Art and "how-to" crafts books with colorful covers and interesting contents should be readily available. These can be borrowed from school or public libraries or purchased from commercial sources. Often they can be obtained quite reasonably from discount booksellers or at tag, yard, and garage sales. Encyclopedias often contain biographical sketches of artists and some reproductions of their works (Rowell p.p.).

4. Additional Art Resources

Materials and activities that can also be used to teach reading creatively through art are:

> field trips to art galleries, museums, places of beauty, and artists' homes
>
> related filmstrips and movies
>
> guest speakers, including artists, models, art historians, local craftspeople, art gallery employees or volunteers

ART TECHNIQUES FOR COMBINING ART AND READING

Students need opportunities to experiment with art techniques and materials. If a technique has been introduced by an art teacher, give students an opportunity to practice it in a way related to reading. After students have completed their work, it is important to display it in an attractive manner. Three dimensional objects could be displayed on window ledges or tables with an eye-catching display card. Flat objects could be mounted against black or colored paper so that a color edge of about a quarter of an inch shows all around. The following art techniques can be used effectively to combine art and reading:

> box sculpture
> calligraphy
> carving with blunt instruments
> chalk drawings
> charcoal sketches
> clay sculpture
> cloth pictures
> collage
> combination of several media, such as crayon and chalk, crayon and paint,
>   paper and chalk, crayon and magazine cutouts
> crafts including stitchery, pottery
> crayon drawing
> crayon wash
> cut paper
> dioramas
> finger paint
> mobiles
> montage (incorporating paper into a painting)
> mosaics from cut paper, letters, pictures
> murals
> painting
> paper cutouts
> paper strip sculpture
> papier maché
> photography

potato prints
puppets (sock puppets, paper-bag puppets, cutouts mounted on cardboard
    strips, hand puppets, finger puppets)
sponge prints

Throughout this chapter when the terms *illustrate* or *illustration* are used, students should be encouraged to use a variety of materials including crayons, paint, chalk, charcoal, cut paper, and combinations such as crayon, paint, and chalk. Art techniques should be chosen with the capabilities of the students in mind. These experiences should be pleasurable and not frustrating or embarrassing because of undeveloped art skills.

FINDING STUDENTS' INTERESTS

When using art to teach basic reading skills, it is important to use materials and art works that are appealing and interesting to the students. Students usually enjoy working with most types of art materials, and as they develop expertise with various techniques, they will enjoy the activities even more.

It is possible to get an indication of the type of art works students enjoy by showing them a variety of pictures and asking them which ones they like best and why. Works by Klee, Matisse, Manet, Van Gogh, Gauguin, Chagall, and Seurat seem to appeal to most students; paintings of the developing American West by Remington and Russell are favorites of many students. General interests can also be found by administering an "interest inventory" or by listening to students talk at relaxed times such as recess and lunch. If students are interested in animals, outer space, the ocean, or sports, for example, it might be wise to begin art appreciation and reading activities with art works related to these topics. It is best to start with types of pictures that interest most of the students and then to gradually expand their artistic horizons (Rowell p. p.).

Artistic Reading-Readiness Activities

What is art but life upon the larger scale?[1]

Many reading-readiness skills can be strengthened through art activities. Since most young children enjoy art, the reading-readiness period can be made more interesting by including some art-related activities. Additional ideas for increasing young children's phonic awareness, word-meaning skills, and comprehension can be adapted from activities given in those sections of this chapter.

[1]Elizabeth Barrett Browning, *Aurora Leigh.*

VISUAL SKILL DEVELOPMENT

1. Finding the Colors

Have a word for the day, such as *red*. Ask the students to locate objects in the room that are red. Then have them talk about other things that are red. Let them draw or paint a picture of objects that are red, using only red paint or crayons.

2. Noticing Similarities and Differences

Show students two art prints of the same subject, such as clowns or dogs. Ask them to describe how they are alike or different.

3. Shapes in Things

Give each student a piece of paper on which is traced a triangle, square, rectangle, or circle. Discuss shapes of familiar objects. Then have them make pictures with the shapes.

4. Visual Matching Bingo

Give students a bingo board with different colors and shapes of objects. Have them cover a square when shown a card with the same object and color. The first person with three in a row wins.
example:

5. Sorting the Objects

Give students magazine pictures, art prints, or objects to sort by color, shape, size, or topic.

6. Matching the Sequence

Show students a sequence of color strips, beads, or blocks. Have them arrange similar objects in the same sequence.

7. Sequencing Pictures

Display prints that show a sequence in nature, such as prints of the seasons. Then have students draw their own sequence pictures, dictating appropriate captions to be written under each illustration.

8. Finding What Is Out of Order

Show students a series of pictures that are out of sequence and have them arrange them in order.

9. Noting the Differences

Draw a simple figure on the chalkboard. Tell the students to look carefully at it. Then have them close their eyes while you change the figure. Ask them to describe the change. Gradually progress to more subtle changes.
example:

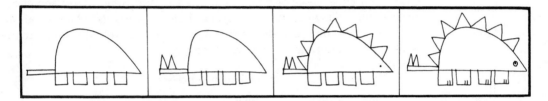

10. Art Works and Visual Discrimination

While students are looking at an art print or object, have them note the different colors and shapes and find the same colors or shapes in objects in the classroom. They could then dictate comments about the different colors or shapes.

11. Art Works and Visual Memory

After students have looked carefully at a print or art object, take it away and ask them to describe it. Write their descriptive comments down. Then show them the print again and compare it with their comments.

AUDITORY SKILL DEVELOPMENT

1. Listening and Doing

Give students oral directions for an art project.
example:
> Draw a brown house.
> Put a green tree beside it.
> Put a bird in the tree.

2. Listening and Matching

Show students an art print or picture. Then give them a sentence about the picture and ask them to decide whether it is correct or incorrect.

example:

> The clown is sad.
> (incorrect)

> The clown has dots on his hat.
> (correct)

3. Finding the Right Picture

Put three different art prints in front of the students. Tell them to listen carefully while one of the pictures is described. Then have them point to the picture that was described.

4. Colorful Responses in a Group

Give each child a set of strips of colored paper. Read aloud sentences such as the following that are missing their color words. Students are to select and hold up the appropriate strips of colored paper to complete the sentences. Encourage every pupil to respond.

examples:

> We have a _____ chalkboard in our classroom.

> Janice has on a _____ shirt.

> The sky is _____ today.

Artistic Language Experiences

The secret of life is in art.[1]

Students will usually converse naturally and informally about their experiences with art because they enjoy them. The activities in this section use experiences with art as springboards for experiences with recording language. For example, art can provide the framework for a group-experience story that can be dictated to someone. When the story has been recorded on a large sheet of paper it can then be reviewed in a variety of ways. While watching their very own words being written down and hearing them read, the students will be learning that written symbols stand for spoken words.

Children will also enjoy dictating information about their individual drawings and paintings to be written on the same pages with their creations. This experience of individual dictation about an art work can be a special sharing time between the child and the person taking down the

[1]Oscar Wilde, *The English Renaissance.*

words. The art work and story can then be taken home and shared with parents; or student-created stories can be bound into a large class booklet entitled "Our Stories about Art." Each child could illustrate at least one of the stories and make a contribution to the cover design. Students will usually be interested in reviewing these materials because they deal with enjoyable events they have experienced and contain their own thoughts and words.

1. Language Experience and Art Production

After students have worked on an art project, let them dictate information for a language-experience chart on such topics as the sequence of steps in the activity, their feelings about what they created, or stories or poems about their creations.

2. Language Experience and Famous Art Works

Encourage students to look carefully at an art print and discuss their reactions to it. Elicit facts, opinions, and ideas about the art work from the students. Then have them dictate their opinions of the painting or make up a story about it. Place the written copy of their impressions underneath the art print.

3. Art Works and Guided Language Experience

Gradually introduce students to new art terms that are relevant to a specific work of art, such as *texture,* or *color.* Have them practice using these words in meaningful sentences. Then have them dictate sentences using these new terms.
example:

Van Gogh's *Sunflowers*

He used bright *colors* to make the sunflowers.
The *colors* he used were orange, yellow, brown and green.
His picture has a rough *texture.*
The *texture* looks like little bumps and hills.

4. Art Works and Related Words

After studying and discussing an art print, have students look through magazines and cut out related pictures. For example, after studying Van Gogh's *Sunflowers,* the students could cut out pictures of other flowers. These pictures with their labels printed underneath could then be posted around the art print to provide more exposure to the printed word.

5. Puppets and Language Experience

After reading a story to students, have them dictate the story in their own words while someone records their dictation. Then have the students act out the story with stick or paper-bag puppets they have made while someone reads the story they have dictated.

6. Photography and Language Experience

Let older students who are having difficulty with reading take photographs, dictate corresponding stories, and create a display for their photographs and stories. The photographs could be a collection of prints dealing with one topic, such as transportation, or deal with a sequence of events, such as building a model or taking a trip.

Decoding via the Artist's Touch

The temple of art is built of words.[1]

The ability to decipher words in print is one of the most basic skills of reading, and research indicates that students who are taught how to decode words will show greater growth and will be better readers (Chall 1967). Moreover, children need to learn a variety of word-attack skills and to select the most appropriate technique in any given situation. To learn to use these skills automatically requires much practice. The activities in this section provide students with an opportunity to practice important decoding skills in a variety of ways that involve art.

SIGHT-WORD RECOGNITION

1. Word-Card Color Paintings

Give students several cards with color words on them. Ask them each to paint or draw a picture using only these colors. Then have them write the color words at the bottom of the picture.
example:
　　Paint a picture using the colors on these cards.

red	brown

2. Word-Card Object Paintings

Give student cards with the names of objects on them and let them each create a picture using these things. Have them write the names of the objects under their pictures.
example:
　　Make a picture with the words on these cards.

cat	house	flower

[1]Josiah Gilbert Holland, *Plain Talks on Familiar Subjects: Art and Life.*

3. A Picture to Remember

Ask students to think of something they could draw that would help them to remember abstract words, such as *of, the, if,* or *was.* Have students draw or paint the pictures and then write the words on them in meaningful sentences.
example:

4. Bumpy-Word Art

Give each child a sheet of writing paper on top of a small piece of screen wire. Have the students use crayons to copy words that give them difficulty onto the paper. The screen wire beneath the writing paper will create a bumpy surface. Students can trace over the word's bumpy surface while they are looking at it and saying it. This will help them to remember the word. Students could also make an appropriate illustration on the same sheet of paper.

5. Clay Words

Let the students make clay letters to spell out difficult words. As they are making the words, have them pronounce them.

6. Illustrating Phrases

To give additional review of words, print out short phrases for the students to illustrate.
examples:
    in the house, by the tree, on the horse

7. Making Word Games

Let students make their own games to review words. Stress that they must be carefully made so that the words and pictures can be understood. For these games, the students must match words with pictures.
    Examples of word games students could make themselves:

Bingo Cards | Bingo Leader Cards

PHONICS REVIEW

1. Comparing ABC Books

Direct students to compare the illustrations in different *ABC* books. Ask them which they like best and why. Have an *ABC* Book-of-the-Week and/or -Month contest. Reviewing these books will not only help the students to appreciate illustrations more, but will also give them additional exposure to the letters and their sounds.

2. Painting Letter-Sound Pictures

Have each student paint a large picture covered with things that start with a certain letter's sound. (For example, for the letter *p*, they might include peanuts, paper, pencils, and popcorn.) Students should dictate the names of the objects so that they may be written down on the paintings.

3. Art Techniques Alphabet Book

Have students make individual sound books using a different art technique for each letter. The books could be centered around themes, such as "animals," "things we like," "things that move," or "funny things."

4. Making a Phonics Picture

Print letters on a ditto in appropriate places. Give students a theme, such as "a park," "the beach," or "the zoo," and have them draw pictures in the proper places.
examples:

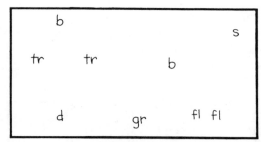

The Park

Draw a picture of something you could see in the park that starts with each of these letters.

Example of student's work

5. Studying Different Shapes and Sizes of Letters

Have students cut different sizes and shapes of the same letter from magazines and newspapers. Compare the different ways the same letter can be made. Then have the students cut out pictures of things that start with this letter's sound. Make a large bulletin board collage composed of the different sizes and shapes of the same letter and objects that start with its sound.

6. Potato Letter Printing

Have each child cut a potato in half and, using a dull knife, cut a letter design on the smooth, peeled surface. When working with very young children, prepare potatoes in advance. Dip the letter section of the potato in paint and then stamp it on paper. Have students say the sounds of the letters as they make the design.

7. Illustrating a Letter Picture Story

Write silly phonic sentences on the board. Have the students listen to each sentence, review the letter sounds, write the sentence, and then illustrate it. They could also write or dictate additional sentences.
example:
   Felix, the fat fish, fought a fierce fight with five foxes in a forest lake.

8. Letters and Textures

If students are experiencing difficulties learning a letter-sound combination, have them make a letter with a texture that they can trace over and feel while looking at the letter and saying its sound. This extra reinforcement can help them to remember the association. Textured letters can be made of clay, of sand sprinkled over glue, cut from textured fabric, or traced in a box of sand.

9. Famous Paintings and Sounds

After students have carefully looked at a slide or large reproduction of a famous painting, have them name all the objects in it that begin with a specific letter-sound. Write the names of these objects on the chalkboard.

10. Phonic Game Making

Let students make their own materials for games such as "Fish," "Bingo" or "Concentration." Review sounds to be included and their representative words or pictures. Have students make the cards carefully to ensure that the pictures are understandable. When they play the games, they must match the appropriate pictures to the letters. Game cards can be protected by laminating or by putting clear "contact" paper over them.
examples:

Concentration Pairs

Bingo Cards   Bingo Leader Cards

Say initial sound   Give sound and
                     word that begins
                     with the sound

Fish Cards

STRUCTURAL ANALYSIS

1. Making Compound-Word Picture-Riddles

Have students draw pictures of the various parts of compound words and
have others guess which compound word they have illustrated.
examples:

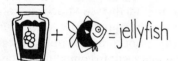 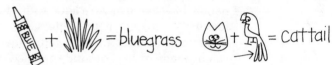

2. Picturing Compound Words

Give each student a rectangular piece of unlined paper. Students are to
fold the paper in half, then unfold it and lay it flat on the desk.

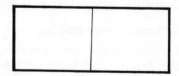

Have them fold the right end of the paper toward the center crease, and
then fold the left end to the center crease.

100

Have each child choose a compound word, such as *football, anthill, goldfish, beehive, basketball, flagpole,* or *battleship* (see list on page 15 for more examples). Children are to write and draw the first part of the compound on the outer left flap and the second part on the outer right flap, then open the flaps and write and illustrate the compound on the inside.

3. Illustrating Comparative Endings

Have students divide a sheet of paper into three sections. Have them write words with comparative endings *er* and *est* and illustrate each word.
examples:

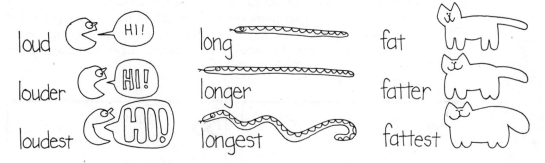

loud
louder
loudest

long
longer
longest

fat
fatter
fattest

CONTEXT-CLUE USAGE

1. Pictures and Context Clues

Give each student a dittoed paragraph in which some words are deleted. Ask each to read the entire selection carefully and then draw pictures to represent the missing words.
example:

Mark and his _____, Spot, went for a walk in the _____. Spot saw a

baby _____ that had fallen from its _____ in a tall _____. Spot

barked and barked at the baby _____.

2. Picturing the Meaning

Have students read a paragraph in which a new word is defined in the context and ask them to each draw an illustration that matches the description given in the context. Then have them look up the new word in an illustrated dictionary or encyclopedia to check the accuracy of their drawings.

example:

> A deciduous tree loses its leaves in autumn. It lives through the winter without any leaves. In spring tiny new leaves begin to grow on its branches. In summer the tree is filled with beautiful green leaves. Draw a picture of a deciduous tree in autumn, winter, spring, or summer. Then look up *deciduous* in the dictionary. Did your illustration resemble the one in the dictionary?

DICTIONARY PRACTICE

1. Alphabetical-Order Mural

After students have mastered all their letter-sounds, have them make an alpabetical-order mural. They should paint, draw, or cut and paste individual pictures, label the subjects of their works, and then attach their contributions in alphabetical order to a large sheet of mural paper.

2. Making Picture-Dictionaries

Let students draw or cut out pictures of objects that begin with each letter of the alphabet and then paste each picture onto a piece of paper labeled with the appropriate letter. Then have them write the name of each object next to its picture, put the pages in alphabetical order, and staple them together.

examples:

3. Personal Art Dictionaries

Have students compile personal art dictionaries in which they define new art terms and write brief descriptions of each art activity they do. This will help them to remember not only the new terms but also the art activities they have experienced.

4. Illustrated Word Lists

Illustrated word lists can often help students to understand and retain content-area vocabulary. Have students write brief explanations and draw pictures for new words, such as *toga, plateau,* and *mesa,* in their notebooks or for a large class word-list to be posted on the bulletin board.

5. Dictionary Noun-Pictures

Let each student pick a noun that is not already illustrated from the dictionary and illustrate it according to the definition. Have others guess what the word is and then check the reference to see if an accurate illustration was made.

6. Finding Information About Art in the Dictionary

Have students see what they can learn about art by using different dictionaries. Have them look up terms such as *texture, line,* and *paint* and select the meanings that apply to art; or they can look up artists such as Michelangelo, Picasso, and Renoir to find brief biographical sketches.

Vocabulary Growth Through Art Activities

A picture is a poem without words.[1]

The development of an extensive and accurate vocabulary is a necessary phase of learning to read. By engaging in various art-related activities, students can learn many new words—by associating words with visual images as well as by using descriptive and technical terms when they discuss and write about art. Vocabulary developed in this way will not only extend students' ability to read but will also help them to appreciate, enjoy, and interpret works of art. The activities in this section can be used to arouse students' interest in the meanings of words through enjoyable and interesting experiences with art.

1. Learning Technical Terms

Art terminology is best learned through actual participation in art activities. Choose technical terms and words for media and materials, words that refer to the subjects of paintings, or words relating to the physical or cultural setting in which a painting was created. Write the words on the chalkboard, discuss them in relation to the art activity, and continue to use them frequently during the lesson. At the end of the lesson, have the students define the words in their own terms and use them in meaningful sentences to describe what they did. It is important to use the new words again and again in reference to other art works to make sure that students understand and retain them. New art terms could also be listed on an attractively decorated bulletin board or in a student-maintained class art-dictionary with pictures illustrating the terms.

[1]Quintus Cornificius, *Auctor ad Herennium.*

examples:

Technical Terms

balance	line
color	mass
composition	perspective
complementary color	repetition
contrast	rhythm
distortion	shade
hue	space
intensity	texture

Terms for Media and Materials

chalk	paint
charcoal	paper
clay	pastels
collage	paste
crayons	sketch
montage	wash
oils	watercolor

2. Art-Word Bingo

Review new art terms occasionally by playing games such as "Art-Word Bingo," in which the students have to locate the proper word from a description given by the teacher or game leader.

example:

Teacher reads: "a smooth, soft, thick mixture used to join light materials such as paper and cloth." Students must then locate and mark the word *paste.*

perspective	line	chalk
clay	repetition	paste
model	glaze	paint

3. Writing Artistic Captions

Have students write their own captions using designated terms for art displays. Select several of the best captions, write them on the board, and have students select the best one to use in the display.

4. Vocabulary Expansion Through Great Art

Encourage students to look carefully at a painting and name all the objects in it, or all the colors they see, or the things that might be alive or edible. List these things on the chalkboard. Then point to a word and have a student locate the object in the picture.

5. Parts of Speech and Paintings

Have students look at a painting and list all the objects that they see (nouns). Then list all the words that tell what these things are doing (verbs). Then list the adjectives that describe the objects and the adverbs that help describe the actions.

6. Prepositional Pictures

Have students show that they understand the meanings of prepositions by making appropriate illustrations for words such as *up, down, inside, outside, together, apart, in,* or *out.*

7. Picturing the Meaning

Give students a new word, such as *obese, pompous, perceive, exceedingly,* or *endeavor,* and ask them to look through a magazine to find a picture that illustrates it. Have them write the word, give its pronunciation and meaning, and write a sentence using the word on the page with a picture. A variation of this activity would be to let students look through the dictionary to find a word that intrigues them and then select an appropriate illustration.

8. Colonial Sign-Making

Tell students that colonial sign painters painted signs on wooden boards for merchants to hang outside stores. These signs had to include pictures as well as words because many colonists couldn't read. Discuss some of the vocabulary and expressions of those days, such as "Steak and Brew" or "Food and Grog." Then have students make a sign using paint on a board or piece of cardboard that includes both words and pictures and can be understood by someone who can't read.

9. Thematic Word-Picture Collage

Have students pick a topic and then look through magazines and newspapers to collect words and pictures to make a thematic collage. Have them arrange the designs in a pleasing pattern on a sheet of paper and then paste the objects down.

examples of themes for collages:

the seasons, animals, occupations, the senses, the outdoors, myself, sports

10. Shades of Colors

Divide students into small groups to list all the synonyms or shades they can think of for different colors. Discuss their results. Then have them go to a dictionary to find even more. Have students look at crayons and paint samples to see the different shades of colors. Discuss any unfamiliar terms. Encourage them to use some of the new terms.

examples of synonyms and different shades of various colors:

Red

brick, burgundy, carmine, carrot, cerise, cochineal, copper, coral, crimson, garnet, rose, ruby, ruddy, sanguine, scarlet, terra-cotta, vermilion

Blue

aquamarine, azure, indigo, navy, sky-colored, ultramarine

Brown

auburn, bay, bronze, fallow, fawn, hazel, mahogany, musteline, russet, smoky, snuff-colored, sorrel, tabac, tan

Purple

damson, heliotrope, lilac, magenta, mauve, puce, violet

Yellow

amber, buff, cream, flavescent, jaundiced, khaki, nankeen, saffron, sandy

Green

chartreuse, emerald, forest, grass, jade, moss, olive, pistachio

11. Color Words

Display paintings that contain predominantly shades of the same color, such as works of Picasso's "blue period" or Rousseau's "green jungle." Have students discuss all the shades of blue or green. List these words and look for other color words in the dictionary. Have a color chart for the words.

12. Vocabulary and Paint-Sample Cards

Obtain paint-sample cards from a local store and have students speculate possible reasons for the names of colors such as *cactus white, buttermilk, veggie green, shetland brown, summer sand, heavenly pink, raspberry jam, paprika red, tomato, mountain blue, waterway blue, hot mustard,* or grapefruit (Sherwin Williams paint samples). Separate the names from the colors of some of the paint or carpet samples. Encourage them to use descriptive words. Then select the best name for each sample.

13. Make Up a Color-Name

Let students make up their own names for paint or carpet samples. Encourage them to use descriptive words. Then select the best name for each sample.

14. Homonym Montage

Montage is the technique of making a picture by arranging a number of pictorial elements around a central theme. Encourage students to think about the different meanings of a word such as *light*: they might include *light bulb, daylight, light work,* or *lightheaded.* Then give them each a homonym that has one spelling but a variety of interpretations, such as *saw, run,* or *strike.* Let them draw different interpretations of the word or cut out appropriate pictures from magazines and use the cutouts to produce a montage. Underneath each part of the montage, have them write a sentence using the homonym correctly.

15. Picturing the Homophones

Have students draw pictures of homophones (words that are pronounced the same but have different meanings and spellings). Then have the other students guess the words and use each one correctly in a sentence.
examples:

Homophones: son   sun

Sentences   _____   _____

              _____   _____

Homophones: hare   hair

Sentences _____   _____

_____   _____

MORE HOMOPHONES

break/brake	blew/blue	meet/meat	flower/flour
tail/tale	flee/flea	ate/eight	buy/by
read/red	road/rode	sail/sale	rain/reign/rein
steak/stake	weak/week	stare/stair	night/knight
haul/hall	sea/see	pain/pane	dear/deer
			heard/herd

16. Artistic Antonyms

Give students a word such as *work*, and ask them to determine its antonym and illustrate each word.

17. Paintings and Feelings

Have students look closely at a mood-provoking painting and describe how the painting makes them feel. These words can be listed on the chalkboard and students can write a story or poem about their feelings concerning the painting.
examples of mood words:
gloomy, excited, perplexed, peaceful, sad, happy, confused, angry, joyous

18. Emotional-Word Pictures

Let students make an illustration to show how a word makes them feel; use words such as *hate, love, sad, cry, hot,* and *cold.* Then have them write a story or poem to go with their illustration.

19. Colors and Feelings

Give students a sheet of paper containing descriptive words, such as *warm, cool, angry,* or *happy.* Have them match a color-word to each descriptor. Discuss the reasons for their choices. Have students look for uses of color in pictures and discuss how color can create feelings of sadness, happiness, excitement, anger, and fantasy. The warm colors—red, red-orange, orange, yellow-orange, and yellow—may express sunshine, joy, heat, or excitement. Red often indicates anger; yellow, sunshine. The cool colors—green, blue-green, blue, blue-violet, and violet—express coolness, calm, peace, grandeur, and moodiness. Green often indicates jealousy; blue, sadness or despair.

20. Colors in Heraldry

Discuss the meanings of colors in heraldry and shields used by knights. Make sure that students know the meanings of all terms. Then have them design a shield for the class, school, or for themselves, using appropriate colors and symbols.

Color	Signifies
Yellow or gold	Honor and loyalty
Silver or white	Faith and purity
Red	Bravery and courage
Blue	Piety and sincerity
Black	Grief and sorrow
Green	Youth and hope
Purple	High rank and royalty
Orange	Strength and endurance
Red-purple	Sacrifice

From *The World Book Encyclopedia* © 1981 World Book–Childcraft International, Inc.

21. Scary Words

Have students write some words they think of as scary words on paper with a dark, shiny yellow crayon. Then have them apply a wash of thin black paint to make a scary picture.

22. Artistic Similes

Explain that a simile is a figure of speech in which one thing is expressed in terms of another by using the words *as* or *like*. Share some commonly used similes involving colors.

BLUE	RED	WHITE
blue as the ocean	red as a beet	white as snow
blue as the sky	red as a rose	white as a ghost
like a blue streak	red as a lobster	white as a sheet

23. Colorful Phrases or Visual Descriptions

To encourage more "colorful" speech, introduce students to the many idioms and colloquial phrases using colors that have been incorporated into the English language. Discuss the meanings of these expressions. Encourage the students to illustrate them in a variety of ways and use them in sentences and stories of their own.

Colors

to come off with flying colors (to be successful)
to paint in bright colors (to emphasize the best aspect of something)
to see a thing for its true colors (to see something as it really is)
to show one's true colors (to reveal oneself)
to stick to one's colors (to adhere to one's principles)

Blue

blue blood (of royal or noble birth)
blue ribbon (highest prize or honor)
have the blues (to be depressed)
once in a blue moon (something that happens very rarely)

talk a blue streak (talk without stopping)
true blue (loyal, reliable)
out-of-the-blue (quite unexpectedly)

Green

green-eyed monster (jealousy)
greenhorn (a beginner at something—refers to the undeveloped horns of a
    male calf)
green with envy (jealous)
green around the gills (sick)

Red

paint the town red (celebrate)
red flag (signal to indicate danger)
red-faced (embarrassed)
red herring (an attempt to divert attention by introducing some detail of no
    importance; refers to the old trick of drawing a dried red herring across
    the path to destroy one's scent when being followed by bloodhounds)
red-letter day (an important occasion—from the custom of indicating holidays
    in red letters on calendars)
red tape (official formalities—from the old custom of tying up government
    papers with red tape)
to see red (to be very angry)

Developing Comprehension Skills
Through Art Activities

*A room hung with pictures is a room hung
with thoughts.*[1]

The processes for understanding art works and reading materials are very
similar: The eyes see words or colors and shapes, and then the mind
interprets what the eyes have seen. Thus, as students are learning to
understand works of art they are further developing skills and processes
that are necessary for understanding printed matter.

Remember that each person views the world through his or her own
eyes and experiences. Students should not all be expected to have the
same reactions to the art works they study. They should also be allowed to
be creative in their own artistic endeavors.

The activities in this section are arranged by comprehension skills
and include experiences that encourage many levels of thinking while
working with art.

[1]Sir Joshua Reynolds, *source unknown.*

FOLLOWING DIRECTIONS

1. Purposeful Directions

The fun of art activities can provide students with genuine purpose and motivation for following directions accurately. Students should be encouraged to follow directions accurately, although there should always be some room for creativity.

2. Testing for Directions

Give each student a direction sheet of easy-to-read, concise directions for an individual art project. Provide enough time to read the sheets; then have them answer a brief questionnaire about the directions. When the questionnaires are completed, let students proceed with their projects. This type of activity will help students learn to interpret printed directions for arts and crafts activities they do at home, as well as refining their abilities simply to follow instructions.

GETTING THE MAIN IDEA

1. Finding a Picture's Main Idea

Ask students to look carefully at an art print and then discuss the main idea of the painting.

2. Main-Idea Book Jacket

Have students design a book jacket that conveys the main idea of a book or story they have been reading that does not already have an illustrative cover.

3. Determining the Main Idea

Ask students to look carefully at a picture without talking about it. Then have each one write what he/she thinks is the main idea of the picture. Compare responses; then have them do the same type of activity with something they have read.

4. Studying Titles for Art Work

Show students titled art work and ask them to hypothesize about the artist's reasons for selecting that title. What does the title mean? Does it seem to go with the painting? What might be another choice? A variation on this activity would be to show students the art work and have them suggest titles for it before informing them of the artist's title.

5. Visualizing the Idea

Have students illustrate something from a story they are reading for which there is no illustration.

6. Correlating Paintings and Newspapers

Show students a painting and then have them search through newspapers to find headlines or want-ads that they think might correlate with the painting.

RECOGNIZING DETAILS

1. Listing Details in Paintings

Have students list all the details they actually *see* in a painting. Have them work in small groups, with the group listing the most items being declared the winner. Then have the students list all the things that can be learned from a painting. This same type of activity could be repeated using a textbook illustration.

2. Deciding What Is in a Painting

Project a slide of a painting on a screen. Give students a list of objects that do and do not appear in the painting and have them identify the ones that appear. You may also want the students to do this type of activity with an illustration in one of their textbooks.

3. Reading and Drawing

Write a sentence or paragraph on the chalkboard and have students read it carefully and make an illustration that shows all the details.
example:
> The sun was shining on the little blue house with red windows and a yellow door. Two little girls were playing catch outside with a green ball. A boy with a blue plaid shirt was sitting in an apple tree reading a book with a red cover.

4. Stories and Details

After having read or listened to a story with lots of details, discuss the importance of significant details and have students create an illustration that recalls some of the most important details of the story.

5. Artists, Authors, and Details

Explain to students that artists and authors usually show some aspect of their culture in their works. Explain to them that the more they know about an artist or author, the more they will be able to understand and appreciate his/her works. Tell students briefly about Toulouse-Lautrec, Van Gogh, or Chagall, using encyclopedias for quick background information, and then study some of these artists' works. Then tell students some pertinent things about some of the authors and illustrators of the books they are reading so that they will be better able to appreciate their works. Helpful reference books are:

Mahoney, et al., *Illustrators of Children's Books, 1744–1945.*
Viguers, et al., *Illustrators of Children's Books, 1946–1956.*
Kingman, et al., *Illustrators of Children's Books, 1957–1966.*
Fuller, *More Junior Authors.*
Hopkins, *Books Are by People.*
Hopkins, *More Books by More People.*
Cianciol, *Illustrations in Children's Books.*

SEQUENCING

1. Remembering When It Happened

Ask students to think of three events in a story they have been reading. Ask them to draw a picture of each thing and then paste the pictures on a sheet of a paper in the order in which they occurred. Then have them write or dictate something about these events.

2. Cartoon-Strip Sequencing

After students have read a story, have them create a cartoon strip which shows the main events of the story in sequence.

3. Filmstrip Sequencing

Divide a story into a meaningful sequence of paragraphs, pages, or events and ask different students to illustrate each part. Then have students write or dictate a brief caption for each event. Arrange the illustrations with their captions in sequence on a long sheet of paper. These can be shown on a classroom "TV set" (see page 53). A variation of this would be to omit the written captions and have students read their portions of the story sequentially as their illustrations are shown.

4. Making Murals

Murals can be used to illustrate concepts in many content areas. They are fun to make and give students the experience of working together to complete a project. One type of mural that can be effective is the sequential mural that relates a complete story, such as the story of the process of evaporation or the story of the westward movement. Careful planning will be necessary and students should research aspects of the topic in preparation for their parts of the mural.

Following is a suggested plan for making a class mural:
- Choose a subject

- Plan the mural features and layout

- Give each student an assignment

- Use chalk or pencil to outline the mural features

- Complete the mural

CHARACTERIZATION

1. Studying Characters in Great Art

Direct students to look carefully at a portrait, such as Picasso's *Weeping Woman* or Wyeth's *Christina's World.* Have students suggest adjectives which describe the character. Write the adjectives on the chalkboard. Then have the students write a description of the person. Later, when the students are reading a story, have them carefully analyze illustrations of the characters and discuss whether the illustrations match the descriptions given in the text.

2. Illustrating the Characters

After reading or listening to a story with no pictures, have the class draw, paint, or make a clay model or puppet of what they think one of the human or animal characters might have looked like. Encourage students to make their model resemble not only the physical traits of the character, but also the personality characteristics. Have students list all the descriptive words found in the story pertaining to the character and then evaluate the art works as to which best portrays the character.

3. Making a Character Collage

After reading a story, have students discuss the characters. Then ask them to make a collage of one of the characters from magazine pictures that they feel resemble the character, his/her personality traits or interests.

4. Newspaper Characterization

Read to students or have them read a newspaper article description of a person, or read an advertisement describing a lost animal. Then have students draw this person or animal based on the description given. Compare results.

5. Book-Character Charade Art

Divide the class into groups. Have each group member write the name of a book or story character on a card to be given to a member of another group. Exchange cards and give students one or two minutes to make a brief drawing of the character. As the students show their drawings, they can give answers to questions only by shaking their heads. The team that supplies the most correct answers wins the game.

Little Miss Muffet

Huckleberry Finn

6. Drawing Character Pictures

Have students draw a large picture of one of their favorite story characters. Then write about the character within its body.

7. Settings and Personalities

Show students paintings or magazine photographs of room interiors devoid of people. Talk about how rooms can reflect the personalities of the people who use them. Point out that the students' own personalities might be reflected in rooms such as the classroom or their rooms at home. Have them discuss what types of people might live in the pictured settings. Then have them draw an interior design of a room for a character in a story they are reading. Let the other students guess for whom the room was intended. Have them discuss why the room matches the person's personality as described in the story.

RECOGNIZING POINT OF VIEW

1. Paintblots and Viewpoints

Let students make paintblot pictures by blowing paint with a straw onto one half of a sheet of paper and then folding the paper over to make a blot of it on the opposite side. Have them ask three different people what they see in the same blot prints. Then discuss with the class why people can see different things in the same picture. Explain to them that people's perceptions can be influenced by their previous experiences, current needs, and the things they have been taught to see or want to see. Then have them analyze an event in a story from three different viewpoints.

2. Through Different Eyes

Ask students to look at an art print or photograph of a city street scene and note what things would be important to the following people: an architect, a grocer, and a young child.

3. Artistic Comparisons

Have students compare how different artists painted the same subjects, such as dogs, flowers, or people reading. Then have them each consult encyclopedias for two different biographical sketches of the same artist and then discuss how these differ.

4. Analyzing Different Perceptions

After students have had several art and reading activities dealing with point of view, have them write a story in which a mistaken perception or prejudice determines what two people see in something. Have students include character sketches of both people and give the reasons for their misunderstanding. Have them include illustrations showing each person's viewpoint.

MAKING PREDICTIONS

1. Discussing What Happened Before and After

Show students a picture. Ask them to hypothesize about what could have happened before and after the picture was made.

2. Picturing the Next Event

Have students read or listen to a story and then make an illustration of what might happen next.

3. Artistic Predictions

Before showing students a painting, tell them the title and then let them predict what the painting will be about. Encourage them to use vivid descriptive words in their predictions. Write their predictions on the chalkboard. Then show them the painting and let students compare their predictions with the actual painting.

4. Predicting from the Illustrations

Let students read the title of a selection and then thumb through the story looking only at the illustrations. Ask them to predict what they think the story will be about. Write their predictions on the chalkboard. Then have them read the story and see whose prediction was most accurate.

INTERPRETING SYMBOLS

1. Making a Symbol Dictionary

Explain to students that a symbol is something that stands for something else and that the use of symbols can sometimes make communication easier. Ask students to bring in sketches of common visual symbols such as traffic signs, the Texaco star, or McDonald's golden arches. Have them discuss the meanings behind these symbols. Then have the class make a dictionary of common neighborhood symbols using photographs, sketches, and pictures along with written explanations of the symbols.

2. Interpreting Art Symbols

Guide the students to realize that just as words can be symbols of objects, artists sometimes use pictures of objects to convey symbolic messages. Show students some paintings in which figures are used in symbolic ways, such as Dali's misshapen watches that show the passage of time; or show older paintings in which books are used to indicate knowledge, or dogs are used to symbolize loyalty, or the sun is used as a symbol of truth. More able students might enjoy reading about art symbols in *Symbols and Legends in Western Art* (Whittlesey 1972).

3. Knowing the Pennsylvania Dutch Hex Signs

Explain to students that the Pennsylvania Dutch settlers thought that hex signs would protect their farms and animals. Each type of sign had a symbolic meaning. Have them give examples of good-luck signs, such as horseshoes, four-leaf clovers, and rabbits' feet. Have students study the meaning of hex signs in encyclopedias and then make up their own. Have them discuss the meanings of their signs and the reasons that only certain signs or symbols were used.

4. Symbolizing Personal Interests and Values

Ask students to think of their personal interests and then make a collage using pictures from magazines to show what their interests are. For example, someone interested in the outdoors, reading, tennis and cooking might include pictures of trees, books, tennis rackets and food. Then have students think of symbols to represent a character in a story they are reading and make a personality collage for that character. These could be displayed anonymously and the other students could attempt to identify the owner or the story character.

CRITICAL/CREATIVE THINKING

1. Writing a Critique

Let students write their own critiques of art work and compare theirs with others in the class. Then have them compare their critiques with those of professional art critics.

2. Analyzing Artistic "Propaganda"

Have students bring in advertisements that use art and print to get people to purchase items or to disseminate information. Discuss the persuasive techniques used in magazine advertisements, handbills, billboard designs, buttons, posters, T-shirts, and bumper stickers. Have students notice the elements that attract attention and appeal to the viewer, such as layout, lettering, bright colors, and clever illustrations. Have them make up their own advertisements to announce a school event or to suggest a book to read.

example:

How is art being used in this advertisement to encourage people to make a purchase?

COMBINING COMPREHENSION SKILLS
THROUGH ART ACTIVITIES

Although it is important for students to study specific comprehension skills, it is also necessary to provide them with opportunities to use a variety of comprehension skills as well as different levels of thinking while working with one piece of material. The following activities will give students an opportunity to use a combination of different types of comprehension skills to understand art or printed material.

1. Reading a Painting at Three Different Levels

It would be best to do this type of activity first with a realistic painting, such as one by Remington, Brueghel, Stuart or Harnett, and then repeat it with a more imaginative painting, such as one by Chagall, Dali, Monet, Klee, or Picasso.

A. **Literal Level**   Ask students to carefully look at an art print projected on a screen. Have them list and describe the things they actually see. Ask them questions relating to the artist's choice of colors, medium, type of paint, models or objects, and setting. Have students compare the painting with things they have actually experienced.

B. **Inferential Level**   Then ask students what they think the painting means. Help them to realize that the visual images can be used to convey many types of messages. Some artists use symbols to convey thoughts, as Picasso used animals in *Guernica* to portray war, anger, or peace. Symbols can carry profound messages, just as words can have deeper meanings.

C. **Higher Levels**   Now ask students why the artist may have painted the picture or what he/she might have been thinking while painting. Help students to realize that an artist creates with paint and colors as a poet or author creates with words. Have students explore reasons the artist may have used certain colors, materials, or techniques and his/her feelings while using them. For example, why did Cassatt often use pastel colors? Why did Rousseau paint so many vivid jungle scenes? Why did Picasso go through a blue period and a cubist period? Have students relate what they believe the artists were thinking about or feeling while creating their art works to what the writers were thinking about or feeling while creating poetry or fiction. Why were particular words chosen by the authors?

2. Putting Art Appreciation and Comprehension Skills Together

List several comprehension skills on the chalkboard, such as the following:

- Getting the facts
- Noting important details
- Getting the main idea
- Drawing conclusions
- Predicting what will happen next

Show students an appropriate art print and then elicit information from them for each comprehension category. Have them list facts and details about the picture. Then have them discuss what the picture is mainly about or pick a good title for it. Ask them to draw some conclusions as to why the picture was painted or why the specific theme was chosen. Then have them predict what might happen next to the items in the picture. Give students a similar type of activity to do with a short paragraph. Have them read it, list the facts, determine the main idea, draw conclusions as to why it was written, and make some predictions based on the paragraph.

3. Looking and Reading for a Purpose

When students are given specific reasons for studying a picture or a piece of print, they will be more likely to direct their thinking to determine the answers. Have students look carefully at a painting and try to answer the following questions: Who painted it? Why? Where? When? How? What does it mean? Then direct them to do some reading about the artist to try to find answers for these specific questions or others.

Art and the Study Skills

There is an art of reading, as well as an art of thinking, and an art of writing.[1]

Just learning how to read is not enough to equip today's students to cope with informational materials. Reading for information requires special reading study skills which must be developed and practiced early enough so that students will be able to read and learn in any subject area. Art projects and art works can be used to teach students some basic study skills in unusually enjoyable ways that emphasize visual learning.

1. Careful Picture Observation

Without proper guidance, students are likely to just look quickly at art prints, as well as pictures in their textbooks, without really stopping to examine them. Encourage students to take enough time to look carefully at a picture. Help them to understand that they can learn more as they look more closely. Have them look at details—perhaps even using small magnifying glasses, describe interesting items, and then analyze or interpret what they have discovered. Ask them questions related to purpose, mood, details, setting, situation, and importance. Good questioning can usually promote sound thinking. Then have the students turn to an illustration in one of their content-area texts. Have them look at it and discuss it. Point out again that the more carefully they look at the picture, the more they will see and learn.

[1]Isaac D'Israeli, *Literary Character.*

2. Paintings and Research

Have students do research in encyclopedias and other appropriate books and report on an artist, art medium, or subject of a painting. Explain the importance of using the table of contents and index to locate information. Go over the steps for making an outline and preparing a report.

3. Studying a Painting's Historical Context

Direct students to study a painting of life in a certain time and place, such as a painting by Remington of the American West or a work by Brueghel of Belgium. Then have them do research about that period of time and geographical area to see if the painting seems realistic.

4. Comparing and Creating Time-Lines

Have students study different time-lines found in social studies and science books. Encourage them to compare them for visual appeal, information given, and readability. Then have students make a time-line that uses the best features to show a sequence of significant events in a story they have read.

5. Map-Making

Encourage students to analyze maps not only for their content, but also for their aesthetic appeal. Have them discuss why some maps are more appealing, interesting, and informative than others. Then have students make a map that employs only the best features.

6. Illustrating and Interviewing Techniques

Invite an illustrator to come to speak to the class. It is often possible to get an illustrator's address by writing the appropriate publishing company. Many towns also have an illustrator living in the area. Encourage the speaker to discuss his/her career and the problems of harmonizing the illustrations to a written text. Before the speaker comes, study his/her art work and discuss listening skills and appropriate interviewing techniques. After the speaker has left, discuss information presented and have students write appropriate thank-you notes.

Putting Art into the Language Arts

Art is the desire of a man (woman) to express himself (herself).[1]

Most children have a natural inclination to communicate. However, sometimes they do not fully grasp the connection between reading and communicating. Students should learn early that any form of communication, including reading, involves a person who has something to share, whether

[1]Amy Lowell, *Tendencies in Modern American Poetry.*

it is spoken, written, drawn, painted or gestured, and a person to receive.

Creative art work, then, is also a form of communication. Children who create with figures, objects, and colors are telling those who look upon their finished products what has happened to them or what they have observed or felt.

The ideas in this section can be used to develop students' ability to transmit and receive communication through activities that revolve around art and language arts.

1. Writing and Art Works

Let students use a painting or piece of sculpture as the basis for a creative writing assignment about what story it tells, their personal interpretations and reactions, what they think it would have been like to create the art work or to pose for it, or how they would have designed the piece of art differently.

2. Art-Work Captions

Have students look at an art-work and then create new titles for it or write or dictate captions for it.

3. Magazine Art and Writing

Have students each cut out a picture of one item from a magazine, such as a car, book, or person, then paste the item on construction paper, and build a scene around it. Then have them write a caption, story, or poem about their creation.

4. Writing About Photographs

Explain to students that photographs can show us familiar things in different and unusual ways. Show students some newspaper photographs or collections of photos that portray familiar things in unusual ways. Then have them write descriptions of a photograph that is especially appealing or find photographs to illustrate a story they are reading.

5. "Found-Art" Writing

Encourage students to see art in everyday things, such as automobiles, tennis rackets, food, flowers, or the sky. Have them write descriptions of the art of these objects.

6. Appreciating Beautiful Things

Create a special spot in the room where students can bring things they think are beautiful, such as pottery, flowers, carvings, or feathers. Have students write descriptions of the objects and include comments as to why they think they are beautiful.

7. Describing an Interior Design

Have students write descriptions of their ideal color scheme for the interior walls of the classroom, school, or their rooms at home. Have them include the reasons for their selections.

8. Writing Magazine Picture-Stories

Have students write letters or stories using pictures from magazines to replace some of the words.

9. Creating Words for Wordless Books

Give each student a book that contains no words, only pictures. Have them study the illustrations and then write a narrative for the book.

10. Writing a Book and Illustrating It

Have students write and illustrate their own books. They could be on personal topics, such as "My Most Embarrassing Moment," or "A Funny Thing That Happened to Me," or the books could be fictional. The students could then bind the books, decorate the covers, and add them to the class library.

11. Imaginary Logging

After studying a painting and its artist, have students write an imaginary daily log of an artist's thoughts as he/she created the work of art.

12. Making Posters

Bring in posters or reproductions of posters by Chagall, Toulouse-Lautrec, or other famous artists. Have students compare them as to appeal, attractiveness, clarity, and effectiveness in getting the message across. Then have students select a topic for a poster, such as "reading," "health," "safety," or an upcoming event, such as a science fair, book sale, or carnival. Discuss key words and slogans to be used and the necessary information to be included. Remind students that the written message must be brief and dramatic and that all necessary information should be condensed as much as possible. Encourage students to use legible, well designed, and properly spaced lettering and simple but effective pictures. Have them plan their posters by first making small pencil sketches.

13. Designing Stationery

Ask students to bring in samples of stationery. Discuss design, appeal, and practicality. Then have students design their own stationery for the next activities.

14. "Dear Illustrator"

Study techniques of letter-writing by having students write letters to their favorite living illustrators complimenting them on their work. They could also ask them some questions related to reading, such as: "Do you like to read? What is your favorite book? Which book did you most enjoy illustrating?

15. Composing Invitational Letters

Let students compose a class letter to invite a local artist to come visit the class to demonstrate, lecture, or be a guest teacher.

POETRY AND ART

Because a poet uses words to express ideas much as an artist uses shapes and colors, poetry is one of the best media for correlating language and art. When students experience a poem aesthetically, they must recreate its images in their "minds' eyes" as well as respond to the sounds and rhythms of the words. But the figurative language in poetry can cause problems if students lack visual imagnation or are unable to understand poetic imagery. The ability to experience visual imagery can be developed early in school years by encouraging students to respond artistically and aesthetically to poetry.

When selecting a poem for students to illustrate, make sure the poem is pleasing to listen to or read, that it can stimulate feelings and emotional responses through visual images, and that its images and feelings are within the scope of children's experiences. Poems that are appealing to children usually contain surprise, action, humor, or mystery. The activities in this section are designed to develop the student's visual imagination and aesthetic sensitivity through experiences with poetry and art.

1. Group Poetry and Art

Read a poem to the students, have them discuss it, and then ask them to shut their eyes and think about it. Let students draw or paint what they saw in their "minds' eyes" about the poem.

2. Individual Poetry Reading and Art

Give each student a poem to read and illustrate. Encourage them to read their poems several times to make sure they have drawn all the things mentioned. Then let them read their poems to the class while showing their illustrations.

3. Making a Poem/Painting

Have each student write an original poem and then create a painting for it. After their paintings are dry, have them letter their poems neatly on the paintings so that the poems become part of the paintings.

example of a *cinquain* poem painting (see also page 236):

The Sun
Hot - Far Away
Warming Up the Cold Earth
Blazing Bright Like a Yellow Star
Our Life

4. Correlating Poetry and Art

Show students an art print of a subject such as a clown or dog, and then read them poems about clowns or dogs. Ask students which poem reminds them most of the painting and why? Post relevant poems on a bulletin board surrounding the painting. A variation of this would be to provide several poetry books and have students each select a poem to go with a specific painting. Have them practice reading their poems aloud and then read them to the class while standing near the painting.

5. Writing Poems About Art Works

After students have spent some time viewing and discussing an art work, have them each write a poem about it. Let them read their creations to the others and then post all the poems on a bulletin board surrounding the art print.

6. Creating Colorful Poems

Have students make up a class poem entitled "Color Is" with each writing a line about a favorite color for the poem.

7. "My-Favorite-Color" Poem

Have students draw pictures using only their favorite colors or make collages of magazine pictures in their favorite colors. Then have them make up poems about their favorite colors to attach to their art works. The poems could be written with ink or crayon of the appropriate color.

8. Poetry and Calligraphy

Have students select a favorite poem, design decorative letters that are consistent with the meaning of the poem, and then copy the poem using the special letters.

9. Brush Painting and Haiku

Haiku—unrhymed poetry about natural things, based on a particular scheme of syllabication—is usually illustrated with watercolors or simple sketches. Read samples of Haiku from books and show students the accompanying illustrations. Then have students write their own Haikus and illustrate them appropriately. (For more about Haiku, see page 236.)

10. Silhouette Pictures and Poetry

Have students read poems about shadows, such as "My Shadow" by Robert Louis Stevenson, and then make silhouette pictures by cutting out shapes of shadows from black paper and attaching them to white paper. The students could also create and illustrate their own poetry about shadows.

Creating an Interest in Reading Through Art

*The habit of reading is the only enjoyment in which
there is no alloy: it lasts when all other pleasures fade.*[1]

One of the goals in teaching students basic reading skills is to equip them to read with enough ease so that they will enjoy and learn to value reading. Art plays a significant role in many children's lives and many activities that involve art can help students to become more personally interested in reading. Such activities can motivate students to want to read for information about how to do an art project, to learn more about an artist, or to look for interesting related ideas in books.

Acquainting children with the various types of illustrations used in books can help them to appreciate both art and literature. Books with colorful covers and illustrations often attract students and, due to the increasing use of modern media techniques, the illustrations in today's children's books are particularly exciting.

The activities in this section can be used to help get students excited about reading. When using these activities, the pleasures and joys of reading and art should be stressed to stimulate students' interest. This chapter also contains a section on artistic book reviews.

1. Story-Painting Match

After students have listened to or read a story or poem, direct them to

[1]Anthony Trollope, *Speeches.*

look through a collection of prints or art books to find a painting that would correlate with it.

2. Art and Literature

Biblical events, legends, and myths have often been used as themes by artists. After studying such literary works, have students view related art works. Discuss whether they agree with the artist's interpretation.

3. Art in the News

Encourage students to bring to class information about art from newspapers and magazines and "found art" from advertisements and calendars. Set aside time to discuss their contributions. This can help students to become interested in reading materials which have art reviews, such as Sunday newspapers and selected news magazines.

4. Art and Reading Learning-Center

Set up an art and reading learning-center where students can work independently on activities that combine art and reading. They could view an art print and then be asked to answer questions concerning what is pictured, the colors used, the meaning of the picture, or they could do some research about the subject or the author. Directions and materials for simple art projects could be included. Materials should be changed periodically to maintain interest.

5. Guests from the World of Art

Invite guest speakers such as local artists, art historians, and museum guides to discuss art and its relationship to reading. For instance, a museum guide might discuss titles of art works, maps of museums, or collection labels. A local artist might discuss favorite reading materials; or an art historian might discuss how one uses printed materials to learn about artists and their works.

6. Reading Visit to an Art Gallery

If possible, take a reading-related visit to an art gallery. Have students prepare for the trip by studying a road map and planning the way to get there. Have them study floor plans of the gallery, help plan the sections to visit, and read literature about the museum and types of collections there. While at the gallery, point out titles of art works and the printed information that is given about many of the paintings. Have students find the location of certain works in the museum. After returning to the school, have them read more about their favorite artist or painting, share the information with the class, and write an evaluation of the field trip.

7. "Our-Favorite-Artist" Display

Have groups of students pick a favorite artist and plan a bulletin board display with appropriate materials. Students could first read about the artist in art books or encyclopedias and then arrange a display that would be meaningful to the other students. Their display could have a theme, such as different ways the artist used color, or different subjects painted by the artist, or how the artist changed throughout his or her life. Underneath the display, arrange appropriate reading materials.

8. Reading Through a Famous Artist's Eye

Many painters, such as Gauguin, Van Gogh, Picasso, Renoir, and Cassatt, have included readers and reading materials in their works. Show students some reproductions or slides of these paintings to help them see different ideas about reading. Ask students questions about these works of art and the artists' possible reasons for including reading materials in the paintings. Have students make hypotheses as to what is in the reading materials, the reader's opinion of the materials, and the physical properties of the reading matter itself.

9. Reading Through a Student-Artist's Eyes

Have students discuss ways in which reading is important to them, places they like to read, and the types of things they like to read. Have them draw, paint, or use cut paper to make a picture that shows someone reading in a special place or for a special reason. Then have them write an essay on the importance of reading to them or why they like to read. Pictures and essays could be posted together.

10. Techniques of Illustrators

Help students to see that illustrations are not only a way of enhancing a story, but are also something to be valued and appreciated for their own sake. After reading and discussing the illustrations in a book, show students other books illustrated by the same artist. Ask them what makes the artist's style unique and easy to recognize, what media and techniques does the artist use, and what colors occur frequently. Display a collection of books by the same illustrator. Discuss their similarities and differences. Also discuss the types of books that are illustrated. Does the artist usually illustrate outdoor books, books about children or fairy tales? Have the students write to the illustrator in care of the publishers of the books to obtain more information.

11. The Caldecott Winners

Let students read or listen to the books that were awarded the Caldecott Medal for the most distinguished illustrations of an American book for children. Remind the students that although the prize is awarded primarily for the illustrations, the pictures must be compatible with the text. Have groups of students or the entire class carefully study all of the Caldecott nominees for a certain year. To do this, they must read the books as well as look at the illustrations. Have them choose their own award winner and give reasons for their choice (Rowell p. p.).

12. Comparing Illustrations for the Same Story

After students are familiar with Mother Goose Rhymes, fairy tales, or stories such as *Alice in Wonderland,* bring in versions of these stories illustrated by different artists. Ask students to compare the different styles, types, and contents of illustrations: color versus black and white; the medium used, such as collage, water color, or line drawing; and fantasy versus realism.

13. Meet the Author/Illustrator

Before reading a book to students, introduce them to some information about the illustrator. Interesting tidbits about an artist's life, such as knowing that Maurice Sendak often creates to music, can help the students to better appreciate an artist's work. Information about illustrators can be found in the books listed on page 113.

14. Studying the History of Books

Review with students the history of writing and have them make their own old-fashioned books. Students could make their own clay tablets or they could dip paper in tea to make it look like old parchment and write on it with pens fashioned from turkey or seagull feathers; or they can make scrolls by gluing pictures to sheets of paper and rolling and tying them with colored string. Students could look up more about the history of writing in the encyclopedia and suggest other ways to illustrate it.

15. "Read-All-About-It" Art Corner

Have a "Read-All-About-It" art corner in the room with attractive prints and colorful art books where students can read more about the art activities they are doing, about artists whose work they admire, or art history. Encourage students to spend time in this part of the room.

16. Pleasure-Reading About Art

To encourage students to read about art, have an occasional period in which they can read anything they want about art. After a ten- or fifteen-minute period, students could discuss some of the things they learned or enjoyed while reading. Materials could include art magazines, art books from a class collection or school or public library, or relevant articles in encyclopedias that are listed and indexed for the students.

ARTISTIC BOOK REVIEWS

Students usually enjoy sharing information about books through art activities, and "artistic book reports" can often help students to recall, translate, or interpret what they have read. However, care should be taken to ensure that the art activity is not so time consuming or demanding that students will lose their initial enthusiasm about a book during the project. Students should also have an opportunity to share verbally their reactions to the books they have read. Experience with verbal expressions will better prepare them for sharing their opinions about what they have read in social situations outside of school.

The read-and-share artistic ideas in this section can be done in reasonable amounts of time. It is important that the type of activity selected be appropriate for the book. Each activity also requires the student to discuss some aspect of the book. Students could all be assigned the same type of activity or they could each select an artistic way in which to share their books.

1. Favorite-Book T-Shirt

Let students each design and make a T-shirt showing an important event or character in a book. The design could be made on an old white T-shirt using colorfast marking pens. The students could wear the shirts while explaining why others would enjoy reading their books.

2. Favorite-Books Quilt

Have each student design a square for a paper or cloth quilt of favorite books. Have each student discuss the reasons for his/her design and its relationship to the book.

3. Come-and-Read Poster

Encourage each student to make a poster urging others to read a particular favorite book. Then have students stand next to their posters as they encourage people to select their books.

4. Book Jackets

Display book jackets in the room and discuss the information included on each—the titles in prominent letters, authors' names, and attractive pictures or designs. Have students each make a book jacket for a favorite book. The book jacket should include all necessary information and also reveal something about the book. Then let students discuss the reasons for including the cover pictures or designs in relation to their particular books.

5. Book Marks

Discuss the importance of using bookmarks—or have the librarian lead such a discussion. Then let the students each make a bookmark representing a book they have just read. Emphasize that the marker should be flat and made with fast colors that will not rub off on the pages. Then have students discuss the ways the bookmarks relate to their books.

6. Book Puppets

Have students each make a sock-, paper-bag-, stick-, finger-, or hand-puppet of a favorite character from a book. Then have them discuss their books from their characters' point of view.

7. Character, Object or Event Models

Let students each make a soap carving or clay model about an important event, character, or object in their book. Have students tell about the significance of the model to the story.

8. Character Masks

Have students each make a paper-bag mask of a character in a book. Then have them wear the masks and tell about the books from the vantage points of their characters.

9. Significant-Objects Mobile

Let each student make a mobile with significant items related to a story and then tell about the importance of these items to the plot.

10. Cartoon-Strip Events

Have each student make a cartoon strip of a book and then tell about important parts of the story.

11. Book Movie

Let each student draw a series of pictures in sequence on a long strip of paper. Attach the ends to rollers and place in a cardboard box (see page 53). The students could print simple dialogues to accompany the pictures or they could tell about important scenes from the story.

12. Additional Illustrations

Have students make two or three illustrations that they think should have been included in their books and tell why they should have appeared.

13. Flannel-Board Characters

Let students make flannel-board characters and use them on a flannel board to tell about their stories.

14. Meaningful-Quotation Collage

Have students make a collage of meaningful quotations from their books. Have them write the quotations with different styles of print and then discuss the significance of several of the quotations.

15. Pictorial Time-Line

Let students make pictorial time-lines of events from their books and discuss the importance of the time-line.

16. Book Map

Have students make maps for their books and discuss where significant events took place.

17. Book Advertisements

Display a variety of book advertisements and discuss the ways art and print are used to capture one's attention. Have students make attention-getting advertisements for their own books. Then let them try to "sell" their books to others.

18. Book-Mood or -Theme Collage

Have each student make a collage of magazine pictures that relate to the mood or theme of a book, then discuss reasons for the pictures selected. Include a discussion of color and mood effects.

19. Book-Setting Diorama

Discuss the importance of the setting or scene to a story. Have each student select one setting from a book and make a three-dimensional diorama in a shoe box. Then let students explain the significance of their scenes to the stories.

20. "My Favorite Picture in the Book"

Let each student select a favorite book illustration to share with the class and explain how it relates to the subject of the book.

21. Book Picture-Postcards

Have students each make a picture postcard illustrating a favorite scene from a book. Then have them write descriptions of the books on the other sides of the postcards. Suggest that they send their cards to each other or to friends or relatives outside of school.

22. Book-Reading Travel Agents

Let each student present an illustrated review, using appropriate post-cards, photographs, slides, and pictures, of a travel book he or she has read. A large poster could be used as the background.

Art is everywhere, from museums to posters on subway walls. It is attractive to the eye and stimulates thought and discussion. Since it is easy to become involved in art on a personal and creative level, art can serve as a special and attractive resource for stimulating student interest in reading and in the acquisition of basic reading and language skills.

Readings and References

CHALL, JEANNE. *Learning to Read: The Great Debate.* New York: McGraw-Hill, 1967.

CIANCIOL, PAT. *Illustrations in Children's Books.* Dubuque, Iowa: William C. Brown, 1970.

EVANS, RALPH. "Characteristics of Color." *World Book Encyclopedia,* Vol. 4. Chicago: Field Enterprises, 1980.

FULLER, MURIEL. *More Junior Authors.* New York: H.W. Wilson, 1963.

HALL, BARBARA ANN. "The Arts and Reading—Coming to Our Senses." *Claremont Reading Conference,* Claremont, California: Claremont Graduate School, 1979, pp. 60–67.

HOPKINS, LEE BENNETT. *Books Are by People.* New York: Citation Press, 1969.

HOPKINS, LEE BENNETT. *More Books by More People.* New York: Citation Press, 1974.

KINGMAN, LEE; JOANNA FOSTER, and BEULAH FOLMSBEE. *Illustrators of Children's Books* (1957–1966). Boston: Horn Book Inc., 1968.

MAHONEY, BERTHA E.; LOUISE LATIMER, and BEULAH FOLMSBEE. *Illustrators of Children's Books* (1744–1945). Boston: Horn Book Inc., 1947.

National Assessment of Educational Progress, "Art Zeal High: Knowledge Lacking." *NAEP Newsletter,* No. 6, December 1977.

ROWELL, ELIZABETH H., "Developing Reading Skills through the Study of Great Art." *Fine Arts and Reading Monograph,* Newark, Delaware: IRA (publication pending).

SEIFERTH, JOHN C. "Guggenheim Museum Children's Program: Learning to Read through the Arts," *ED* 137–460, 1975.

TWAIN, MARK [Samuel Clemens] *The Adventures of Huckleberry Finn.* New York: Macmillan, 1962.

VIGUERS, RUTH HILL; MARCIA DALPHIN and BERTHA MILLER. *Illustrators of Children's Books (1946–1956). Boston: Horn Book Inc., 1958.*

WHITE, E.B. *Charlotte's Web.* New York: Harper & Row, Pub., 1952.

WHITTLESEY, EUNICE. *Symbols and Legends in Western Art: A Museum Guide.* New York: Scribner's, 1972.

chapter four

learning to read
via the sounds
of **MUSIC**

Introduction

*Music produces a kind of pleasure which human
nature cannot do without.*[1]

More than at any other time in history, music is a part of our environment. In this age of transistor radios, portable headsets, car stereos, and TV and movie sound tracks, there are very few places one can go without hearing some kind of music.

Music is also very important to children. Regardless of their background or levels of musical ability, they all have some form of music in their daily lives. They have favorite singers and musical groups and they collect records and buy posters of their favorites. The National Assessment of Educational Progress survey of musical interests and abilities has indicated that most students enjoy music. Over 95 percent of the individuals surveyed said they enjoyed listening to some type of music. Eighty percent said that they also enjoyed singing, and either played or would like to play a musical instrument (Rivas 1974). Many youngsters are virtually "hooked" on rock, country, or folk music, and Americans of all ages are spending more money than ever before on musical instruments, accessories, sheet music and self-instructional aids (Benner 1975).[2]

The importance of music in the growth and development of the child has often been underestimated. Because children get pleasure from it and can respond to it in a variety of multisensory ways, music can be a wonderful addition to a school day. It can provide a change of pace, furnish a release from tension, and help students to relax. Music can also reduce the boredom of the repetition and drill that is often necessary in learning to read and music-related reading activities can often get students more interested and involved.

[1]Confucius, *source unknown.*
[2]Chapter readings and references appear on page 184.

Students can improve in valuable skills important to reading while working on musical activities. Music can stimulate them to think ahead and anticipate, and help to develop attention span, perception, conceptualization, imagination, insight, and creativity (Taylor 1973). When singing or reading lyrics, children must also read at a given rate of speed in order to participate, put words properly into syllables, and speak or sing with proper inflection, pronunciation, and emphasis. Musical activities can also be used to develop new vocabulary, word meanings, auditory acuity, and rhyming ability. While involved in music-related activities, students often feel freer to experiment with different sounds and new words and can get the kind of repetitive practice they need without being judged.

Many students who dislike reading or find it difficult enjoy music and can show improvement in reading through music-related activities. Although poor readers are often easily distracted and seem to have brief attention spans, it is often possible to hold their attention and discover their ability to remember through music.

Music-related activities can provide group experiences for children who would be too shy to speak or read aloud by themselves. Music is especially helpful for foreign students who are learning to speak and read English. The multisensory musical experience can be an aid in mastering new vocabulary and language patterns. Sometimes the rhythm of music can help students who have comprehension problems because they read unevenly. People who stutter when speaking or reading aloud often have no trouble when they sing. Music-related learning can also carry over throughout all of adult life because of the presence of music in the everyday world.

Research indicates that there is a strong positive correlation between language-reading and music-reading abilities (Dalton 1952). Studies have also noted that children who receive musical instruction or participate in music-related reading activities frequently perform better in reading and have better study habits than children who do not (Kokas 1969; *Time* October 1965; Pelletier 1963; Movesian 1969; Anderson 1971; Harper 1973; Turnipseed 1974).

Research done with preschoolers and first graders showed that children who participated in musical activities developed better auditory discrimination skills, were better able to coordinate their senses of hearing and seeing, and had greater ability to handle instructional tasks. They also improved their self images (Turnipseed 1974). Several studies showed that students from preschool through junior high could learn reading vocabulary and comprehension skills through musical activities such as singing, dancing, listening to records, and learning to play instruments (Pelletier 1963; *Time* 1965; Movesian 1969; Seides 1967). Research with slow learners showed that they also gained in reading skills as a result of special music programs (Pelletier 1963; Seides 1967; Nicholson 1972).

At one school where reading was taught once a week with music, teachers noted that the students grew in self-esteem and confidence, were

138

more willing to volunteer, and improved in reading expression and vocabulary. Students said this approach was "fascinating," put them in a good mood, and made their whole day better. Some said they knew more "what words were," read a lot better and faster, and had greater smoothness in reading (Gibbs 1970). At another school where disadvantaged students learned new vocabulary words through folk songs and dance, the students jumped four months ahead of a class using standard methods. The principal stated that the students were not afraid to learn how to read because they didn't know they were doing it (*Time* 1965).

Music can be used in many imaginative ways for teaching reading skills. Most students find listening to music or working on music-related reading activities extremely enjoyable. Often they get so engrossed that they do not realize they are learning reading skills while participating in musical activities. In short, music can enable students to have pleasure while learning to read.

MATERIALS FOR MUSIC AND READING ACTIVITIES

A lack of musical training need not be a deterrent to providing interesting musical reading activities. The important thing is for a teacher to display enthusiasm and interest in music. A recording can be used to give melody and tempo, and a tuning fork, pitch pipe, or toy xylophone can be used to find the first note of a song. Librarians can suggest appropriate music-related books and local musical stores can provide information about suitable records.

Every child brings with him or her a background of music and it is important to begin where the student is to keep interest alive when working on musical reading activities. Most students enjoy music whether musically talented or not. Materials, devices, and techniques should be matched to the students' interests, vocal development, singing range and musical skills. The materials and activities used should not call for a level of proficiency in musical skills which the students do not have.

Students must also be helped to realize that it is not so much how they sound when they sing, play an instrument, or how they look when they do a movement, but it is the spirit behind the effort that is important. Those students who are talented or play an instrument could participate in a special way. This can often be a boost to their self confidence.

It is important to vary activities to avoid predictability. Reading activities could be centered around a number of different musical experiences, including singing, listening, dancing, doing movements, playing instruments, or creating new music. Materials should be presented in such a way that children will enjoy the activity as they develop reading skills.

The following are materials that can be useful for music-related reading activities:

1. Record player and headsets

2. Cassette tape recorder and headsets

3. Records and cassettes
   (It is best to encourage students to bring in only specific titles. Some songs might deal with subjects unsuitable for study with a particular class.)

4. Music books and lyric sheets
   (Often lyrics are printed on record jackets or can be obtained by writing to the record company.)

5. Books about music and musicians
   (Many of these can be obtained from the school or public library or from students' private collections.)

6. Posters of composers or musicians
   (Sometimes these can be obtained inexpensively or at no cost from music companies.)

7. Pictures of musical instruments and/or actual instruments
   (Sometimes these can be borrowed from the music teacher or band director.)

8. Tapes of TV specials, commercials, and theme songs

9. A wide variety of musical instruments

piano	resonator bells	tambourine
autoharp	tune glasses or bottles	jingle clogs
guitar	cymbals	triangles
ukulele	wood blocks	sand blocks
banjo	drums	maracas
xylophone	rhythm sticks	castanets

10. A wide variety of musical selections

country and western music	opera
electronic music	patriotic songs
folk music	popular music
jazz	rock music
sound tracks of musicals or movies	songs from other countries
nursery rhymes	soul music

SELECTING APPROPRIATE MUSIC

It is important to pick music in which students will be interested that also has possibilities for reading development. It is wise to check the vocabulary and subject content of a song before using it for a musical reading activity. Songs do not usually have a graded vocabulary and many children's songs and popular tunes do not lend themselves to beginning reading instruction due to the range in vocabulary. However, these songs might be appropriate to use with upper grade students who may need to be highly motivated. Some traditional songs contain words which can be explained to students but are seldom part of their experiences, such as cobbler's bench and weasel in "Pop Goes the Weasel." Songs used with beginning readers should be relatively simple. It is often possible to substitute pictures for words in the lyrics that students might not know how to read.

The style of music is also important because students need to hear the words distinctly. Some music blends the words too much, pronunciation is poor, or the tempo is too fast for the students to hear the words separately. It is important to use different types of music to expand students' musical experiences. At times it may be desirable to select music based on holidays, weather, poems, or special experiences.

To find out what students are interested in, keep up with the current trends by listening to popular radio stations or get lists of the top hits from record shops. Much can be learned about students' musical preferences by listening to them talk about music at informal times during the school day, such as before or after school or during lunch or recess. It can also be helpful to question them either orally or through the following type of written questionnaire:

1. What kind of music do you enjoy listening to the most?
    _____ classical   _____ movie or musical sound tracks
    _____ country-western   _____ rock
    _____ electronic   _____ religious
    _____ folk   _____ soul
    _____ jazz   _____ other _____

2. List your three favorite musical selections or songs.
    _____ _____ _____

3. List your two favorite singers.
    _____ _____

4. List your two favorite musical performers or groups.
    _____ _____

5. List the two songs you sing the most often for pleasure.
    _____ _____

6. Do you play an instrument? If so, which one? _____

7. If you could play an instrument, which one would you like to play?
    _____

8. What kind of music would you like to know more about?
    _____ Why? _____

Reading Readiness via Musical Activities

What will a child learn sooner than a song?[1]

Since most young children enjoy listening to music, singing, and playing rhythm instruments, the beginning stages of learning to read can be made more pleasurable by using musical activities. Many reading readiness skills can be strengthened through musical experiences. Visual skills such as visual discrimination, visual memory, and visual-auditory association can be developed through musical activities and music is a natural medium to use to develop the auditory skills that are necessary prerequisites for learning phonics.

Additional activities for increasing prereaders' word knowledge and for getting them enthusiastic about learning to read can be found in the vocabulary and interest portions of this section. Ideas for working on comprehension skills can be adapted from those presented in the comprehension section.

VISUAL SKILL DEVELOPMENT

1. Making Descriptions

Show students a musical instrument and have them describe how it looks and differs from other instruments. Then remove the instrument and ask them to describe it or draw a picture of it.

2. Noting the Notes

Have students look carefully at a page of music and discuss the differences among the types of notes. Then have students look to see if the notes are going up (ascending) or down (descending).

3. Going from Left to Right

While students are listening to a new song, project a copy of the lyrics with an overhead and then use a pointer stick as a marker to show students the left-to-right, top-to-bottom progression in reading.

4. Music and Visual Imagery

After students have listened to a song with a story, such as "Go Tell Aunt Rhody," ask them to describe what they saw in their "minds' eyes" while the music was being played. Encourage them to use descriptive words.

142

[1]Alexander Pope, *Imitations of Horace: Epistles.*

5. Seeing and Doing

Draw a rhythm pattern on the chalkboard for students to play by clapping
or using rhythm instruments. A simple line-dash pattern or a combination
of large and small objects could be used to designate short and long
sounds.

examples:

6. Picturing the Rhythm

Beat or clap out a rhythm for the students and have them illustrate it with a
picture so they can keep it and play the rhythm again. Then have them
play the rhythm from their drawing.

7. Associating Sounds with Pictures

Give students each a rhythm instrument and have them produce a sound
only when given a visual stimulus for their instrument. For example, the
visual stimulus for drums might be a picture of a woodpecker; bells—a
picture of a bird; and blocks—a picture of a horse.

AUDITORY SKILL DEVELOPMENT

1. Describing the Music

Have students listen to different musical sounds and/or instruments and
then describe what they heard.

2. Hearing Musical Differences

Play two sounds on the piano, guitar, xylophone, drum, or on two
different instruments and ask students whether they sound alike or
different. If they are not alike, have them describe how they are different.
Develop the concepts of high-low, same-different, and soft-loud. Then
play chords and single notes and have students listen and describe
whether and how these differ. Next play two simple sequences of sounds
and ask the students to compare how they are alike or different. Develop
the concepts of like-unlike, fast-slow, and even-uneven. Play a record of
the same song sung or played by two different people or instruments.
Have students listen carefully and then compare how the two versions are
similar or different.

3. Hearing the Differences

While playing a record, the piano, or a rhythm instrument, have students
close their eyes. Occasionally change the volume of the sound. Have

students raise their hands when the volume is different. Have them tell whether the music is softer or louder. A variation of this would be to have the students walk to the music and stomp when the music is loud and tiptoe when the music is soft. Change the volume occasionally.

4. Playing Musical Chairs

Have students sit on chairs in a circle facing out. When the music begins, have them walk around the group of chairs. Remove one chair. Then stop the music. When the music ceases, each must find a chair and sit. The student who does not have a chair is out of the game. Repeat the process. Remove one chair each time after the music has resumed. Vary this activity periodically: Instead of merely stopping the music, turn the phonograph to a faster or slower speed or make the volume much louder or softer.

5. Music and Rhyming Words

Learning rhyming words can be more enjoyable when students find words that rhyme in songs they enjoy listening to or singing. Have students locate all the words that rhyme in a song and then if possible make pictures of the rhyming pairs. Older students with more advanced phonetic backgrounds could list the rhyming words and study the various spellings.
examples:

> Rhyming words in "Hush Little Baby":
>
> bird—word
> sing—ring
>
> Rhyming words in "Twinkle, Twinkle, Little Star":
>
> high—sky
> star—are

6. Supplying the Missing Rhyming Words

After students have heard a song with rhyming words, sing it for them again, omitting the final rhyming word in a pair. Let them supply the missing word.
example:

> "Twinkle, twinkle little star,
> How I wonder what you _____."

7. Composing Rhyming Lyrics

Encourage students to make up extra verses containing rhyming words for songs, such as "Hush Little Baby," "Row, Row, Row Your Boat," "Sweet Betsy from Pike," or "Twinkle, Twinkle Little Star."

8. Making Auditory Predictions

After studying the sounds of many different instruments, show the students a new instrument and have them predict the sound it will make. Then play the instrument and compare its sound with their predictions.

9. Careful Listening

Before playing a short piece of music, ask students to listen carefully for the story in the song or what they think the music is telling them. Then have them listen again so that they can describe or hum the melody. Have them listen another time so that they can describe the instruments used. Telling students to listen for something specific prior to playing the music will help them to listen for a purpose and improve their listening skills.

10. Following the Leader

Sing or play a single musical sound and have students copy it. Then sing or play a short simple tune or rhythm and have students reproduce it. They could also take turns being the leader to make the sounds that the others must reproduce.

11. Passing a Musical Message

Softly sing a simple short tune into a student's ear so that no others can hear it. Then have the student quietly sing the tune to the person next to him or her and continue to pass the "message" around the room in this fashion. Compare the original "message" with the concluding one.

Musical Language Experiences

Music is well said to be the speech of angels.[1]

The transition from prereading activities to reading can be quite difficult. One way to make this transition easier is through language experience activities in which students respond to some form of stimulus and then freely dictate sentences about it. Musical experiences can provide activities that can stimulate students to describe what they did, heard, or imagined. These thoughts can then be written down and read back to the students to help them begin to see that print parallels speech. While listening to and watching someone else read their sentences, students can learn that words are read from left to right and they will also be gaining familiarity with the printed forms of a few words.

1. Saying a Song

Have students say or sing very slowly the words to a familiar song while someone writes them down on the chalkboard. Then have the students follow the lines and try to say the words as someone reads the words aloud while pointing to them.

[1]Thomas Carlyle, *Essays: The Opera.*

2. Using Music's Technical Vocabulary

Explain to students the meaning of a new musical term, such as *rhythm, tempo, beat,* or the name of an instrument or composer. After playing an appropriate selection, ask them to dictate sentences using the new term.
examples:

The Clarinet

The *clarinet* makes high sounds and low sounds.
The *clarinet* can squeak like a mouse.
The *clarinet* is black and shiny.
The *clarinet* looks like a black stick with silver jewelry.

Tempo

The *tempo* was slow and fast in this record.
The slow *tempo* made me sleepy.
We marched when the *tempo* was fast.

3. Dictating a Musical Story

After students have listened to music that tells a story, such as "Peter and the Wolf" (Prokofiev), or a favorite song, such as "She'll Be Comin' Round the Mountain," have them dictate a story about it. Put these into a class music story booklet.

4. Dictating a New Song

Have students dictate other words or another verse to a favorite tune, such as "Old MacDonald" or "Row, Row, Row Your Boat," and then sing it.

5. A Musical Filmstrip

Let students draw pictures to go with a song and then dictate individual stories that can be written on their pictures. Arrange the pictures and stories sequentially on long shelf or mural paper, and show the story on a homemade "TV set" (see page 53).

Decoding via the Joys of Music

The language of tones belongs equally well to all mankind (humankind).[1]

Word-attack skills enable students to recognize which word in their oral repertoire a printed word represents. To be able to figure out words in print, students need to have a large base of words they know instantly at

[1]Richard Wagner, *Beethoven.*

sight as well as proficient skills in phonic analysis, structural analysis, and contextual analysis. For aid in deciphering words that are not in their oral repertoire, students need to be able to use a dictionary accurately. A great deal of practice is required to be able to recognize words instantly at sight and to use word attack skills proficiently. This practice and drill can often seem very monotonous and dull. This section includes ways to capitalize on students' interest in music to develop important word-recognition skills.

SIGHT-WORD RECOGNITION

1. Singing Sight-Words

When children are singing songs such as "Old MacDonald," hold up cards with animal names and sounds to introduce a new refrain.
examples:

Cow	**Duck**	**Pig**
moo-moo	quack-quack	oink-oink

When singing "So Early in the Morning," show students action and noun cards.
examples:

wash	**iron**
clothes	shirts

When singing songs such as "Looby Lou" or "Hokey Pokey," hold up flashcards for left and right to indicate which hand, arm, or foot students should hold up.

2. Moving to Words

While playing a record or tape, occasionally ring a bell and hold up a card containing a movement word. Have students indicate that they know the meaning of the word by using the appropriate movement in time to the music until the bell is rung again.
examples of movement words:
> march, skip, step, walk, run, sway, hop, jump, leap, prance, glide, dip, swirl, twirl, dart, swing, slide, bend

3. Learning the Lyrics

After students have learned to sing a song from memory, give them the lyrics written on paper without the musical notations and symbols that might be distracting. Have students follow the lyrics while singing or listening to the song. This will help to reinforce some words by sight. After students have done this several times, ask them to locate certain words or phrases.

147

4. Repeating the Refrain

Some songs have refrains that are repeated many times. Copy the phrases from a song that are similar and have students mark the words that are alike.

examples:

"This is the way we wash our clothes.
This is the way we dry our clothes."

"This land is your land.
This land is my land."

5. Showing the Words

Give students some cards containing isolated words from a song. Have them raise the proper card when they hear the word in a song. Phrases or sentences from songs could be reviewed in the same way.

examples:

Isolated words from "Twinkle, Twinkle Little Star":

star	are	far	sky

Phrases from "Jingle Bells":

Jingle all the way	one-horse, open sleigh

6. Learning Song Words

Write isolated words from songs on shapes suggested by the lyrics. Halloween songs might be on ghost shapes and sea chanteys on boat shapes. Have students review the words first in isolation and then by saying them in a sentence that relates to the theme represented by the shape.

examples from "Old MacDonald":

7. Matching Words

Make two identical sets of word cards from a song. Have small groups of students play the game *Concentration* with the word cards. The person with the most pairs wins the game. (See page 99 for a description of *Concentration*.)

8. Isolating Words from the Lyrics

Let students copy the lyrics from a favorite song on small cards, putting one word on each card. Have them mix up the cards and then make new sentences from the cards or form sentences to match the lyrics.

9. Finding Frequently Used Words in Popular Songs

A large percentage of the words in popular songs are frequently used words (see list on page 11). Have students match these words that they need to review with words in the lyrics of their favorite songs.

10. Word-Song Mural Making

Give each student a word or a phrase from a song to use in making an illustration. Put the resulting pictures on a bulletin board or mural. List the different words or phrases on a chart beside the bulletin board or mural. Have students read the words and then point to the objects in the illustration that depict them.

example words taken from "Hush Little Baby":

mockingbird
billy goat
horse and cart
dog
baby

11. Musical Word Pictures

Select words from a song, such as *boat, stream,* and *gently* from "Row, Row, Row Your Boat," and ask students to look through magazines and find pictures that illustrate these terms. Have students cut out and paste each picture on a corresponding word card.

12. Completing Sentences

On index cards, write sentences from a song and cut the sentences into two parts like a jigsaw. Have children read the phrases and reassemble the sentences.

examples:

You are ♪ my sunshine   You make ♪ me happy

PHONICS REVIEW

1. Musical Instruments, Musicians, and Key Words

Have students make up their own key words to help them remember letter-sound associations by using musical instruments or performers. Have them draw or collect suitable pictures and put them with their beginning letters in prominent places in the room. When students need help in remembering the sound of a letter, encourage them to refer to the appropriate picture.

examples:

A accordion, autoharp	**A** Abba
B bongos, banjo, bass	**B** Beatles, Beachboys
C coronet, cymbals	**C** Cash, Johnny
D dulcimer, drums	**D** Denver, John

2. Phonics and Song Lyrics

After students have sung a song several times and they are familiar with the lyrics, have them identify words in the song that start or end with a certain sound or contain a specific vowel sound. For example, in "Sunshine on My Shoulders," which words start like *soup, shot, money,* and *heart*? Which words end like *pan, try,* and *baby*? Which words have vowel sounds like *try, pond, rub,* and *now*? List these words on the board. A variation would be to give students copies of song lyrics they enjoy and work sheets that contain phonic activities.

SUNSHINE ON MY SHOULDERS

Words by John Denver*

Sunshine on my shoulders makes me happy,
Sunshine in my eyes can make me cry.
Sunshine on the water looks so lovely,
Sunshine almost always makes me high.

If I had a day that I could give you,
I'd give to you a day just like today.
If I had a song that I could sing for you,
I'd sing a song to make you feel this way.
If I had a tale that I could tell you,
I'd tell a tale sure to make you smile.
If I had a wish that I could wish for you,
I'd make a wish for sunshine all the while.

Sunshine on my shoulders makes me happy,
Sunshine in my eyes can make me cry.
Sunshine on the water looks so lovely,
Sunshine almost always makes me high.
Sunshine almost all the time makes me high,
Sunshine almost always makes me high.

1. Add the missing vowels.

   sh—ld–r   h–pp–

2. Cross out the silent letters.

   sunshine   makes

3. Unscramble these words.

   ym   skema

4. Find three words with short vowels.

   _____   _____   _____

5. Find three words with long vowels.

   _____   _____   _____

6. Find three words with digraphs.

   _____   _____   _____

3. Phonetic Lyricists

Write new lyrics containing sounds students need to review to the tunes of simple songs. Students may also enjoy the challenge of composing their own new lyrics.

examples:

"Max the Cat,"
to the tune of "Row, Row, Row Your Boat"
(Review short *a* (a) sound)

Max, Max, Max, the Cat,
Had a fat black rat.
Happy, happy, happy, happy,
Max, the happy cat.

"Five Short vowels,"
to the tune of "Three Blind Mice"
Five short vowels
Five short vowels
Hear how they sound,
Hear how they sound:
a,e,i,o,u; a,e,i,o,u; a,e,i,o,u;
Five short vowels.

4. Singing Nonsense Words

For practice with phonic skills, make up some nonsense words such as *trime* and *flope* (silent e), *sleam* and *frain* (two vowels together), *flug* and *trat* (short vowels in a closed syllable). Put the nonsense words into the lyrics of a familiar song. Then have the students pronounce the words correctly and sing the song.

example:

To the tune of "Row, Row, Row Your Boat"
Trime, trime, trime your frain,
Fluggingly down the flope.
Tratting, tratting, tratting, tratting,
Flug is just a sleam.

5. Noting Nonsense Words

Many songs contain nonsense words or phrases, such as "hey deing dong doodle alley day" in "Sourwood Mountain." Have students pronounce these nonsense words using their word analysis skills.

STRUCTURAL ANALYSIS

1. Beating Out the Syllables

Let students use rhythm instruments, such as bells, drums, and maracas, to beat out the syllables in their names.

examples:

Rob-ert Da-vis   Wil-lie Mae Han-sen

2. Musical Patterns in Poetry

Have students use rhythm instruments to sound out each syllable in a nursery rhyme or short poem.

example:

> Hump-ty Dump-ty
> Sat on a wall.
> Hump-ty Dump-ty
> Had a great fall.
> All the king's hor-ses
> And all the King's men
> Could-n't put Hump-ty
> To-geth-er a-gain!

3. Syllables and Song Beats

Let students sing, clap, walk, skip, or jump to the syllables of a song while either singing or listening to the lyrics. Then have them clap or tap out the syllables without the music. Have them clap harder on the accented syllables.

example:

> "SUN-shine on my SHOUL-ders makes me HAP-py."

4. Music and Word Parts

Give students the lyrics to a favorite song and ask them to mark on the song sheet where the words should be divided.

examples:

> "Sun/shine on my shoul/ders makes me hap/py"

5. Lyric Compound Detectives

Have students list the compound words they find in a song and separate them.

6. Musical Contractions

Ask students to locate all the contractions on a lyric sheet and list the two words that made the contraction.

7. Prefixes and Suffixes in Songs

Have students find all the words with prefixes or with suffixes in a song and list them. Then have them write the words they found in sentences.

CONTEXT-CLUE USAGE

1. Using the Context-Clues

Prepare song sheets with the lyrics in the form of a poem. Underline potential problem words. Have students read the song lyrics silently paying particular attention to underlined words to see if they can identify the words and their meaning from the context.

2. Cloze and Songs

After students are familiar with a song, give them exercises with some of the words in the song deleted. Have them fill in the blanks with the correct words.
example:
> "Sunshine on my _____ makes me _____."

3. Maze and Songs

This activity is similar to Activity 2 except that the words from which the students can select are given at the bottom of the page.
example:
> "Sunshine on my _____ makes me _____."
> *(arm, shoulders, head, foot) (sad, angry, ugly, happy)*

DICTIONARY PRACTICE

1. Deciphering Unknown Words

Pass out copies of song lyrics to students. Have them write the words they do not know on a card and then look them up in a dictionary to find the meanings as used in the song. Have them rewrite the song phrases containing the unfamiliar words using synonyms.

2. Musical Alphabetizing

Students can practice their skills in alphabetizing by putting items from the world of music into alphabetical order.
examples of musical items to alphabetize:

- all of the song titles in a favorite record album

- favorite pop artists (last name first)

- musical instruments that the class can play

- ten favorite songs

3. Lyrical Alphabetical Order

Have students write the lyrics of one of their favorite songs on small cards—one word to each card. Then have them arrange all of the word cards in alphabetical order.

4. Making a Class Musical Dictionary

Have students make a dictionary of musical terms including pronunciation, meaning, and a sentence. They could also include musicians and instruments they have studied.
example:

> opera (op′rə, opər-ə) . noun . An opera is a play in which all the people sing instead of speaking.
> We saw part of an opera called *The Marriage of Figaro.*

Musical Activities for Building Reading Vobaculary

Music is the universal language of mankind (humankind).[1]

Musical activities can be used as very effective vocabulary builders. Most song lyrics can tells tories or present information. Songs usually provide a great deal of repetition, and when the music is also slow enough, students can begin to become aware of many new words and their proper pronunciations even if they are not yet fully aware of their meanings. Enriching students' vocabularies by discussing the meanings of the words in favorite songs can be a very enjoyable and rewarding experience. The music-related activities in this section illustrate a variety of ways to increase students' vocabularies.

1. Questioning the Lyrics

Ask students questions about the meanings of words in songs. As many students sing songs and don't know what the words mean, this type of exercise will help them to improve their vocabularies as well as better understand the lyrics. The following types of questions can be asked about most songs to increase students' vocabularies. The examples are based on "The Star-Spangled Banner."

THE STAR-SPANGLED BANNER

Words by Francis Scott Key

Oh, say, can you see,
By the dawn's early light,
What so proudly we hailed
At the twilight's last gleaming?

Whose broad stripes and bright stars
Through the perilous fight,
O'er the ramparts we watched
Were so gallantly streaming?

And the rockets' red glare
The bombs bursting in air,
Gave proof through the night
That our flag was still there.

Oh, say, does that star-spangled banner yet wave
O'er the land of the free and the home of the brave?

[1]Henry Wadsworth Longfellow, *Outre-Mer: Spanish Ballads.*

Definition.	What does the word *ramparts* mean in this song?
Synonym.	What word could be substituted for *perilous* without changing the meaning of the sentence?
Antonym.	What word can be substituted for *proudly* to make the sentence mean the opposite of what it does now?
Homophone.	What word do you know which sounds the same as *see* but is spelled differently and has a different meaning?
Semantic.	What other meanings do you know for the word *hail*?
Phrase Meaning.	What do the phrases "twilight's last gleaming" and "dawn's early light" mean?

2. Supplying the Missing Word

Delete some words from the lyrics and give definitions for them. Then let students figure out what is missing.
example from "Sunshine on My Shoulders":

"Sunshine on my _____ makes me _____."
(part of your body)   (a good feeling)

3. Mood Words

Let students review the lyrics of a song to find the words used to create a mood. List the mood words in isolation and in phrases on the chalkboard. Encourage students to use the words in their own conversations.

4. Dialect and Regional Expressions

Discuss different dialects and the meanings of regional expressions, such as "get along little dogie" or "down yonder"; discuss also any double meanings of words in songs. For example, during the Civil War, the word *train* was used to refer both to a "train to heaven" and to the "underground railroad" of people who helped slaves escape to freedom.

5. Descriptive Words and Songs

Have students underline all the descriptive adjectives and adverbs in a song. Discuss how these modifiers add to the meaning. Encourage student to suggest other descriptive words that would change the meaning of the song.

examples from "Red River Valley":

From: "We will miss your <u>bright</u> eyes and sweet smile"
To: "We will miss your <u>dull</u> eyes and sour smile."

examples from "Row, Row, Row Your Boat":

From: "Row <u>gently</u> down the stream"
To: "Row <u>roughly</u> down the stream."

6. Music and Parts of Speech

Give students the lyrics of a short song and ask them to list the different parts of speech. Then ask them to underline all nouns, circle all verbs, draw boxes around all adjectives, articles, and possessive pronouns, put triangles around all adverbs, lines through all prepositions, and an "x" through every conjunction.

examples from "Row, Row, Row Your Boat":

Nouns: boat, stream, life
Verbs: row, is
Adjectives, Articles, Possessive Pronouns: your, a, the
Adverbs: gently, merrily, but
Prepositions: down

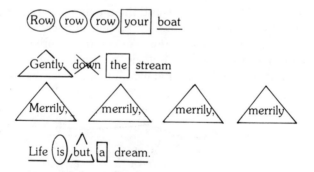

7. Categorizing Musical Words

Discuss the meanings of different musical terms. Then have students group words into appropriate categories.

examples of musical words and categories:

Types of Dances

polka, waltz, minuet, gavotte, jig, hora, mazurka

Rhythmic Movements

up, down, forward, back, over, under, round, square, right, left, small, large, fast, slow, even, uneven, clockwise, counterclockwise, walk, run, hop, skip, jump, curtsey, bow, circle, sway, march, step, prance, glide, dip, swirl, twirl, dart, swing, slide, bend

Musical Terms

melody, rhythm, tempo, form, dynamics, harmony, pattern, beat, syncopation, tone, score, improvisation, accent, meter, crescendo, diminuendo.

Instruments

Stringed: violin, viola, cello, double bass, banjo, guitar, lute, lyre, mandolin, sitar, ukulele, zither, dulcimer, harp

Woodwind: flute, piccolo, bassoon, oboe, English horn, clarinet, saxophone

Brass: trumpet, bugle, trombone, French horn, sousaphone, flugelhorn, tuba, baritone, cornet

Percussion: kettledrum, bongo drum, snare drum, bass drum, timpani, vibraphone, triangle, cymbals, sleighbells, chimes, gong, claves, maracas, castanets, tambourine

Keyboard: piano, accordion, organ, harpsichord

Types of Music

jazz, folk, classical, pop, rock, electronic, spiritual, religious, soul, calypso, bluegrass, opera, musical comedy

Musicians

conductor, player, performer, singer, instrumentalist, soloist

Singing Ranges

soprano, alto, tenor, bass, baritone, contralto, mezzo-soprano

Composers

Bach, Beethoven, Brahms, Chopin, Mozart

Conductors

Bernstein, Caldwell, Fiedler, Levine, Previn, Toscanini

Instrumentalists

Woody Herman, Al Hirt, Andrés Segovia

Singers

Johnny Cash, John Denver, Mahalia Jackson, Dolly Parton, Luciano Pavarotti

8. Antonyms and Synonyms in Songs

Give students words from familiar songs for which they can list antonyms and synonyms. Then have them rewrite the song using either the antonyms or synonyms.

example:

Find an antonym and synonym for each of the following words in "Row, Row, Row Your Boat":

Song Words	Antonyms	Synonyms
row	drive	propel
boat	tank	craft
gently	roughly	placidly
merrily	sadly	pleasantly
stream	hill	liquid solution
life	death	existence
dream	reality	illusion

Now rewrite the song using antonyms and then synonyms.

Drive, drive, drive your tank
Roughly up the hill
Sadly, sadly, sadly, sadly,
Death is all reality.

PROPEL, PROPEL, PROPEL YOUR CRAFT PLACIDLY DOWN THE LIQUID SOLUTION PLEASANTLY, PLEASANTLY, PLEASANTLY, PLEASANTLY EXISTENCE IS BUT AN ILLUSION!

9. Paraphrasing Song Titles

Get lists of the most popular songs from a local record store or have students submit their own lists of favorites. Read the song titles and review any difficult terms. Then have students paraphrase the titles.

examples:

"Sunshine on My Shoulders" to "Solar Heat Warms My Body"
"Three Blind Mice" to "Three Sightless Rodents"

10. Moving to the Antonym

Discuss word opposites with the students and have them show that they know the antonyms of common words by making appropriate movements to music. For instance, play a record and have students move up and down, forward and backward, fast and slow, take even and uneven steps, go clockwise and counter-clockwise, walk and then run.

11. Learning Instrumental Names

Encourage students to learn the names of musical instruments by showing them pictures, having people demonstrate the instruments, and listening to instrumental records. To help them retain this vocabulary, show them pictures of the instruments and ask them to name them and to describe how they are played and what they sound like. They can categorize instruments by whether they are blown, hit or struck, have a keyboard, or have strings. Simple games can also be played, such as "What Instrument Am I?" in which an instrument is described and the students must supply the correct name, or "Instrumental Bingo," in which students are given cards with names of different instruments and a space is covered up when the appropriate instrument is shown or described.

example of "Instrumental Bingo" Cards:

drum	violin	tuba
flute	cymbals	bass
oboe	clarinet	piccolo

12. Musical Crossword Puzzles

Make a crossword puzzle of words from the lyrics of a song. Write the definitions and have students find the appropriate words. Encourage students to make up their own crossword puzzles.

example based on "Sunshine on My Shoulders":

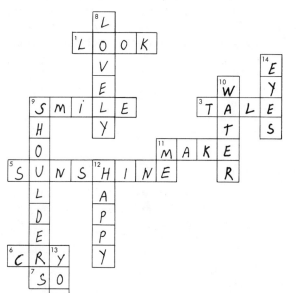

ACROSS

1. To see
2. A happy expression
3. A story
4. To create something
5. What the sun gives
6. What you do when you are sad
7. Homophone for "sew"

DOWN

8. Something very pretty
9. Part of the body
10. Something to drink
11. A name for yourself
12. Good feeling
13. Not me but _____
14. What you see with

Developing Comprehension Skills with Music

Music sweeps by me as a messenger carrying a message.[1]

Like language, music is a form of communication. But music can communicate feelings and emotions in ways that words cannot. Music without lyrics is a nonverbal way of communicating thoughts and feelings. Music with lyrics communicates through both the musical sounds and the words.

The words and sounds of their favorite music mean a great deal to students. Many songs tell stories that have sequences of events or include detailed descriptions of characters, places, or events. Thus the information presented in music can easily become the basis for many kinds of comprehension-building activities.

Musical activities can be used in a variety of interesting ways to develop students' reading and thinking abilities. The activities in this section are arranged by specific comprehension skills. Suggestions are also given for conducting a directed music and reading activity.

FOLLOWING DIRECTIONS

1. Directional Movements

Write on the chalkboard movement patterns for students to read and respond to while listening to music. The patterns could contain words for movements, such as *step, walk, run, jump, hop, creep, gallop, skip, leap, slide,* and *bend.* Directional words, such as *left, right, back,* and *front,* could also be included in the directions. The movement patterns must match the music.
examples of movement patterns:
> Walk, walk, jump
> Walk, walk, jump
> Skip, skip, jump and bend
> Skip, skip, jump and bend
> Walk, walk, jump.

2. Rhythmic Directions

Write on the chalkboard or on individual worksheets rhythmic patterns for students to tap out with their hands, pencils and/or drum sticks. Use words such as *clap, tap,* and *rest.*
examples of rhythmic patterns:
> clap, clap, tap, tap
> clap, rest, clap, rest
> tap, tap, rest, clap

[1]George Eliot, *The Spanish Gypsy.*

3. Reading Directions and Making Instruments

Write on the chalkboard or on a worksheet easy directions for making simple musical instruments, such as maracas from hollowed-out gourds or light bulbs covered with *papier maché*, or tambourines made from paper plates and bottle caps. Directions for making these can be found in many music books.

GETTING THE MAIN IDEA

1. Summarizing the Main Idea

Have students read the lyrics to a song carefully and then in one sentence tell what the song is about. List student summaries on the chalkboard and select the best one.

2. Understanding the Musical Theme

Many songs have themes or messages about such topics as patriotism, love, pollution, war, or death. Have the students study the lyrics of a song to determine its theme or message. Then have them discuss the theme and the way it is developed through the words and phrases used in the lyrics.

3. Picturing the Main Idea

Have students design a record cover for a song that shows they understand the theme or main ideas.

4. Finding the Correct Title

Put some titles for unfamiliar songs on the board and then pass out the lyrics without the titles to the students. Have the students read the lyrics and then select the title they think fits best.

5. Matching the Music to the Title

List titles of instrumental musical selections on the chalkboard and ask the students to predict what the music will be about. Then play a short but representative selection of each piece and ask the students to select the correct title. Use recordings of music such as *Danse Macabre* and various selections from the suite *Carnival of the Animals* by Saint-Saëns or *La Mer* by Debussy.

SEQUENCING

1. Singing and Sequencing

Some songs, such as "Frog Went a Courtin'," "The Grey Goose," and "The Fox," present definite sequences of events. Have students sing a song of this type and then repeat its sequence. Ask them what happened first, second, or third or have them list the events that happened in the correct order. Explain that the number of events will probably differ from the number of verses.

THE FOX

American Folk Song

The fox went out on a chilly night,
Prayed for the moon to give him light,
For he'd many a mile to go that night
Before he reached the town-o,
The town-o, the town-o,
For he'd many a mile to go that night
Before he reached the town-o.

He ran till he came to a great big pen
Where the ducks and the geese were put therein,
"A couple of you will grease my chin
Before I leave this town-o,
This town-o, this town-o,
A couple of you will grease my chin
Before I leave this town-o."

He grabbed a gray goose by the neck,
Threw a duck across his back;
He didn't mind their quack, quack, quack,
And their legs all dangling down-o, down-o, down-o,
He didn't mind their quack, quack, quack,
And their legs all dangling down-o.

*Then old mother Flipper-flopper jumped out of bed,
Out of the window she cocked her head,
Crying, "John, John, the gray goose is gone,
And the fox is on the town-o, town-o, town-o,"
Crying, "John, John, the gray goose is gone,
And the fox is on the town-o."*

*Then, John went up to the top of the hill,
Blew his horn both loud and shrill:
The fox, he said, "I better flee with my kill
Or they'll soon be on my trail-o, trail-o, trail-o,"
The fox, he said, "I better flee with my kill
Or they'll soon be on my trail-o."*

*He ran till he came to his cozy den,
There were the little ones eight, nine, ten.
They said, "Daddy, Daddy, better go back again,
For it must be a mighty fine town-o, town-o, town-o,"
"Daddy, Daddy, better go back again,
For it must be a mighty fine town-o."*

*Then the fox and his wife without any strife,
Cut up the goose with a fork and knife;
They never had such a supper in their life,
And the little ones chewed on the bones-o, bones-o, bones-o,
They never had such a supper in their life,
And the little ones chewed on the bones-o.*

Where did the fox find the ducks and geese? | Why is John blowing his horn? | What is old mother Flipper-flopper saying? | What did the foxes eat for supper?

2. Remembering What Happened Before and After

Mention to students an event that occurred in a song that stresses sequential order. Ask them to state what happened immediately before and after the event.

examples from "The Fox":

    What happened just *before* John blew his horn?
    What happened just *after* the fox got to his den?

3. Mixed-Up Sequencing

List out of order several things that happened in a song. Have students arrange them in the order in which they occurred.

examples from "The Fox":

Number these events in the order in which they happened.

_____ The little ones chewed on the bones.

_____ Old mother Flipper-flopper jumped out of bed.

_____ The fox threw a duck across his back.

_____ The fox came to a great big pen.

INFERRING THE MOOD

1. Recognizing the Mood from the Lyrics

Have students silently read the lyrics of a song that is predominantly
happy, sad, funny or patriotic. Ask them what they think the mood of the
song is and give reasons to back up their answers from the lyrics.

SONGS THAT PORTRAY DIFFERENT MOODS OR IDEAS

Happy Songs: "She'll Be Comin' 'Round the Mountain," "Camptown
Races," "When Johnny Comes Marching Home Again," "Sunshine on My
Shoulders."

Humorous Songs: "Billy Boy", "The Boll Weevil," "The Grey Goose," "Frog
Went a Courtin'."

Sad Songs: "Streets of Laredo," "The Minstrel Boy," "Red River Valley."

Patriotic Songs: "The Star-Spangled Banner," "This Land Is Your Land,"
"You're a Grand Old Flag," "The Power and the Glory."

2. Matching the Mood to the Lyrics

After students have studied the lyrics to determine the mood of a song,
have them listen to a recording of the song or sing it as originally intended to see if the music does match the mood of the lyrics. For example,
the lyrics of "Red River Valley" are very sad, but the music does not seem
so somber; however, both the words and music to "Minstrel Boy" are very
sad. Have the students give reasons for their opinions.

RED RIVER VALLEY

American Folk Song

From this valley they say you are going,
We will miss your bright eyes and sweet smile,
For they say you are taking the sunshine
That brightened our pathway awhile.

(Refrain)
Come and sit by my side if you love me;
Do not hasten to bid me adieu,
But remember the Red River Valley,
And the cowboy that loved you so true.

Oh just think of the valley you're leaving,
Oh, how lonely, how sad it will be,
And just think of the fond heart you're breaking,
And the grief you are giving to me.

(Repeat refrain)

RECOGNIZING POINT OF VIEW

1. From Another Viewpoint

After students have studied the lyrics for a song, have them discuss the song from another viewpoint. For example, they could suggest a different set of lyrics for "Red River Valley" written from the viewpoint of someone who is glad to be leaving, or for "The Erie Canal" written from the viewpoint of Sal, the mule.

2. Describing the Event

Have students describe an event in a song from different characters' viewpoints. For instance, after singing "Go Tell Aunt Rhody," they could describe the death of the old gray goose from the perspectives of Aunt Rhody, the gander, or the goslings; or after singing "The Fox," they could describe the scene from the perspectives of old mother Flipper-flopper, John, the fox, the vixen (female fox), or the young foxes.

MAKING COMPARISONS

1. Comparing Song Variations

Explain to students that most folk songs have different forms partly because they were first passed on orally. For example, "Barbara Allen," one of the best known ballads brought over from England, exists in over two hundred versions. Give students the lyrics of a folk song that has different versions to study. Have them speculate as to why the changes were made and if the changes significantly altered the meaning of the song. After an experience of this type, encourage the students to look through several books of folk songs to find other songs with different versions.

example:

Read the two sets of lyrics for "Go Tell Aunt Rhody." What differences in the lyrics can you find? List them. Decide if each difference changes the meaning of the song. How do you think these variations occurred?

GO TELL AUNT RHODY

American Folk Song

Go tell Aunt Rhody (3 times)   The old gander's weepin' (3 times)
The old gray goose is dead.   Because his wife is dead.

The one she's been savin' (3 times)   Goslings are mournin' (3 times)
To make a feather bed.   Because their mama's dead.

She died on Friday (3 times)   Go tell Aunt Rhody (3 times)
With an achin' in her head.   The old gray goose is dead.

GO TELL AUNT RHODY

American Folk Song

Go tell Aunt Rhody (3 times)   The old gander's mourning (3 times)
That the old grey goose is dead.   Because his wife is dead.

The one she's been saving (3 times)   The goslins are crying (3 times)
To make a feather bed.   Because their mother's dead.

She died in the millpond (3 times)   Go tell Aunt Rhody (3 times)
Standing on her head.   That the old grey goose is dead.

Do you see any differences between the two musical notations? If so, what are they?

2. Comparing Class Favorites

Encourage students to bring in a list of songs sung by their favorite musical artists. Have them list the titles on the board under the performers' names. Discuss the following types of questions: How are the titles for each singer alike? Do the titles contain common words or themes? Does each performer tend to sing a certain type of song? Have them classify the performers by the types of music they sing. The students might discover that some stars are in more than one category. A chart for the bulletin board could be made listing the category, star, and titles of representative songs.

3. Categorizing Songs

Give students lists of song titles and have them categorize the songs by subject or musical style.
examples of categories suitable for younger students:
   animal, farm, holiday, home, patriotic, play, weather.

examples of categories for older students:
   ballad, blues, country-western, folk, jazz, pop, rock, spiritual

Have groups of students analyze the lyrics of some songs in each category and list the common qualities, such as subject, common words, and length. Have the different groups report on their findings.

DRAWING CONCLUSIONS

1. Finishing the Song Another Way

After students have sung a song with a story line, such as "The Fox," ask them to write a different ending for the song. Emphasize that the ending must fit in with the rest of the lyrics.
example of a different ending for "The Fox":

AN ORIGINAL VERSION

*Then the fox and his wife without any strife,
Cut up the goose with a fork and knife;
They never had such a supper in their life,
And the little ones chewed on the bones-o, bones-o, bones-o,
They never had such a supper in their life,
And the little ones chewed on the bones-o.*

STUDENTS' VERSION

*Then the goose and the duck with lots of good luck,
Ran and hitched a ride on a farmer's truck.
Crying, "Fox, Fox, Don't come back again
You're not wanted in the town-o, town-o, town-o."
Crying, "Fox, Fox, Don't come back again
You're not wanted in the town-o."*

2. Drawing Conclusions from Song Lyrics

Ask students questions that will cause them to draw conclusions from facts given or implied in song lyrics.

examples from "Go Tell Aunt Rhody":
Was the old gray goose a pet?
(No, Aunt Rhody was saving her to make a feather bed.)

How did the goose actually die?
(From drowning while standing on her head in water in the millpond)

How did the gander feel about the gray goose?
(He must have loved her because he was crying because she was dead.)

SENSORY READING

1. Singing and Sensing

After students have sung or listened to a song that tells about a particular event, such as "The Star-Spangled Banner," "The Ship Titantic," or "The Streets of Laredo," ask students to imagine that they were there. Ask them to sing or listen to the music again and imagine what they can see, hear, feel, smell, and perhaps taste. Write their sensory perceptions on the blackboard.
example based upon "The Star-Spangled Banner":
See: rockets, bombs bursting, dawn's early light, soldiers, flag, ramparts
Hear: bombs bursting, soldiers, guns, silence
Feel: bomb fragments, mist, breeze
Smell: gun powder, smoke

2. Reading Aloud with Feeling

After students have determined the dominant mood of a song, have them practice reading the lyrics aloud and using their voices effectively to portray the mood of the song. Have students take one song, such as "Red River Valley," and read it first in a sad tone at a slow pace and then in a happy tone at a more rapid pace to see how their voices and tempo can be used to change the mood of the words. Encourage them to use appropriate voice quality and facial expressions when reading or singing to add more meaning to the lyrics.

MAKING PREDICTIONS

1. Making Predictions from Song Titles or First Lines

Have students read just the title of a song they are unfamiliar with and predict what the song will be about. List their predictions on the board. Then have them read the lyrics as they listen or sing to see if their predictions were correct. A variation of this would be to write the first line of a song on the board and have students make predictions from it. Many song books contain an index of first lines.

2. Predicting What Could Happen Next

If a song does not end with a definite conclusion, ask students to predict what could happen next.

example:

> How do you think Aunt Rhody will get her feather bed now that the old gray goose is dead?

CRITICAL/CREATIVE THINKING

1. Advertising the Music World

Ask students to look through newspapers and magazines and bring in advertisements for musical instruments, concerts, records, tapes or equipment, such as stereos and radios. Have them analyze each for advertising techniques used. (See list of advertising techniques, page 68). Have students compare the ads for information given and appeal to the reader.

2. Getting the Jingle's Message

Explain to students that the singing commercials they hear on radio and TV are urging them to buy products. Ask them to list any singing commercials they can remember. Have them try to write down the lyrics from memory. Then record some of the more popular commercials on audio tapes and transcribe the lyrics. Have students analyze the lyrics to note how they encourage people to make a purchase. Let the class determine what kinds of advertising techniques are used. Then have them listen to the singing commercials again to notice how the music is particularly designed to be easy to remember, with catchy phrases, and much repetition.

DIRECTED MUSIC AND READING ACTIVITY

Song lyrics can provide exciting, inexpensive sources of reading material that is interesting to students. Lyrics can tell unusual tales, describe journeys or characters, give vivid descriptions of places or events, or arouse emotions and feelings. The following section gives a framework and specific activities for presenting a directed music reading activity. It is important to remember that music is to be enjoyed, and these activities should be enjoyable.

1. Introduction and Motivation

The initial introduction should be geared to the interest and development level of the students. Motivate them to want to listen to, sing, or study the lyrics of a song through brief anecdotes, background information, remarks about unusual aspects of the title, lyrics, mood, or information about the history of the music, the composer, performers, or instruments used. Write an interest-arousing sentence on the board.

examples:

How would you write a song that shows you love your country? ("This Land is Your Land")

What do you think we can learn about people by studying a song from another country? ("Waltzing Matilda")

What do you think we can learn about the history of our country by studying a song that was written many years ago? ("Sweet Betsy from Pike")

As an alternative, have students predict what the music will be about from studying the title.

2. Introducing New Vocabulary and Concepts

Depending upon the age and developmental level of students, discuss factors that might be helpful in studying the music, such as the types of instruments used, style of music (folk, pop, rock, spiritual), and use of musical elements such as rhythm, melody, and tempo. Also explain any new words in the lyrics that might be confusing; for example, in "Waltzing Matilda" students will encounter such words as *coolibah, billy, jumbuck, tucker,* and *squatter*. Write the new words on the chalkboard, discuss their meanings, and then have students explain them in their own words.

♪ DOWN CAME A JUMBUCK TO DRINK AT THE BILLABONG, UP JUMPED THE SWAGMAN AND GRABBED HIM WITH GLEE, AND HE SANG AS HE SHOVED THAT JUMBUCK IN HIS TUCKER BAG: "YOU'LL COME A-WALTZING MATILDA WITH ME." ♭

3. Directed Listening or Reading

Give students some specific things to focus on as they listen to, sing, or study the lyrics for a piece of music. For example: What happened at the beginning or end? Did the music have a message? What types of instruments were predominant? What phrases are repeated over and over? The students could write down their reactions. Encourage them to listen or read carefully and to respond imaginatively.

4. Follow-Up Discussion

Have students compare their predictions based on the title with what they heard. Ask questions about the music on literal, interpretive, and critical or evaluative levels.

examples of questions based on the lyrics of "Go Tell Aunt Rhody" (see page 166):

Literal

Who were the main characters?
Why was Aunt Rhody saving the goose?
How did the goose die?
Why is the gander mourning?
What color was the old goose?

Vocabulary

What is a *gander*? a *gosling*?
What is a *millpond*?
What does *mourning* mean?

Interpretative

Is this song sad or happy? Why?
After the old grey goose died, how did the gander and her goslings feel? How do you know?
What do you think Aunt Rhody will do after learning of the death of the old grey goose?

Critical or Evaluative

Why would a goose stand on her head in a millpond?
How does this version of the song compare to others you have heard?
How does this song about a goose compare to other songs about animals you have sung?
Is this song fact or fiction? Could these events have really happened?

5. Expanding Reading Interest Through Music

Have students:

- Read the lyrics aloud with expression.

- Write a critique of the music.

- Find songs on similar topics. Write the titles down and post them on a bulletin board.

- Write a poem, story or summary of the song.

- Write another set of lyrics for the song.

Using Music to Teach Reading Study Skills

Music is a science, an art and a language:
Science is to know, art is to do and language
is to communicate.[1]

Students need to be taught a variety of study skills so that they will know how to locate material, gather information through a variety of means, use general reference books, select and organize important items, and then translate them into their own words. To maintain these skills, students need instruction and practice through the school program with materials that are meaningful to them. Since most students respond eagerly to music, practicing these study skills with music-related activities can add interest and motivation. This section contains a variety of music-related activities to strengthen study skills.

1. Learning Map Skills Through Music

Have students mark on a map the location of all songs they are familiar with that mention a place name, such as Laredo in "The Streets of Laredo" or California in "California Here I Come." If a song like "This Land Is Your Land" mentions several places—California, New York Island, Gulf Stream waters, and Redwood Forests—have them estimate the distance between the different places by using the map's measurement scale. Then let them discuss appropriate means of getting from one location to another.

2. Making a Musical Time-Line

Have students make a time-line of their favorite songs. This will require them to look at publication dates on contemporary songs and look up the history of some of the folk songs in folk music books.

3. Outlining Musical Items

To refine students' outlining skills, have them make outlines of types of musical instruments, performers, or composers. Give students skeletal outlines to fill in, and then eventually let them make the entire outline.
examples:

Musical Instruments

I. Strings	II. Woodwinds
A. Violin	A.
B. Bass	B.
C.	C.
D.	D.

[1]Wayne Bloomingdale, "Creston's Songs: The Art of Communication."

Favorite Musicians

I. Rock   III. Jazz
  A.   A.
  B.   B.
  C.   C.
II. Country Western
  A.
  B.
  C.

4. Skimming the Lyrics

Have students practice their rapid reading or skimming skills by quickly looking over the lyrics of a new song to locate a particular phrase or word.

5. Using a Table of Contents

To develop students' skills in using a table of contents, have them look in the table of contents of a songbook to locate the page number for a particular song or type of song.

6. Practicing Index Skills

Review index usage by having students use the index of a songbook to locate songs about a particular theme, such as patriotism, the weather, or a specified holiday. Many song books also index the first lines of songs. Give students a first line and ask them to find the song; or give them a theme, such as the sun or moon, and ask them to find this mentioned in the first line of a song.

7. Doing Field Research

Have students find examples of how music is used in different ways:

- To cover or mask noise (dentist's office, store)
- To fill in gaps of silence (TV programs)
- To set a mood or provide atmosphere (restaurant)
- Provide continuity (movies, musicals, TV programs)
- To provide dramatic background or support (TV, radio)

Students could also write letters to companies to find out more about their use of music or go to the library and do research on the use of music. Have students summarize their findings and share them with the class.

8. Conducting Musical Survey Polls

Review the skills necessary in survey research by having the students make a survey questionnaire and then poll other students in the school to determine their opinions. Questions could be asked about their favorite types of music, favorite musicians, favorite songs of the week or month, or instruments played. Have students make a chart to show the results of the survey.

9. Reviewing Interviewing Techniques

Review interviewing techniques by having students invite guest musicians from the community to perform and talk to the class. Encourage students to question them about their musical skills. Have students summarize the interviews and write appropriate "thank-you" letters to the guests.

10. Doing Musical Library-Research

Go over with students the skills needed to do library research on a topic, including using a card file, table of contents, and indexes to locate information. Also review techniques for note-taking, organizing, and summarizing information. Then give them an opportunity to do research about something that interests them in music. When they present the results of this research to the class, encourage them to play recorded musical excerpts.

examples of musical topics to research:

- Favorite instruments, their origin, use, or well known players

- The composers of favorite pieces or types of music

- The life of a favorite musician, such as Elvis Presley, Dolly Parton, Isaac Stern, John Denver
  (Research on contemporary stars will need to be done from current sources, including magazines.)

- Music in another country or culture

- The origins of various types of music, such as jazz, folk, rock, electronic, pop, and spiritual

- Different careers in music, such as performing, composing, instrument repair, publishing, manufacturing records and instruments, managing or booking artists, producing records or events, music reporting and reviewing, music librarians, disc jockeys, announcers, writers of musical commercials.

11. Testing the Hypothesis

Play recordings of several works by the same composer, such as movements of Beethoven's Third ("Eroica"), Fifth, or Sixth ("Pastoral") symphonies, or Woody Guthrie's "This Land Is Your Land" and "So Long, It's

Been Good to Know You." Ask students to hypothesize and then write about the sort of person they think the composer was. Then have them read about the background of the composer and compare their hunches with the factual information. It would be helpful to have the music available on records or cassettes for students to refer to as they are doing their research.

Music and the Language Arts

*A man (woman) should hear a little music, read a little
poetry and see a fine picture every day of his (her) life,
in order that worldly cares may not obliterate the
sense of the beautiful which God implanted in the
human soul.*[1]

The language arts—listening, speaking, reading, and writing—as well as music are all forms of communication. Students can improve all of their communication skills through music-related activities.

Music can be a great stimulus to many forms of creative expression. By making use of the emotional power of music in connection with poetry, stories, and dramatization, students can be made much more receptive to the beauty and mood of language. Music-related activities can also encourage students to express themselves through their own writing.

Many students can learn to enjoy poetry when it is introduced through the lyrics of songs such as "Wayfaring Stranger" or "Blowin' in the Wind." Ask students to suggest songs that they feel have poetic elements; or bring in recordings of songs by Bob Dylan, Joan Baez, Peter, Paul and Mary, Paul Simon, Pete Seeger, and Arlo Guthrie. Students will continue to listen to the radio, buy records, and go to concerts throughout their lives. Their understanding of how to read poetry can be enhanced by the experience of working with poetry in the music they enjoy so much.

This section is divided into the following parts: Writing and Music, Poetry and Music, Drama and Music.

WRITING AND MUSIC

1. Musical Letter-Writing Activities

Let students practice techniques of letter writing through music-related activities:

[1]Johann Wolfgang von Goethe, *Wilhelm Meister's Apprenticeship.*

- Write a favorite musician to see what he/she likes to read.

- Write a favorite author to find out what kind of music he/she prefers.

- Write letters to record companies requesting song lyrics, pictures of stars, and copyright information.

2. Penmanship and Song Lyrics

Have students improve their penmanship while copying favorite song titles or lyrics.

3. Writing It in Their Own Words

Give students the lyrics for a song, such as "The Star-Spangled Banner," and have them rewrite the lyrics in their own words.

4. Musical Phrases

Write phrases from a song on the chalkboard and ask students to put the phrases into sentences that differ from the original ones.

examples:

"Sunshine on my shoulders makes" ___me get sunburned___ .

"This land is" ___good for growing tomatoes___ .

"Twinkle, twinkle little star, how I wonder" ___if you really are like our sun___ .

5. Isolating a Musical Moment

Have students write a story about an incident mentioned in a song, such as why Aunt Rhody was saving a grey goose to make a feather bed, in "Go Tell Aunt Rhody."

6. Stories About Song Characters

Encourage students to make up a story about a character in a song, such as Mother Flipper-Flopper in "The Fox" or the goose in "Go Tell Aunt Rhody."

7. Updating an Old Favorite

Have students write a modern version for an old song, such as "Daisy, Daisy" or "Sweet Betsy from Pike." For instance, today Daisy might be on a moped or motorbike, instead of on a bicycle built for two, and Betsy might be traveling across the big mountains on a jet instead of in a wagon with two yoke of oxen.

8. When I Was a Clarinet

Let students write stories about their existence as a violin string, saxophone reed, drum head, one of a pair of cymbals, conductor's baton, record, or piece of recording equipment. Emphasize that although their stories will be fictitious, they must be based in fact.

LET ME INTRODUCE MYSELF...

9. My Favorite Music

Encourage students to write an essay about what their favorite piece of music, kind of music, instrument, or musician means to them. They could also make their own musical scrapbooks with illustrations, stories, and critiques about different songs, musicians, and instruments.

10. Listening and Writing

After students have listened to a piece of music, have them write a story based on the music. For example, they might write a scary story after listening to *Danse Macabre* (Saint-Saëns), *Night on Bald Mountain* (Moussorgsky), or *In the Hall of the Mountain King* (Grieg); or they might write a peaceful sea story after listening to *La Mer* (Debussy). To encourage even more creativity, don't tell students the title of the music before they listen to it. Have them guess what the music is supposed to represent. Experiment with familiar and unfamiliar music, such as classical selections, TV or movie themes, and popular music.

11. Descriptions in Musical Terms

Have students listen to a piece of music and then write about what was heard using musical terms, or have them do a musical critique of a recording or song patterned after those in newspapers or magazines.

12. Same Tune—Different Song

Encourage students to bring in lyrics from songs they like. Write the lyrics on the chalkboard or on a transparency and have students discuss them. Then have students write a different type of song for the same lyrics. For example, instead of a humorous song, they could write an animal song. Display the new versions and let students sing them.

13. Song-Writing Unit

Have a song-writing unit and encourage students to compose their own music and write appropriate lyrics. They could also compose their own commercial jingles to sell something or to publicize a school event.

14. Planning a P.A. Announcement

Help students plan the script and music for a spot announcement on a school P.A. system. The entire announcement should not take over thirty seconds. Suggest a format such as the following:
1. Music (ten seconds)
2. Announcement
3. Music—fade (ten seconds)

example:

1. **Music:** ten seconds of "This Land is Your Land"; music fades to soft, wordless music during the announcement.

2. **Announcement:** "Tomorrow is Arbor Day. At nine o'clock tomorrow morning, a tree will be planted in the front of the school by the 6th grade class. All classes are invited to attend the ceremony at nine o'clock."

3. **Music:** ten more seconds of "This Land is Your Land" and then fade.

POETRY AND MUSIC

1. Matching Lyrics and Poetry

Have students take turns reading the lyrics for a song aloud like a poem. Then have them find or read several poems on the same theme or subject and compare how they are alike or different. Have them discuss the meanings of the words in both the song and poems and note phrases used to create mental images. Then have students write their own poem on the same theme.

2. Adding Another Verse

After students have studied the poetic elements in the lyrics for a song, have them write an additional verse. Have them test the rhythm of their verse with the rhythm of the song by singing their words into a tape recorder while the song is being played or hummed by others in the class.

3. Rearranging the Song

Give students the lyrics of a song in an unarranged form and have them rearrange the lyrics as a poem, supplying capital letters and punctuation.

4. Rhythm and Poetry

Let students listen to poems and study their rhythms. Have some students use rhythm instruments, such as drums, cymbals, or castanets, to emphasize the rhythm while others read a poem aloud.

5. Correlating Poetry, Music, and Dance

Have students write an original poem or choose a favorite poem, select appropriate music for it, and then create a dance or movement to go with both the poem and the music. Have some students read the poem aloud as a group while others play the music or recording and some dance or dramatize it through creative movements. For example, students could write a poem about the ocean, play a recording of *La Mer* (Debussy), or sing a sea chantey and do movements that resemble the waves, fish, or sailors. Or students could write about life in the West, play portions of the *Grand Canyon Suite* (Grofé) or of cowboy ballads such as "Get Along Little Dogie," and do a square dance or movements that resemble cowboys.

6. Creating Poetry About Music

Encourage students to write poems about music they have heard, instruments, songs, or musical compositions, or write a poem about some object and compare that object to music.
examples:

THE WIND

The wind sounds like a quiet tunes
It whispers softly in my ear
And goes away too soon.

MY DOG

My dog makes a clarinet sound
when he is lost
and wants to be found.

7. Finding Poems About Music

Have students look up musical items in the indexes of poetry books to locate poems about music. Have them select poems with musical themes to read aloud to the class, to copy and put on a musical poetry bulletin board, or to include in a classroom anthology of poems about music.

8. Writing Poetry to Music

Play softly some music without words and have students write poems as they listen to it.

DRAMA AND MUSIC

1. Reading Lyrics with Expression and Meaning

Let students perfect their oral reading skills while reading lyrics aloud, working individually and in groups. They should avoid reading in a monotonous or sing-song fashion. Encourage them instead to read with expression, good diction, clear pronunciation, and to vary the pitch, tone, and speed, to best convey the meaning of the song.

2. Acting Out the Music

Some songs tell a story that can be acted out, such as "Three Blind Mice," "Waltzing Matilda," "The Fox," or "Streets of Laredo." Have some students act out the lyrics while others sing or read them aloud. Other students could use rhythm instruments to create effects.

3. Musical Dramatizations

Let students perform their own class musical combining spoken and sung parts. The students could use a musical that is included in the class music books, or they could write their own dialogue and select appropriate songs to sing or selections of recorded music to play.

4. Songs and Mime

Discuss with students the effects of facial expressions and body gestures in portraying thoughts and emotions. Then have students act out or pantomime a song and see if others can guess the name of the song. When this activity is first used, it might be helpful to list some possible song titles on the board and see how quickly students can guess the appropriate one. This can also be done as a team game similar to charades.

5. Original Playwrites

Have students write their own play about music and select appropriate music to accompany it. For example, they could write a play based on a piece of music such as the *Carnival of the Animals* (Saint-Saëns), *The Nutcracker Suite* (Tchaikovsky), or *Peter and the Wolf* (Prokofiev); or they might write a play about a musical instrument, such as the history of drums, the problems of playing a guitar, or of being a violin; or their play could be about the life of a real musician, such as Stephen Foster or Elvis Presley, or the origin of a type of music, such as rock, jazz, or country-and-western.

Creating an Interest in
Reading Through Music

Music is the literature of the heart.[1]

Motivating students to want to read is often as important as teaching them how to read. Most students are very responsive to learning from materials that interest them and find listening to music, talking about music, or reading about music in the classroom extremely enjoyable. They are usually eager to listen to and read the lyrics of songs, and many also enjoy reading about their favorite musicians and musical styles.

Music can also be studied as a form of literature. Many musical works have been derived from literary sources. When students gain more familiarity with the legends, myths, fairy tales, literary classics, stories, and poems that have inspired the writing of music, they will get more out of both the music and the literary works.

This section contains suggestions for helping students become interested in reading through music-related activities.

1. Setting a Musical Reading Mood

Sing or play on the record player or tape recorder a few notes from a favorite melody to call students to a reading group or to announce story time. Each reading group could have its own special song and the music for story time could be selected to go with the story that is to be read.

[1]Alphonse M. L. Lamartine, *source unknown.*

2. Musical Interest Reading

Encourage students to read a book about some aspect or type of music, such as jazz, country-and-western, folk, or the music of other countries. Then have students report on what they have read in a musical way by singing a song about it or by softly playing an appropriate recording while giving their reports.

3. Musical SSR (Sustained-Silent-Reading)

Occasionally set aside a fifteen- or twenty-minute period during which students can quietly read about music. They may choose from collections of songs, stories of music or operas, biographies of musicians, or articles in encyclopedias. During this time, a background record of "music to read by" could be played softly.

4. Music and Reading Interest-Centers

Set up a center in the room with a record or cassette player with head-sets; records or tapes of different types of music; colorful pictures of instruments, music, composers, pop singers; a bulletin board or scrap-books for students to add pictures and clippings; and books about musical composers, plots of operas, or ballads. Let students contribute their favorites. In a prominent space, write a few interest-arousing questions to encourage students to read. Have students write a few comments about each item they add to the center.

5. Thematic Music and Reading Activity-Centers

Set up a thematic music activity center where all the posters, pictures, album covers, songs, books, and task cards revolve around a central theme. For each center, include music-related reading activities for vocabulary, word attack, comprehension, and study skills. Also, have some activities for pleasure reading and language arts.
examples:

THE MOON IN MUSIC AND READING

Include recordings and lyrics of songs about the moon, such as "Shine On Harvest Moon," "When the Moon Comes Over the Mountain," "How High the Moon" and "It's Only a Paper Moon".

Include books and poems about the moon and relevant reference materials.

On activity cards shaped like the moon, encourage students to read portions of specified books or materials and answer question about the moon, or write poems or stories about the moon, or listen to a recording and study the lyrics of a song to pick out a description of the moon or how the moon made someone feel.

PATRIOTIC MUSIC AND READING ACTIVITY-CENTER

Include recordings of patriotic music, such as marches by John Philip Sousa and songs such as "This Land Is Your Land," "The Star-Spangled Banner," and "My Country 'Tis of Thee."

Include the lyrics of patriotic songs, a map of the United States, a flag, patriotic posters, books about great patriots, and poems.

Include activities structured around the patriotic theme.

6. Student-Designed Music and Reading Activity-Centers

Encourage students to design their own thematic music and reading center. Have them first select a theme and then bring in appropriate items, such as tapes or records, posters, books, and copies of the lyrics. Have them write activity cards that direct students to read something in the center and answer appropriate questions or to write an appropriate story.

7. Determining the Musical Story

Some music, such as folk songs and ballads that tell a story, can be studied as literature. Have students study the lyrics of appropriate songs to note the introduction, plot development or theme, conclusion, characterization and setting.

examples of songs that could be studied as literature:
  "Go Tell Aunt Rhody"
  "Frog Went a Courtin'"
  "The Fox"

8. Matching Music to Stories

Have students find music to go with their favorite stories or books. Discuss ways in which they could be related, such as by theme, topic, or historical era. For example, for *Little House on the Prairie* (Wilder 1953), they could select an American folk song such as "Sourwood Mountain"; for *The Little Engine that Could* (Piper 1954), they could choose songs that have a railroad theme, such as "Little Red Caboose" or "This Train."

9. Selecting Musical Backgrounds

Have students select music and sound effects to use as backgrounds for plays, oral readings, or slide shows. Let students select or compose music to match the mood of the material and then tape relevant selections. Sound effects that they could produce might include thunder (beating on pans, gongs, or cymbals), walking or horse trotting (sand blocks), rain (dripping or pouring water on tin), and wind (electric fan).

10. Knowing the Story Behind the Music

Point out to students that many musical compositions are based on literary works (see the list that follows). First familiarize students with the literary work on which the music is based. Then ask them to describe how they think the music will sound. Encourage them to be as descriptive as possible. Write their predictions on the board. Then play selections of the musical work. Question students afterwards as to how accurate their predictions were. Ask them if the music helped them to see, feel, and hear the story. Which parts were loud, soft, quiet, lively, slow—and why? Did they feel the music was appropriate? Have them compare the literary work with the music. They might need to read portions of the literary work and hear parts of the music again to make better judgments as to the appropriateness of the music. Students could then dramatize stories from which the music has been taken using recordings of the music as background.

Music Based on Folk Tales and Legends

Beowulf (Hansen) from British folktale
The Story of Peer Gynt (Grieg) from Norse Legend
Peter and the Wolf (Prokofiev) from Russian Legend
Till Eulenspiegel's Merry Pranks (Strauss) from German and Flemish Legends
The Firebird (Stravinsky) Russian Legend
Swan Lake (Tchaikovsky) German Legend

Music Based on Fairy Tales

The Nightingale (Stravinsky) (Anderson 1965)
The Three Bears: A Fantasy (Coates) (Rojankovsky 1948)
Cinderella (Prokofiev) (Perrault 1955)
Mother Goose Suite (Ravel) from four French tales: "Sleeping Beauty,"
    "Hop o' My Thumb," "The Green Serpent," "Beauty and the Beast"
    (Grimm 1977) (Perrault 1967) (Aulnoy 1923) (Pearce 1972)

Music Based on Classics

Scheherazade (Rimsky-Korsakov): *1001 Arabian Nights* (Colum 1953)
A Midsummer Night's Dream (Mendelssohn): Shakespeare's play of the same
    name (Shakespeare 1968)
Through the Looking Glass (Taylor): poem by Lewis Carroll (Carroll 1975)
Afternoon of a Faun (Debussy): poem by Mallarmé (Mallarmé 1952)
Sorcerer's Apprentice (Dukas): *Der Zauberlehrling* by Goethe (Hosier 1961)

(Bailey 1969)

Broadway or Hollywood Musicals Based on Earlier Works of Fiction and Non-Fiction

The Wiz: The *Wizard of Oz* (Baum)
Annie: "Little Orphan Annie" comic strip (Harold Gray)
Oliver: Oliver Twist (Dickens)
The Sound of Music: The Trapp Family Singers (Trapp)
Camelot: Tales from King Arthur's Court

Music is everywhere in our daily environment in one form or another and adds much enjoyment to our lives. Music is popular with young people and their interest in it can provide a natural resource that can easily and effectively be tapped to help stimulate interest in reading and in the improvement of basic reading skills.

Readings and References

ANDERSON, HANS CHRISTIAN. *The Nightingale.* Translated by Eva La Gallienne. New York: Harper & Row, Pub., 1965.

ANDERSON, JOHN. "Improving Reading Skills for the Non-Musical Teacher." *Claremont Reading Conference 35th Yearbook,* Claremont, California: Claremont Graduate School, 1971, pp. 179–180.

AULNOY, MARIE. "The Green Serpent." *Fairy Tales.* Philadelphia: David McKay, 1923.

BAILEY, EVELYN HOPE. "Symphonic Music from Literary Sources: A Selected Bibliography and Critical Analysis of Musical Works Derived from Legends, Myths, Fairy Tales, Literary Classics, Other Stories, and Poems and Their Appropriateness and Utility with Elementary School Children." *ED 034–789,* 1969.

BAUM, FRANK. *The Wizard of Oz.* New York: Dover, 1960.

BENNER, CHARLES H. "Dough'-re-mi Can Put Students on Key in Other Subjects." *American School Board Journal* (March 1975), pp. 38–40.

CARROLL, LEWIS. *Alice in Wonderland.* New York: W. W. Norton & Co., Inc., 1975.

COLUM, PADRAIC. *The Arabian Nights.* New York: Macmillan, 1953.

DALTON, RUTH SHUMWAY. "A Study of the Relationship between Music Reading Ability and Language Reading Ability." Unpublished master's thesis, Syracuse University, 1952.

DICKENS, CHARLES. *Oliver Twist.* New York: Signet Classics, 1966.

GIBBS, MARY ELLEN. "The Coach Teaches Reading through Music." *Journal of Reading.* Vol. 14, No. 1 (1970), pp. 23–25.

GRIMM, BROTHERS. *Sleeping Beauty.* Boston: Little, Brown, 1977.

HARPER, ANDREW. "Education Through Music." *Phi Delta Kappan,* 54 (May 1973), pp. 628–629.

HOSIER, J. *The Sorcerer's Apprentice and Other Stories.* New York: Henry Z. Walck, 1961.

KOKAS, K. "Psychological Tests in Connection with Music Education in Hungary." *Journal of Research in Music Education,* 8 (3) (1969), pp. 102–114.

MALLARMÉ, STEPHEN. "Afternoon of a Faun." *Little Treasury of World Poetry.* Edited by H.A. Creekmore. New York: Scribner's, 1952.

MOVESIAN, EDWIN R. "Reading Music—Reading Words." *Journal of the National Education Association* LVIII (January 1969), pp. 42–43.

NICHOLSON, DIANA, "Music as an Aid to Learning." Unpublished dissertation, City University of New York, 1972.

PEARCE, PHILLIPPA. *Beauty and the Beast.* New York: Thomas Y. Crowell, 1972.

PELLETIER, HAROLD. "An Investigation of the Relationship between Training in Instrumental Music and Selected Aspects of Language Growth in 3rd Grade Children." Unpublished dissertation, Arizona State University, 1963.

PERRAULT, CHARLES. *Cinderella, or the Little Glass Slipper.* New York: Scribner's, 1955.

PERRAULT, CHARLES. "Hop o'My Thumb." *Famous Fairy Tales.* New York: Franklin Watts, 1967.

PIPER, WATTY. *The Little Engine that Could.* New York: Platt and Munk, 1954.

"Principal Julius Levine Uses Music and Dance to Help Students Learn to Read." *Time,* October 22, 1965, p. 54.

RIVAS, FRANK. "A Perspective on the First Music Assessment." *ED* 097-276, 1974.

RIVAS, FRANK. "The First Music Assessment: An Overview—National Assessment of Educational Progress Report." *ED* 097-275, 1974.

ROJANKOVSKY, FEODOR. *The Three Bears.* New York: Golden Press, 1948.

SEIDES, ESTHER. "The Effect of Talent Class Placement on Slow Learners in the 7th Grade." Unpublished Dissertation, New York University, 1967.

SHAKESPEARE, WILLIAM. *A Midsummer's Night Dream.* New York: Cambridge University Press, 1968.

TAYLOR, FLORENCE. "Learning Is Learning to Learn How to Learn." *ED* 099-109, 1973.

TRAPP, MARIA AUGUSTA. *Story of the Trapp Family Singers.* New York: Random House, 1960.

TURNIPSEED, J. P. and others. "Effect of Participating in a Structured Classical Musical Education Program on the Development of Auditory Discrimination in Pre-School Children." *ED* 102-089, November 1974.

WILDER, LAURA INGALLS. *Little House on the Prairie.* New York: Harper & Row, Pub., 1953.

WILLIAMS, RALPH L. JR. "Sound-Word-Sentence-Meaning Song Cards." *ED* 106-789, 1973.

ZINAR, RUTH. "Reading Language and Reading Music: Is There a Connection?" *Music Educators Journal* (March, 1976), pp. 70–74.

ZINAVER, EUGENE, Ed. *King Arthur and His Knights.* New York: Oxford University Press, 1975.

chapter five

teaching reading
in the **OUTDOORS**

Introduction

Come forth into the light of things,
Let Nature be your teacher.[1]

Students are fascinated by outdoors. Their thoughts are often drawn to the outdoors even during school hours. They enjoy being outside and are interested in and curious about life in the natural environment. For this reason, the outdoors can function as a uniquely effective learning site. Not only will students relish the change of routine, they will also learn to see reading as a fascinating activity that can take place anywhere, anytime, and be related to any subject. When reading activities take place outside, students often become so engrossed and so excited being outdoors that they do not realize that they are improving their reading skills (Rowell and Goodkind p.p.).[2]

A teacher does not need to have special training in science, ecology or other areas in order to use the outdoors to teach reading. Rather the outdoor environment should be considered as just another special resource that can be used to motivate reading growth. Because they are experiencing more of a natural world around them, the outdoors is an ideal location in which to develop students' ability to learn by using all of their senses and to help them relate in greater depth to their reading.

Many successful reading experiences can take place on the school's steps, sidewalk or grounds, in a park, woods, or field, or throughout the school's surrounding neighborhood. Urban, suburban, and rural settings all offer a great variety of outdoor resources.

Research studies have indicated that students studying in the outdoors made equal or significantly higher gains in basic concepts and in

[1] William Wordsworth, *The Tables Turned.*
[2] Chapter readings and references appear on page 242.

reading and language arts skills than students who did all their studying within the confines of the classroom (Hick 1970; Life Camps 1948; Malcombe County 1974). These studies also found that students were more enthusiastic, more attentive, had a more positive outlook, and were more aware of their surroundings when working in the outdoors.

Many youngsters secretly long for a more meaningful and direct relationship with their environment (Gustafson 1972). While working on reading skills in the outdoors, students can not only improve their basic reading and thinking skills, but can also learn to be more aware of and appreciate the outdoor environment and their relationship to it.

All of the activities in this section can be modified according to pupils' needs and abilities and the available outdoor facilities. Although most of the activities are designed to be done outdoors, many can also take place inside, by bringing a touch of the outdoors into the classroom. One or several of these activities could be done each day, or on one special day a week, or an entire unit could be devoted to reading activities outside of the classroom.

OUTDOOR RESOURCES FOR MOTIVATING READING GROWTH

Many schools have access to nature centers, outdoor education sites, environmental trails and a variety of field trips; and every school has an immediate outdoor area, usually encompassing a playground and a few trees. Even the deepest inner-city school has access to a patch of grass and some form of wildlife—squirrels, ants, and birds, for example. These locations offer countless possibilities for worthwhile outdoor reading experiences. When working outdoors on activities that require writing, it is advisable for students to have writing materials, such as clipboards, masonite sheets, or pieces of heavy cardboard with large paper clips, fasteners or rubber bands to hold their papers in place.

The following is a list of outdoor resources on or near most school sites that can be utilized to stimulate reading growth:

HUMAN-MADE RESOURCES

Buildings—school, shops, factories, farms
Sidewalks, curbs and gutters
Roads and traffic
Views
Playground equipment
Litter
Vacant lots
Fences
Cars, buses, trucks, motorcycles, bicycles, roller skates, skate boards

190

Signs (traffic, parking, advertisement)
Fire hydrants, fire alarms
Parking lots
Chimneys
Fire escapes
Flags, flagpoles
Letters and numbers on buildings
License plates
Street furniture (benches, phone booths, street lights, litter baskets)
Power lines, telephone poles, meters

NATURAL RESOURCES

Water (puddles, lakes, streams, dew)
Trees (leaves, roots, stems, twigs, seeds, cones, fruits)
Insects (ants, grasshoppers, beetles, crickets)
Animals (worms, snails, mice, chipmunks, squirrels, birds)
Plantings (bushes, flowers, grass, shrubs, weeds, ferns)
Noises (wind, animal sounds, flowing water, insects)
Smells (flowers, fruits, dampness)
Weather (rain, snow, hail, fog, wind, clouds, sky, sun)
Soil, rocks

GETTING INSIGHTS INTO
THEIR OUTDOOR INTERESTS

Although most students enjoy any type of outdoor activity, an awareness of their specific outdoor interests can be helpful when planning for initial outdoor reading experiences. It is often enlightening to question them informally about their outdoor interests, or to administer a written questionnaire such as the following:

Outdoor Interest Survey

1. When I am outdoors, I like to _____
2. My favorite outdoor place is _____
3. The most interesting outdoor animal is _____
4. The most interesting outdoor plant is _____
5. The most interesting outdoor insect is _____
6. My favorite spot in the schoolyard is _____
7. My favorite place to read outdoors is _____
8. I would like to know more about the following outdoor things:

   _____, _____, _____

Reading Readiness in
Mother Nature's Classroom

His (Her) daily teachers had been woods and rills. . . .[1]

Young children need a rich variety of stimulating and informative experiences to help them develop the skills necessary for reading; these reading-readiness skills are best developed in an environment that provides optimum conditions for physical, intellectual and social development. Most young children delight in being outside and many visual and auditory skills that are essential reading-readiness skills can be developed while they are outdoors. Many of the activities in this section would also be helpful for older students who need additional work on visual and auditory skills. Additional reading-readiness activities can be adapted from those given in the vocabulary, comprehension, and reading interest sections of this chapter.

VISUAL SKILL-DEVELOPMENT

1. Developing the Technique of Careful Observation

Explain to students that careful observation is a necessary part of what scientists and naturalists do in their work. Bring out the differences between observation and merely looking. Have students carefully study one outdoor item, such as a tree, stoplight, or anthill, and then ask them to describe carefully in detail what they saw.

2. Noting Similarities and Differences

Point out a fence post, rock, shrub, or cloud. Ask students to find another object that is similar. Ask them how the objects are alike and different. Then have them find a similar object that is much larger, smaller, narrower, wider, lighter, or heavier.

3. Picture and Object Matching

Give students pictures of a pine tree, flower, curb, brick wall, or something else found in the schoolyard. Ask them to match the pictures to the real objects.

[1]William Wordsworth, *Song at the Feast of Brougham Castle.*

4. Matching Colors

Give the students small scraps of colored paper. Ask them to find one
thing in the outdoors for each color. Instead of picking or harming a plant
or flower, the students could draw a picture of the object and remember
where they saw it.

5. Taking a Color-Walk

Take walks at the same location during different times of the day or year
and discuss the range of colors found, or look very carefully at one object,
such as a tree or butterfly, and discuss the range of colors seen. Changes
in colors over a period of time could also be noted and discussed.

6. Making Outdoor Color-Associations

Show students a color and ask them of what outdoor item it reminds
them. For instance, green might remind them of grass, leaves, and grasshoppers, while yellow might remind them of the sun, dandelions, or a
butterfly wing. This activity can also be done in reverse: the teacher or a
student-leader names the outdoor object and the other students hold up
the color associated with it. For instance, if the student-leader said "the
sky," the others might hold up *blue*. If students hold up different colors
and can defend their answers logically, such answers should be accepted.
If for example a student held up *gray* for the sky and explained that on
rainy days the sky was gray, the student's answer should be considered
correct.

7. Finding Shapes in Nature

Have students look for geometric figures in natural objects. For example,
show them a circle, square, and triangle and then ask them to find these
shapes in such objects as a cobweb, a rectangular brick, or a tree with a
triangular shape.

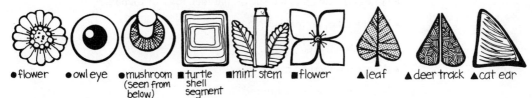

●flower ●owl eye ●mushroom ■turtle ■mint stem ■flower ▲leaf ▲deer track ▲cat ear
(seen from shell
below) segment

8. Taking a Close-Up View

A close-up view often provides a different perspective on things in the
natural environment. Have students closely examine some outdoor item,
such as a tree, shrub, or nearby building. Ask them to give detailed, oral
descriptions. Smaller objects could be studied using a small magnifying
glass or hand lens.

9. Remembering the Disappearing Object

Place a number of objects found outdoors—a rock, piece of wood, a
leaf—in a row in front of the students. Ask students to look the other way

or close their eyes. Remove one item from the row; then ask students which object is missing. The number of items should be increased according to the ability of the students.

10. Building Long-Term Visual Memory

Have students closely examine an outdoor item such as an insect, tree, bush, or sidewalk, and describe it. Later, perhaps when they are back in the classroom, have the students describe the object in detail again. Take down dictation of their descriptions. Then return to the outside object for verification. A modification of this activity would be to have the students draw pictures of the outdoor item when they are inside and then return to the outdoors to compare their drawings with the real objects.

11. Identification Keys

Help to sharpen students' visual skills by showing them how to use pictures in insect, plant, bird, or tree keys to help identify species they encounter. Many excellent paperback identification books are available commercially and others can be obtained from state environmental departments and libraries. Simplified keys could be made of items that the students would be most likely to encounter. Students could match the object to the appropriate picture in the key and then ask an adult to tell them its name.

12. Animal Tracking

One of the most fascinating activities in the outdoors is studying animal tracks. Tracks can be identified and animal trails followed in muddy or sandy soil in the spring or fall and in deep snow in the winter. Close examination of the tracks helps to develop visual discrimination and stimulates inferential and creative thinking. Students can locate tracks and try to answer the following questions.[1]

- How does the animal walk, on flat feet, toes, or toenails?
- What kind of animal is it?
- Where is it going?
- Where has it come from?
- Is it hunting or being hunted?
- Is it moving quickly or at a normal rate?
- Is it large or small, young or old, injured?
- Is it traveling alone or in a group?

TOEWALKERS

Toewalkers are those animals who walk on the toes of each foot. In some cases there will be fewer than five toes appearing in the track and usually a foot pad will appear behind the toes.

[1]Illustrations courtesy of Thames Science Center, New London, Connecticut.

Common toewalkers are the dog, fox, and cat.

DOG	FOX	CAT

TOENAIL WALKERS

Animals that walk up on their toenails include the deer and the horse.

DEER

FLATFOOTS

Flatfoots are those animals who walk on the heels and soles of their feet. Three common flatfoots are the racoon, skunk, and opossum.

RACCOON

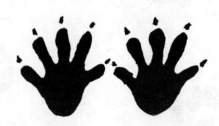

SKUNK

H.

F.

OPOSSUM

F.

H.

196

13. Playing Outdoor Visual Matching Games

Distribute or have students make pairs of cards with the same outdoor-item pictures: two snails, two smokestacks, or two ants, for example. A small group of students could then be given twelve to sixteen pairs in mixed-up order, face down. Each student approaches to turn over two cards at a time. When a student finds a matching pair, he/she gets an additional turn. If the cards don't match, they are replaced, and the next student has a turn. The student with the most pairs at the end of the game wins.

14. Outdoor Dominoes

Make up or have students devise a set of tagboard dominoes with pictures of outdoor items. Some dominoes should have matching pictures. The game is played similarly to regular dominoes.
example:

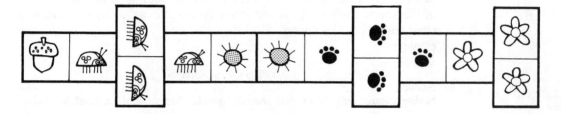

15. Natural Matching Relay

Have groups of students collect a number of nonliving natural items in the area, such as fallen tree leaves, twigs, rocks, or gravel. Have the groups try to locate two of each type of item. Put items into two piles and divide the class into two groups. The teacher or game-leader holds up a rock or calls its name and the first student in each team runs to the team pile and locates the correct object. The first person to locate the object secures a point for his or her team, the object is replaced in the pile, and the team member goes to the end of the line.

AUDITORY SKILL-DEVELOPMENT

1. Outdoor Listening

Have students sit very quietly outside and listen to the sounds they hear. To increase their listening skills, ask them to close their eyes. After a few minutes, have them describe, identify, or imitate the sounds they heard:

birds chirping, leaves rustling, cars honking, a bus stopping, or children playing. Discuss the number and kinds of sound. List the different sounds. How are they alike? How are they different? How do the sounds make them feel? A tape recording could be made and played. If possible, repeat the activity in different types of outdoor locations and compare the sounds heard in the different spots.

2. Describing Specific Outdoor Sounds

Direct students to focus on a single outdoor sound. A tape recording could be made for reference or a commercially available recording of the sound could be played. Ask the students to describe the sound in several different ways and then select the best description.

3. Categorizing Sounds

Have students describe the sounds they have heard, using a variety of descriptive terms. Then let them categorize the sounds by placing pictures of the sound-makers in appropriately labeled boxes, or by or creating a chart such as the following:
example:

TYPES OF SOUNDS

Sound Maker	loud	soft	high	low	harsh	gentle	happy	sad	animal	machine
crow	x			x	x			x	x	
cricket		x	x			x		x		x

4. Outdoor Auditory-Memory Game

After students have spent some time experiencing their outdoor environment, have them sit down in a circle. Then ask them to each think of one thing they heard. The first person tells what he or she observed: "I heard a sparrow chirp." The next person repeats what the first person said and adds his/her own statement. The game continues with each one repeating everything that was previously said and adding something else.

5. Outdoor Sound-Stories

List the sounds students have heard outside, such as bird calls, frog songs, traffic sounds, or children playing. Have students practice imitating these outdoor sounds. Then tell a story and have students make the appropriate outdoor sounds.
example:
> On a warm day in May, I went outside and heard the birds (*tweet, tweet, chirp*) and frogs (*chur-up, chur-up*). I also heard the children (*shout, whistle, sing*) playing in the yard.

6. Improving Listening Skills

When students are outdoors, explain to them the "TQLR" listening technique:

T Tune in, try not to think about anything else
Q Question what or who is making the sound and why?
L Listen; really listen
R Review the sounds you heard (SRA 1974)

Then ask them to use this technique to concentrate on outdoor sounds. When students appear to be having difficulties listening, remind them to "TQLR."

Language Experience in the Fresh Air

Go from the creatures thy instructions take.[1]

One of the most interesting ways to let beginning readers of any age know that print is just speech written down is by having them dictate stories that can be written down and read back to them. In this way they can learn that what they experience can be talked about, recorded in writing, and read back to them exactly as they stated it. An interesting story can be dictated about an outdoor object, such as a bird, flower, or tree, while the students can actually see and perhaps hear, feel, or smell it. Students in an urban setting could dictate a story about the traffic, buildings or clouds seen from the playground. Most students are excited about discussing things that are experienced outside the confines of the classroom. The stories that they dictate can then be used for a variety of reading experiences.

199

1. Group Outdoor Stories

Have students together carefully examine one outdoor object, such as a shrub, tree, animal or building. Ask them to describe how it looks, feels, smells, etc. Their vocabularies can be strengthened by introducing some words such as *needles, roots, bricks,* and *smokestacks.* Then ask each student to think of a sentence to say about the outdoor item. Write down their sentences on lined chart paper and read the story back to them several times.

example:

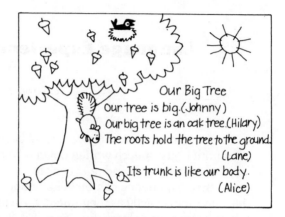

2. Our Favorite Outdoor Things

While the students are outside, have them draw pictures of their favorite outdoor objects and then dictate their own individual stories that can be written down beneath their pictures. These stories could be bound into a booklet entitled *Our Favorite Outdoor Things* and placed in the library corner.

3. Paraphrasing an Outdoor Story

Read the students a story with an outdoor theme while they are relaxed outside. Then have then retell the story in their own words while someone takes their dictation.

Decoding in the Sunshine

Nature speaks in symbols and in signs.[1]

Competent readers use a variety of skills to identify or analyze words. They either recognize a word instantly by sight or use phonics, structural analysis, context clues, or picture clues to decipher the words. When all

[1]John Greenleaf Whittier, *To Charles Sumner.*

else fails, they can go to the dictionary for help. Students at any grade level might need some work on decoding skills. Some might need a great deal of work, others a review of some specific skills, and still others some help in using their skills in a meaningful way. For a change of pace, take the students outside for work with these skills. Activities are included in this section that can help children learn new sight words and different ways to attack unknown words in the outdoors.

SIGHT-WORD RECOGNITION

1. Learning Words Outdoors

Show the students the words for objects in the playground when they are outside. Students are to look at each word, say it, find the real object, and place the appropriate word card on or near the object.

2. Reviewing Words in the Fresh Air

When you go outside, take word-cards for words that the students need to practice, such as *on, was,* or *is* (see list of frequently used words on page 11). Hold up the card for the word *is.* Ask the students to say the word. Then ask them to look around and dictate a sentence of something they see using the word *is.* Write the sentences on chart paper.
example:
> The fence *is* made of wire.
> The white cloud *is* ragged.
> The ant *is* biting me.

The sentence could then be read to the students and they can supply the word *is.*

Although most frequently used words can be reinforced in the outdoors, the following words are particularly appropriate:
> are, as, at, big, can, down, for, from, had, has, have, is, in, little, out, the, this, to, up, was, will, with

PHONICS REVIEW

1. Outdoor Phonics Search

Give students small paper bags in which to put nonliving items they find that start with a specified sound; or give them pieces of paper on which to draw pictures of things they see outdoors that start with a specified sound.

NATURE'S OUTDOOR PHONICS

Regular Consonants

b bat, bark, bear, beaver, beetle, berry, bird, bobcat, bug, bush, butterfly

d daddy longlegs, daisy, dam, dandelion, deer, dell, den, desert, dew, dogwood, dove, duck

f falcon, feather, fence, fern, fish, fog, forest, fox

h hail, hawk, hedge, hedgehog, hemlock, heron, hill, horn, horsefly, huckleberry, hummingbird, hummock, humus

j jack-in-the-pulpit, jay, junco, june bug

k katydid, killdeer, kingfisher

l ladybug, lagoon, lair, lake, land, larch, larva, laurel, leaf, leech, lizard, log

m maggot, mantis, maple, marsh, meadowlark, milkweed, moose, mosquito, moss, moth, mountain, mouse, mud, mushroom

n nest, nettle, newt, nighthawk, nut

p parasite, park, paw, pebble, pigeon, pine, poison ivy, pond, pool, porcupine, puddle, puffball, pussy willow

q quahog, quail, quartz, Queen Anne's lace

r rabbit, raccoon, ragweed, rain, rainbow, rat, redbud, reservoir, river, road, robin, rock, root, rose

s salamander, sand, sap, sassafras, sea, sediment, seed, sod, soil, sun

t tadpole, tail, tamarack, tick, tide, toad, toadstool, turtle

v valley, varmint, vein, vine

w wasp, water, weasel, web, wilderness, willow, wind, wing, wolf, worm, woodchuck, woodpecker

x xenolith, xylem

y yarrow, yucca

z zone, zoology

Hard and Soft "c" and "g"

Hard "c" pronounced like "k" when followed by a, o, u: cactus, caterpillar, cattail, cave, cocoon, cowbird, cockroach, coyote, cub, currant, current

Soft "c" pronounced like "s" when followed by e, i, y: cedar, cement, centipede, cicada, cirrus, cycad, cyclone, cypress

Hard "g" when followed by a, o, u: galaxy, gale, gall, gander, gar, garden, goat, goldenrod, goldfinch, goose, gopher, gulch, gulf, gull, gully

Soft "g" pronounced like "j" when followed by e, i, y: geode, gymnosperm, gypsy moth

Consonant Blends

A consonant blend is a combination of two or three consonant letters blended in such a way that each letter in the blend keeps its own identity.

bl bloom, blossom, bluejay

cl clam, claws, cloud

fl	flower, fly
gl	glowworm
pl	plankton, plant
br	bramble, branch, brick, brook, brush
cr	crab, crayfish, cricket, crow
dr	dragonfly, drake
fr	frog, fruit
gr	grass, grasshopper, gravel
pr	prairie, praying mantis, predator
tr	trail, tree, trout, trunk
sc	scale, scallop, scavenger, scorpion
sk	skeleton, skunk, sky
sm	smelt, smoke
sn	snail, snake, snow
sp	sparrow, spawn, spider, sponge, spore
sq	squid, squirrel
st	star, stick, stone, stump
sw	swallow, swamp, swan
tw	twig, twilight
spl	splash, split
str	stream

Consonant Digraphs

A consonant digraph is a combination of two consonant letters representing one speech sound that is *not* a blend of the two letters.

sh	shade, shadow, shale, shallow, shark, shore, shrub
ch	chigger, chipmunk
wh	whale, whippoorwill
th	thistle, thorn, thunder

Vowels

$\bar{a}$	acorn, cave, hail, lake, rain, snail, snake
$\breve{a}$	ant, animal, apple, bat, clam, grass, plant, rat, sand, sap
$\bar{e}$	eagle, eel, beetle, leaf, sea, seed, stream
$\breve{e}$	den, egg, elk, nest nettle

ī   ice, icicle, slime, spider, tide, vine

ĭ   insect, spring, tick, twig, wind

ō   crow, foam, ocean, opossum, snow, stone

ŏ   octopus, osprey, otter, pond, rock, smog

ū   use, usual

ŭ   brush, bug, duck, scrub, shrub, slug, sun, underground, upstream

Vowel Dipthongs

A vowel dipthong is a combination of two vowel letters representing a sound that is *not* a blend of the two vowels.

oi   moisture, soil

oy   oyster

ou   bough, cloud, ground, mountain, mouse, outside, trout

ow   flower, owl, shower

R-Controlled Vowels

ar   bark, park, star

or   storm

ir   (ər) bird, dirt, fir

er   (ər) fertile, herd

or   (ər) worm

ur   (ər) current, fur

2. Nature's Phonics Stories

Have the students write or dictate phonic stories about objects they have seen outdoors using primarily one letter sound.
examples:
>The *s*limy *s*lug *s*links up the *s*lippery rock.
>The *s*un warms the *s*unflower *s*eed in the *s*andy *s*oil.

3. Phonic Riddles in the Fresh Air

While students are outside, have them use their knowledge of letter sounds to figure out the answers to some phonic riddles.
examples:
>I am thinking of something that starts like *shark*. There is one of these beside Ann. It moves when she does. What is it? (Shadow.)

>I am thinking of a three-syllable word. It is the name of a green insect we often see outdoors. What is it? (Grasshopper.)

1. Outdoor Compound Words

Explain to students that a compound word is made up of two or more words and that it usually has a meaning that comes from the two parts. Use examples such as *bluebird*—a bird that is blue, and *thunderstorm*—a storm where there is thunder. When students encounter something in the outdoors that has a compound name have them identify the two separate words in the compound and discuss the meaning of each part. A list of outdoor compound terms follows:

anthill	dragonfly	ladybug	snowbank
beehive	drawbridge	lighthouse	snowbird
blackberry	earthworm	mailbox	snowdrift
blackbird	evergreen	milkweed	snowflake
blacktop	farmhouse	mockingbird	snowman
bluebell	farmyard	mountainside	snowstorm
blueberry	fencepost	nighthawk	starfish
bluebird	firefly	nuthatch	steamboat
bluegrass	flagpole	outdoors	stonewall
bullfrog	flycatcher	pathway	sunbeam
bumblebee	foxglove	primrose	sunflower
buttercup	foxtail	railroad	sunlight
butterfly	glowworm	rainstorm	sunrise
campfire	goldenrod	redwood	sunset
catbird	gooseberry	rosebug	thunderstorm
catfish	grasshopper	rowboat	toadstool
cattail	graveyard	sagebrush	tombstone
chestnut	groundhog	schoolhouse	topsoil
cloudburst	hailstone	schoolyard	underground
cobweb	hailstorm	seacoast	uphill
cottontail	hardwood	seaside	waterway
cottonwood	haystack	seaweed	wayside
cowslip	highway	shellfish	wildflower
crabapple	hillside	sidewalk	windmill
crossroad	hilltop	skylight	windowpane
crosswalk	horsefly	skyline	windstorm
curbstone	hummingbird	smokestack	woodchuck
daylight	jackrabbit	snowball	woodpecker
dewdrop	jellyfish		

2. Finding the Compound Partner

Give students two columns of words, the list on the left containing the first parts of outdoor compound words, and the list on the right the second parts. Students are to draw lines connecting the words to form the compounds.

example:

Draw a line from the word on the left to the word on the right that will make up the name of something you have seen outdoors.

toad	hill
bull	stool
ant	frog

3. Outdoor Compound-Word Pictures

Give students sheets of paper with a series of three boxes. Have them illustrate that they know the meanings of some outdoor compound words by illustrating the meaning of each separate word and then the combined meaning of the compound word. They could then give the appropriate definition and write a sentence using the term.

example:

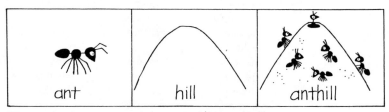

ant	hill	anthill

The ants were scurrying over the anthill.

4. Categorizing Natural Phenomena by Prefixes and Suffixes

Study prefixes and suffixes that are used to refer to objects in the natural world while the students are outside where the meanings will be much more vivid. They could then categorize objects, such as those that are movable and immovable, winged and wingless, living and nonliving, like and unlike, or pleasant and unpleasant (see list of prefixes and suffixes on page 12).

5. Outdoor-Word Syllabication

Give students a list of outdoor words to categorize according to the number of syllables.

example:

Arrange these words according to the number of syllables you hear in each: flower, bird, butterfly, dirt, erosion, caterpillar, water.

One	Two	Three	Four
bird	flower	butterfly	caterpillar
dirt	water	erosion	

6. Practicing Syllabication Rules

Give students a list of outdoor words to divide into syllables.
example:

maple	garden	butterfly
(ma/ple)	(gar/den)	(but/ter/fly)

CONTEXT-CLUE USAGE

1. Supplying the Missing Word

After students have had an outdoor experience, give them dittoed exercises in which they must determine the missing word using the other words in the sentence and their knowledge of the outdoors.
examples:

The oak tree sheds its _____ and has a nut called the _____.

Ants have _____ main parts to their bodies and _____ legs.

2. Correcting the Mistake

Give students factual statements about things they have experienced outdoors. Have an incorrect word in each statement. Ask the students to locate the incorrect word and correct it.
examples:

a. The tree in front of the school is a (*coniferous, deciduous*) tree.

b. There are (*three, two*) bushes beside the flagpole.

c. The school building is made of red and (*black, yellow*) brick.

DICTIONARY PRACTICE

1. Outdoor Alphabetization

Have students put words dealing with the outdoors into alphabetical order.
example:
These are things we have seen outside. Put the words into alphabetical order.

snail	bee	sparrow	june bug
ant	rock	crow	inchworm
toad	grass	elm	katydid
frog	dandelion	horsefly	mouse

2. Picture Alphabetizing

Younger children can put pictures of outdoor items into alphabetical order.

examples:

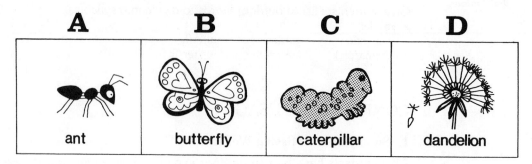

A	**B**	**C**	**D**
ant	butterfly	caterpillar	dandelion

3. Dictionary Pronunciation with Outdoor Words

Give students terms written using diacritical marks for them to decipher, pronounce, and locate outside.

example:

> Write the correct spelling for these words and then find one example of each on the playground. Write a sentence telling where you saw each one.
>
> jōo'nə-pər   dăn'də-līən   spăr'ō   thĭs'əl   pīn

Vocabulary Growth Under the Sun

The language of nature is the universal language.[1]

One of the reasons for failure to understand what one reads is a lack of familiarity with the words that are used. Before students of any age tackle a reading assignment, they should have a grasp of the concepts and the meanings of most of the printed words they will encounter.

Words are often learned best through first-hand experiences, as words connected with these experiences are usually more easily retained. It should not be assumed that students know the meanings of many commonly used outdoor words, such as *twig, insect,* or *bark.* Many children have received very little vocabulary input while playing outside and do not know the meanings of many outdoor terms. The following outdoor activities can be used to increase students' vocabularies.

[1]Christoph Willibald Gluck in Haweis, *Music and Morals.*

1. Environmental Hikes

Take a short walk near the school or a hike around the playground and call students' attention to things in the outdoor world that they have either ignored or to which they have not yet been fully exposed. In a rural setting, there are many obvious possibilities, such as barns, stone fences, ponds, and pond life. In the city, point out clouds, landscaping, signposts, plants growing through cracks in the cement, different types of building materials, roofs, litter, and sources of pollution. Encourage students to carefully examine one object such as a fence. Gradually introduce new terms such as iron, rust, mesh, immovable, or boundary. Encourage them to use the new words to ensure their retention.

2. Color Words

Give students small paper bags and ask them to find two things that are grey, brown, or green. Then discuss and compare the items they find. Categorize them by shades of color or by item type, such as grass, leaves, rocks, or pebbles.

3. Color Wheel

Make a large color wheel. Then have the students go outside and find objects that fit into the various color sections. Write the names of the items in the appropriate color section.
example:

4. Outdoor Classification

Students can classify things they experience outdoors in a number of ways depending on their developmental level. They can draw pictures of objects or write their names down and then classify them in appropriately labeled boxes or lists. The following is a list of possible categories to use when classifying objects outdoors.

animals	flowers	playground equipment
wild animals	wild flowers	transportation
domesticated animals	domesticated flowers	noises
mammals	trees	smells
insects	bushes	living things
birds	rocks	nonliving things
fish	pebbles	natural things
plants	buildings	constructed things

5. Extending Outdoor Vocabularies

Keep a chart of descriptive words and phrases used by students to describe outdoor objects. Encourage them to extend their vocabularies by using these again and by adding new ones to the list.

6. Outdoor Similes

The study of similes, one of the most ancient forms of description, is often more interesting when done outdoors. Similes occur when two essentially unlike things are compared by using the words *like* or *as*. Many similes are based on natural phenomena, such as stars, moon, sun, ocean, flowers, birds, and insects. Share some similes based on outdoor things with the students. Discuss their meanings and then encourage the students to make up their own.
examples:

OUTDOOR SIMILES

angry as a wasp	dainty as a rose
beautiful as a sunset	dance like a withered leaf
beautiful as a rainbow	run like lightning
bend like a willow in the wind	sing like a bird
bent as a rainbow	slippery as an eel
blink like a toad	sly as a fox
busy as a bee	soft as rain
buzzing like a fly	sparkle like snow in the sun
clean as a pebble	speckled as a toad
clumsy as a june bug	speechless as a stone
cold as ice	spread like fog
cozy as the nest of a bird	spreads like ivy
crawl like a snail	still as a mouse
creep like shadows	talkative as a magpie
cunning as a fox	wise as an owl

7. Outdoor Singing

The lyrics of many songs that stress the outdoors take on special meaning when read and/or sung outdoors. Take music books outside and have students suggest songs with outdoor themes. Or if music books are unavailable, words for songs such as "Sunshine on My Shoulders," "Open Up Your Heart and Let the Sunshine In," and "This Land Is Your Land," could be duplicated and given to students to read and/or sing outside. Discuss the meanings of unfamiliar words in these songs.

8. Grammar in the Fresh Air

The study of grammar can be more appealing outdoors. After a discussion of nouns and verbs, adjectives and adverbs, take the students to the playground. Make a list of things they see—nouns. Then list the things the nouns are doing—verbs. Then describe the objects with adjectives and the actions with adverbs.

examples:

nouns	adjectives	verbs	adverbs
bird	gray speckled	flies	slowly
car	little yellow	moves	quickly

These words can be written on individual color-coded cards—red for nouns, blue for adjectives, yellow for verbs, and green for adverbs—so that students can pick a card of each color and make up a sentence.

9. Outdoor Vocabulary Review

New outdoor words can be reviewed by playing games such as *Bingo, Concentration, Charades,* or *Password.*

   a. *Bingo*

   The leader holds up a large picture of the item or reads a definition of it, such as: "This creature has eight legs and spins webs." Students put markers on the identified words. The first student with three spaces in a row wins.

tree	ant	rock
spider	flower	cloud
lake	park	sky

   b. *Concentration*

   Give a small group of students twelve to sixteen pairs of words and matching pictures face down. Have students take turns trying to match the pairs. The student with the most pairs wins.

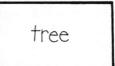

c. *Dominoes*

Students must match the dominoes with the pictures and words. The student wins who first uses all of his/her dominoes.

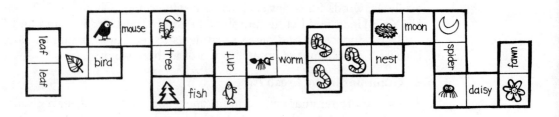

d. *Charades*

One student acts out an outdoor word, such as *smoke, frog,* or *snail*; other students must guess the word.

e. *Password*

Students are given clues to identify the appropriate outdoor word.

NATURAL ETYMOLOGISTS

Etymology, the study of word origins, is often not very interesting to students. However, when the topic is introduced through the study of natural objects in the environment, it is usually more interesting and appealing. For example, one can discuss with students the difficulties of having to find accurate and different names for all the animals and plants in the world. They can learn that all discovered plants and animals have at least two names. One is a *common name,* such as *bluejay* or *daisy,* based upon some special trait of the animal or plant. This is the name commonly used by most people. Some animals, such as the skunk, which is also called a polecat, have more than one common name.

A second name is a *scientific name.* All of the several million known animals *ever* discovered have scientific names. These have at least two words, sometimes three. The first word, a generic one representing the genus, stands for the particular group to which the individual animal or plant belongs. The second word, the species or specific name, stands for that individual animal or plant. The generic name is capitalized while the specific name is not. Greek or Latin words are usually used for generic names as these are the universal languages of science.

Each different animal or plant has a different name; no two share the same scientific name. And, just as common names do, their scientific names usually tell something special about them; but the special traits are harder to discover. Clues regarding characteristics are often given in both the generic and specific names.

example:

> *Chrysemys picta dorsalis* is the scientific name for the southern painted turtle.
>
> *Chrysemys*, the genus name, has two parts—*chrys* means "gold" and *emys* means "freshwater tortoise"; so *Chrysemys* means "a gold freshwater tortoise."
>
> *Picta dorsalis,* the specific name, refers to the red stripe or picture on its back.
>
> *Picta* means "picture" and *dorsalis* means "dorsal" or "back."
>
> (Saxon 1964)

Good sources for budding natural etymologists to use in these activities are:

- Webster's *New International Dictionary.*

- Saxon, Gladys H., *Secrets in Animal Names.*

- Jaeger, Edmund C., *Source-Book of Biological Names and Terms* (for more advanced readers only).

- Books on special animal groups, such as the Peterson and Conant field guides.

The activities in this section can be used to introduce students to the study of word origins in ways that relate to the outdoors.

1. Indian Names

Give students a list of Algonquin Indian names and their meanings and see if they can identify whose common name has the Indian base.

apasum	The white animal	(opossum)
arathcone	He/she who scratches with his hands	(raccoon)
atchitamon	He/she who goes down head first	(chipmunk)
muskwessu	It is red	(muskrat)

(Saxon 1964)

Explain to the students that when the first colonists came to America, they heard the Indians using these names, so they also used them. The early settlers spelled the Indian names the way they heard them. Although there have been some changes in the original Algonquin terms, the special descriptive facts about the animals still remain hidden in their names.

2. Animal Characteristics and Names

Explain to students that animals receive their names in different ways.

a. Have students listen carefully to animal sounds outdoors or to recordings of animal sounds. Explain that many animals get their common names from the sounds they make; creatures in this category include the bobwhite, flicker, whippoorwill, cuckoo, katydid, and cricket. The mockingbird received its name because its song "mocks" the songs of many other birds; the hummingbird's wings hum as they beat; and the bullfrog croaks with a deep voice like a bull.

b. Color is another important factor in names; cite examples of bird names such as *cardinal, bluebird, blackbird, goldfinch* and *oriole* (from the Latin *aureolus,* which means "golden").

c. Some animals, including the following, were named because of their actions:
    beetle comes from Anglo-Saxon *bitula:* to bite its food
    ant comes from Anglo-Saxon *aemete:* to eat its food
    wasp comes from Anglo-Saxon *waest:* to weave its nest
    spider comes from Anglo-Saxon *spinnan:* to spin its nest
    clam comes from word *clamp* because it "clamps down on things"
    polecat comes from *poultry* cat, because it preys on poultry
    slug comes from Middle English *slugge:* lazy or sluggish
    sapsucker drills rows of holes in trees and sucks up sap
    woodpecker pecks wood to find insects
    cowbird waddles among the cows in a barnyard
    thrasher thrashes in the leaves as it searches for food
    nuthatch hacks at nuts in order to get out the meat

(Saxon 1964)

d. Some creatures got their names because they resemble other animals:
    mosquito from Spanish "little fly"; *mosca* means "a fly," *ito* on the end of a word makes the thing it names small

    mussel from Latin (*musculus*) "little mouse"; because mussels were thought to look like little mice (Students might also enjoy knowing that they have little mice in their arms! Muscles were so named because they ripple under the skin like little mice.)

(Saxon 1964)

3. Nature's Common Names

Have students use books such as Charles E. Funk's *Horsefeathers* to look up the origins of some common names of objects in their environment such as *cobweb, dandelion, daddy longlegs, Queen Anne's lace, Jack-in-the-pulpit,* and *daisy.*

examples:
    The term *cobweb* originated approximately six hundred years ago because an ordinary spider was also known as a *cop.* When the term *cop* was combined with *web,* its pronunciation was changed to *cob.*

The term *daisy* originated a thousand years ago when it was observed that the white parts of its flower opened with the rising sun, exposing the golden center part, and folded again in the evening. It was called *days eye.*

A *dandelion* was called *dent de lion,* or "tooth of the lion" in French, because of its deeply indented leaf. The English changed it to *dandelion.*

(Funk 1958)

4. The First Names

Have students hypothesize about how animals and plants were named. Ask them to guess how these animals and plants got their names; grasshopper, measuring worm, cottontail, swordfish, daddy longlegs, toadstool, catbird, and sunflower.

5. Passing It On

Play the game "Gossip" with students using a natural term in a phrase. The first person whispers the phrase into his/her neighbor's ear and each person passes on what is heard in this fashion.
examples:
The fat frisky squirrel likes all acorns.
I saw a crawling crawfish in the middle of the puddle.

Discuss changes between the original phrase and the last one heard. Then give students a list of Anglo-Saxon names that originated between 400 and 1100 A.D., when few people could read or write. See if they can recognize the animal names.

docga (dog)	mann (man)	staerlinc (starling)
hors (horse)	seolth (seal)	swalewe (swallow)
cu (cow)	flea (flea)	snaegl (snail)
beo (bee)	hwael (whale)	snace (snake)
catt (cat)	sceap (sheep)	fisc (fish)

(Saxon 1964)

6. Making Up Animal Names

Have students each draw a picture of a fictitious animal and name it. Ask them if they would name it for its color, method of moving, the sounds it makes, or some unusual characteristic.? To give them examples to work from, explain that the bumblebee gets its name from the *bummmmmmmmm* sound it makes, and that *porcupine* is made up of two Latin words: *porcus,* meaning "pig," and *spina,* meaning "spines."

7. Nature's Intrigues

Explain to students that some mistakes in naming animals came through carelessness in observation or through lack of knowledge. Have them look up some animals in dictionaries or encyclopedias and discover the meanings of terms that are often misused, including the following:

nighthawk—is not a hawk
milk snake—does not drink milk
guinea pig—is not from Guinea and is not a pig
meadowlark—is not a lark
American robin—is not a robin

(Saxon 1964)

Developing Comprehension Skills in the Outdoors

Never does Nature say one thing and wisdom another.[1]

Sometimes it is assumed that students are having reading problems, when in reality they are having thinking problems. Moreover, cognitive difficulties can be hard to detect. It is often easier to get an indication of students' level of thinking when they are outdoors and considering various types of questions about outdoor items or events. An awareness of students' thinking problems without the extra burden of print could be a first step in helping them to improve in reading comprehension.

Lack of interest in a subject obviously will also affect comprehension. As one becomes more familiar with something and learns more about it, the subject generally becomes more interesting. First-hand experiences with things in an outdoor setting can often help to enlarge a student's field of interest and perspective.

Some of the activities in this section give students an opportunity to develop their thinking skills without the distraction of print. Others involve both reading and thinking. All can be done in the outdoors and can be used effectively to stimulate reading comprehension. Activities can be modified according to the reading level of the students or to tie in with the school's outdoor environment.

216

[1]Decimus Junius Juvenal, *Satires.*

FOLLOWING DIRECTIONS

1. Following Directions

Give students cards with simple one-, two-, or three-part directions to read and follow.

examples:

Walk to the oak tree.		Skip to the fence.
Touch the bark.	or	Sit down on the ground.
Turn around.		Sing a song.

2. Outdoor Treasure Hunt

Give students written directions to find certain items outdoors. Give them small bags and plastic bottles in which to put their treasures.

example:

Find a black insect.
Find a grey rock.
Find a pine needle.

3. Self-Contained Activity Packets

Give small groups of students large envelopes that contain directions and all the necessary materials for an outdoor reading activity. Directions could be geared to the special reading needs of a particular group.

examples:

a. One kit might contain small paper bags and directions telling students to find a natural object for each of the following blends and digraphs: *th, ch, wh, sh, tr,* and *fr.*

b. Another kit might contain copies of a short play and direct students to locate an appropriate outdoor location in which to perform it.

c. Another kit could contain a brief passage or a short book along with pencils, paper and questions that direct the students to compare or contrast the natural setting in the passage or book to something in the immediate environment.

4. Reading and Doing

Have students read and follow simple directions for making and maintaining a bird feeder or for planting a tree, shrub, window-box, or garden.

5. Reading and Gaming

Have available to students the rules and regulations for the outdoor games they like to play so that they can refer to them in times of conflict. Introduce new outdoor games by having students read the directions.

6. Outdoor Eating

Give students written instructions on how to prepare food for eating outdoors. They could cook simple recipes using natural foods they have gathered outdoors, such as blackberries, blueberries, nuts, or dandelion greens.

RECOGNIZING DETAILS

1. Answering Yes or No

Give small groups of students the following type of exercise in which they answer *yes* or *no* after each item.
example:

> The largest tree in the school yard . . .
> a. is next to the front door (yes, no)
> b. sheds its leaves in autumn (yes, no)
> c. is taller than the school (yes, no)

2. Finding the Correct Ending

Duplicate this type of exercise for students to do either outdoors or in the classroom based on things they have experienced outdoors.
example:

> Finish each sentence by drawing a line to its correct ending.

> ### OUR SCHOOLYARD

> a. The largest tree is   behind the school.
> b. The smallest tree is   in front of the school.
> c. The swings are   beside the school.

3. Outdoor Discovering

Duplicate on paper this type of lesson and give it to the students outdoors so that they can discover the answers by actual observation.
examples:

> ### WHAT DOES IT LOOK LIKE?

> The fence at the back of the school is made of (wood, wire, brick).
> The surface on the playground is (blacktop, gravel, sand).

4. Sentence Completion

Give students duplicated incomplete sentences. Ask them to make careful observations and then finish the sentences.
examples:

> The weather is _____.

> My shadow is _____.

5. Thinking Outside

Ask questions orally or give students task sheets on which they are directed to carefully observe something outdoors, think about it, and then answer a variety of questions concerning it.

example:

ANTS

Find some ants on the schoolground. Observe them for a few minutes and then answer the following questions:

a. Do all ants look alike? _____

b. What do they eat? _____

c. What are two different things the ants are doing?

    1. _____

    2. _____

d. Did you find an ant trail? If so, where does it lead?

_____

6. Describing Outdoor Items

Give students written descriptions of outdoor items. Have them read the descriptions and then locate each item mentioned.
example:

WHAT AM I?

I am brown and made of wood.
I am taller than you are.
I am on the northeastern corner of the playground.
What am I? _____ *(telephone pole)*

7. Outdoor Questioning and Answering

Give students two different sets of cards. One set contains questions about outdoor objects, the other contains the answers. Students can make observations outdoors in order to match the answers to the questions.
examples:

Question Cards	**Answer Cards**
How does a grasshopper move?	Grass is green.
What color is grass?	Grass is red.
How many trees are in the yard?	A grasshopper hops.
	A grasshopper swims.
	There are three trees in the yard.
	There are five trees in the yard.

8. Read and Identify

Have each student secretly select an outdoor object and print five or six words which describe the object. Other classmates can try to guess the objects by reading the words.
example:

What am I ?

tiny black busy bites insect ant!

9. Outdoor Riddles

Have students make up and write riddles about outdoor objects. Have the writer read the riddle and others guess the answers.

10. Making Sense-Clue Charts

Give students sense-clue charts on which to list all the things they can see, hear, touch or smell, such as feeling coarse particles of dry soil, smelling wet grass, hearing birds singing, or seeing leaves blowing. (Students should not be encouraged to taste outdoor items.)
example:

SENSE-CLUE CHART

Object	See	Hear	Feel	Smell
grass	x		x	x
bird	x	x		
wind		x	x	

11. Polluting Our Senses

Give students a sensory pollutant handout and ask them to search for things that are polluting their sensory perceptions of their natural or human-made environment.
example:

SENSORY POLLUTANTS IN OUR NEIGHBORHOOD

Sense	Pollutants
sight	garbage, graffiti
feeling	gum on sidewalks
hearing	car horns, motorcycles
smell	motorcycles, diesel engine, smoke

12. Appreciating Illustrations and Descriptive Passages

Stretch students' sensory imagery while they are studying illustrations in texts, pictures, and photos, or reading and listening to descriptive passages or outdoor scenes by asking them for details about what they might see, hear, feel or smell if they were in the scene. If possible, refer to the sensations they experienced during some class outdoor experience.

SEQUENCING

1. Outdoor Sequencing

Take the students on a walk to see the environment outside the school. Then have them list in order the things they saw.

2. Mixed-Up Sequencing

After an outdoor experience, give the students a list of the events in mixed-up order. Have them rearrange them correctly.

DISTINGUISHING FACT FROM OPINION

1. Pointing out the Facts

Have each student point out an outdoor item and give several facts about it.
example:
　　Ants: Ants are very small and have six legs.

2. Expressing Opinions

Let each student select an outdoor item and give several opinions about it.
example:
　　Ants: I think ants are clever and interesting to watch.

3. Fact or Opinion

Have students read sentences about outdoor items. Then discuss whether each sentence is a fact or an opinion.

 SNAKES ARE UGLY.
(fact or opinion?)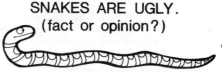

examples:
　　a.　The oak tree is beautiful (*fact, opinion*)
　　b.　The school is made of brick and wood. (*fact, opinion*)
　　c.　Ants have a nasty sting. (*fact, opinion*)
　　d.　Cars make too much noise. (*fact, opinion*)

4. Finding the Emotional Words

Reproduce an editorial, newspaper story, or brief magazine article about the outdoors. Have students pick out all the emotional words and identify all opinions. Have them rewrite the item stating only the facts.

RECOGNIZING POINT OF VIEW

1. My Favorite Place

Have students collect pictures of different kinds of environments, both attractive and unattractive, and compare them. Have students each select the place in which they would most like to spend the day and the place they would like to avoid. Have them give reasons for their selections. Compare the students' choices and have the group discuss the reasons for the different selections.

2. Determining Point of View

If possible, take students to see an area that is in an undeveloped, natural state, or show them a picture of one. After they have enjoyed its beauty, present them with this hypothetical situation. The owner no longer wants this land and plans to sell it. The following people want to purchase the property. Discuss the reasons each might have for wanting the property: a factory owner, the town, a farmer, a contractor, a scientist.

3. Biased Reporting

Have one group of students write a factual description of a designated area. Another group could describe the same area as a group of builders or business people might, and a third group as conservationists might. Remind the students that each report should be based on facts, although they may use descriptive words to attempt to influence others.

MAKING COMPARISONS

1. Natural Comparisons

Have students prepare a chart, showing the similarities and differences of two plants, animals, rocks, or buildings that they have observed.
example:

	Caterpillars	Grasshoppers
1. Size		
2. Color		
3. Movement		
4. Food		
5. Protection		
6. Location		
7. Young		
8. Usefulness		

2. Outdoor Associations

Ask students to identify the things that go together by underlining the correct answers.

examples:

What Goes Together?

Underline the correct answers.

What has leaves? *trees, rocks, flowers*
What can you see in a tree? *rock, squirrel, nest, fence*

3. Locating the Incorrect Item

Have students locate the incorrect item in each list.
examples:

Which Belong in Our Schoolyard?

Cross out things that you do not see in our schoolyard.

Mammals	Insects	Birds	Plants
dog	ants	sparrow	dandelion
elephant	grasshopper	flamingo	grass
mouse	scorpion	crow	orchid
cat	beetle	eagle	rose

DRAWING CONCLUSIONS

1. Outdoor Detectives

Have students find one outdoor thing that might serve as a "clue," such as a broken twig, writing on a sidewalk, a bird's feather that has fallen, or a tiny hole in the ground. Have them try to determine what happened.

2. Reacting to Hypothetical Situations

Pose different hypothetical questions related to the outdoors. These situations could be written on the chalkboard and the students directed to read them and write out their responses.
example:

If the grass and trees in the front of the school were removed and replaced by gravel for a parking lot, what would the front of the school look like? What would be missed next spring when it gets hot? What problems might there be for some animals? What would be the advantages and disadvantages?

3. Reading to Solve Problems

Give students dittoed sheets with real or hypothetical outdoor problems. Have them read the problems and then try to think of solutions. They could look in reference sources to find the necessary information to solve the problems.
examples:

Two children were recently hurt on the swing set. Their legs were badly scratched when they were sitting on the wooden seats. What is the solution?

A shrub next to the back door of the school has not grown much this year. It is turning yellow and losing its leaves. What is the solution?

UNDERSTANDING OUTDOOR ADVERTISEMENTS

1. Advertising About the Outdoors

Ask students to bring to class advertisements that deal with the outdoors. Have them evaluate each advertisement according to its appeal and basis in fact. Then have them write their own advertisement for some type of outdoor item, such as flower seeds, sports equipment, or birdfeeders.

2. Outdoor Advertisements

Have students note how billboards, neon signs, and advertisements in store windows are used to urge people to buy things. Have them draw a picture of one of these advertisements to bring to class. Have students discuss the appeal of different forms of lettering and illustrations. Discuss how the words used in advertisements can be misleading and review the different techniques of advertising used (see pages 68–69).

3. Using the Outdoors in Advertisements

Ask students to collect advertisements from magazines that use pictures of the outdoors to urge people to buy things. Have them analyze the techniques used in each and the relationship of the setting to the product being advertised (as, for example, the use of an outdoor scene to sell soda pop). Discuss how the pictures used in advertisements can be misleading.

Sensory Imagery Under the Clouds

Give us nature's teaching.[1]

Perhaps one of the most important skills for students to develop in reading is the ability not only to see and hear differences in sounds,

[1]John Greenleaf Whittier, *A Sabbath Scene.*

letters, and words, but to actually be able to project themselves into the scene or situation about which they are reading. If they are able to do this now, then in later years when they read a passage about a Civil War battle, a description of a peaceful setting in *Heidi,* or a poem by Walt Whitman, they should be able to see, hear, feel, and even smell it in their minds. The ability to summon up sensory images is an important one. The following outdoor activities can be used to help students make greater use of their senses.

1. Smelling the Great Outdoors

Have students discuss how outdoor items smell. Smells could be classified as bitter, sweet, pleasant, unpleasant, spicy, flowery, fruity, putrid, burnt, and piney.

2. Categorizing by Texture

Have students categorize rocks, stones, bark, and leaves according to their textures or how they feel. They can be classified as being gritty, smooth, hard, soft, rough, sticky, wet, slimy, dry, sharp, pointed, hairy, heavy, light, spongy, crumbly, moist, cold, or warm.

3. Without Sight

Increase students' hearing, feeling, and smelling perceptions by having one or two students take a blindfolded classmate on a short walk to experience as many varied outdoor sensations as possible. Ask students to try to identify what they are smelling, feeling, or hearing without the sense of sight.

4. Sensory Detectives

Divide the class into small groups of three or four. Let each group choose one object in the environment, such as a rock, leaf, fence, or sidewalk. Then have them use their senses to describe the object. How does it feel, smell, sound, look? (Caution them not to taste things in the outdoors as some are poisonous.) Ask them to describe with vivid descriptive adjectives and adverbs what they observed with their senses. They could make up riddles to ask others.

example:
> I have a resinous smell.
> I feel sticky.

I do not make a sound.
I am skinny and green.
I live in clusters.
What am I? (A pine needle.)

5. The Affective Domain

Have students sit alone in a quiet spot for five or ten minutes. Ask them to pretend that they are some living thing they can see from where they are. What would they see and feel as the year passed by? What would they need to survive? Then have them discuss the feelings they had in the quiet spot.

6. Encouraging Imagination

To encourage students to be more imaginative in their thinking, ask questions like the following:

> What would it be like to sit under a mushroom? How would you feel? What would you see, hear, and smell?

> If you were a piece of grass, how would you feel if someone stepped on you?

7. Portraying Feelings

Ask students to show by moving their bodies appropriately how they would feel if they were something in nature.
example:
If you were a dandelion, show how you would feel if

- Hail was falling on you

- It was very hot and dry

- A gentle rain was falling

- A bee was buzzing near you

- A child was smelling you

- A lawnmower was coming near

- Someone picked you

- Your yellow flower turned white and blew away

8. Creative Imagery

Ask students to visualize what it would be like if there were no trees or green grass, or if the earth were completely covered with cities.

Learning Study-Skills with Mother Nature

The volume of nature is the book of knowledge.[1]

Children need specialized skills that will help them to gather and use information about a specific topic. Some students are excellent readers, but lack the basic reference and study skills to be able to locate needed information. They need to know what types of reference books exist, how to locate material in these books, how to read maps and other graphic means used for presenting information, and how to organize the information they have gathered and make use of it.

The information in this section contains ideas for teaching students how to use important study skills. Some of these activities can be done outside, although some may be more feasibly done inside revolving around an outdoor theme.

1. Locating Outdoor Information

Students are usually very curious about their outdoor environment. Have them list a number of questions about outdoor things that they would like to have answered. Then have them look in reference books for the answers. Show them how to use the title of the book, table of contents, and index to determine if a book contains the information needed.

2. Outdoor Reference Sources

Give students time to browse through different types of reference tools. Then list the different types of reference materials on the board and have students discuss the types of information about the outdoors they can find in each:

almanacs	magazines
atlases	maps
dictionaries	newspapers
encyclopedias	pamphlets

Suggested magazines to use for this activity include *Ranger Rick, National Geographic, National Wildlife,* and *International Wildlife.*

[1]Oliver Goldsmith, *The Citizen of the World.*

3. Using the Index

Have students compile a list of items that they have encountered in the
outdoors. Then have them locate each item in the index of one of the
available reference books and list the source and page.

example:

Outdoor Items	Book	Page(s)
ants		
snails		
ladybugs		
worms		

4. Using the Encyclopedia

Give students a list of questions concerning outdoor things that they can
answer by using the encyclopedia.

example:

Look up sparrows in the encyclopedia and answer the following quesitons.

a. Sparrows usually eat _____.

b. The sparrow's nest is made of _____, _____, and _____.

c. The female lays _____ or _____ eggs.

d. The house sparrow was brought to America in _____ from _____.

5. Encyclopedia Detectives

Have students make up questions about outdoor things for others to
answer using the encyclopedia. Emphasize that the answers to the questions must be found in the encyclopedia.

6. Oral Interviews About the Environment

One way to gather information about outdoor items is by interviewing
local birdwatchers, naturalists, hunters, gardeners, geologists, and people
who have lived in the area for many years. Have students conduct oral
interviews with appropriate people and write up their results. They could
research such topics as local parks, flowers, birds, roads, old trees, farms,
farmland, and old buildings.

7. Outlining

After students have categorized items outdoors, have them arrange the
words in proper order in an outline. Encourage them to make an outline
when gathering information for a report.

example:

Things in Our Schoolyard
1. Trees

    A. _____

    B. _____

C. _____

2. Shrubs and Bushes

A. _____

B. _____

C. _____

3. Insects

A. _____

B. _____

C. _____

8. Wildlife in Our Area

Have students each pick one animal in the environment that is of particular interest, such as a mouse, centipede, robin, or lizard. Ask them to collect as much information as possible and list the source of their information, such as observation, interview, or book. They could respond to a series of questions.
example:

Information About My Animal

(Source)

a. Where it lives _____ ( )

b. What it eats _____ ( )

c. How it gets its water _____ ( )

d. What it does in the winter _____ ( )

e. What enemies it has _____ ( )

9. Report Writing

Have students each select one thing in the environment and write a brief report about it. Have them look up information in encyclopedias, field guides, and other references, give the sources of their information, and make sure the reports are written in their own words.

10. Outdoor Careers

Have students research different types of outdoor careers, such as environmentalist, farmer, forester, game warden, geologist, hunter, logger, naturalist, nursery worker, ranger, or tree surgeon. They could read about the careers and interview people employed in these occupations. Have them share their findings in a short report, poster, collage, or mural.

11. Observing, Drawing, Writing, and Verifying

When students are outside, direct them each to find one interesting outdoor object to carefully examine and whenever possible to listen to, touch, and smell. Then ask students to make detailed drawings of their items that will give as much information as possible. Next direct them to write detailed descriptions of their items. The written descriptions should contain the same information as the drawings as well as other information, such as size, texture, color, smell, sound, location, movement, surroundings, and unusual characteristics. When students are back in the classroom, have them look up additional information to verify their observations, identify their objects by their scientific or technical names, and write down additional essential information.

12. Understanding Maps

Give students a map of the schoolyard, or have them make their own map. Then give them specific questions to answer concerning it, such as locations, distances, size, and scale.

13. Logging Outdoor Observations

Explain to students that logs are records of observations done on a regular basis. Have students keep a log of their daily or weekly observations of weather, a plant or tree in the school yard, their shadows measured at the same time each day, or the amount and type of traffic passing by the school. The students could give their reports at the end of the logging period using simple graphs, charts, and tables.

14. Questioning the Reference Book

Help students to realize that informational books are not always absolutely correct by pointing out exceptions to them. For instance, if the bird book states that a particular type of bird is not seen in the school's geographical region, yet some are seen at the class bird-feeder, discuss some possible reasons for the exceptions or inaccuracies that can occur in print.

Language Arts on the Lawn

What Nature wishes should be said she'll find
the rightful voice to say.[1]

Because language skills are complementary and dependent upon each other, effective reading instruction should be based on a total language arts program. Many activities that will help develop students' speaking, writing, reading, and creativity can be adapted for use in the outdoors. When students have stretched their own minds to try to be original, elaborate upon their thoughts, and say or write things in other ways, they will be better able to understand and appreciate the efforts of others.

The activities included in this section can be effectively used to get students interested in both the outdoors and the language arts. A section is also included on poetry in the outdoors.

1. Language Arts Field Trips

Field trips can be a stimulus to learning and lead to greater understanding by providing first-hand observations and direct experiences. On field trips to outdoor areas, students can gain valuable experiences in listening, speaking, and writing down their observations.

2. Solo Field Trip for Feelings

As a homework or schoolyard exercise, have students each go alone to a special outdoor location and stay there for a designated period of time, depending on the age of the group and the circumstances. Then have them each write a brief report about what happened, what was experienced, and their feelings.

3. Picture Stories in the Grass

Have students write stories about something in the outdoors using pictures to replace words they do not know how to spell.
example:

4. Making a Playground Guide

Have students develop a guidebook for the playground or neighborhood to help others become more aware of things in the outdoors. Before writing the guide, have students brainstorm about the information they wish to include.

231   [1]William Winter, *The Golden Silence.*

5. Outdoor Manners Poster

Have students discuss and list proper outdoor behavior. Then have each student pick one idea and illustrate it with a poster. Display these in the school or on the playground.
examples:
> Look at the grass but don't step on it.
> Love the animals and leave them alone.
> Look before you jump off the swing.
> Keep it pretty. Don't litter.

6. Outdoor Penpals

Arrange for students to write to penpals in an area that has a very different type of environment. The focus of the correspondence should deal with the outdoors. Have students describe their own outdoor environment to their penpals.

7. Outdoor Newspaper

Have students gather information about an outdoor area, such as the schoolyard, adjacent empty lot, or surrounding school environment, for a periodic newspaper. Students could interview the people who maintain the schoolyard, oil the blacktop, or plant the trees or shrubs. Information could include types of animals sighted, average or highest and lowest temperatures, student's nature poems, stories, and cartoons.

8. Interpretive Trail Sign Construction

Self-guiding trails have been used in many schools and nature centers. Their purpose is to help visitors interpret the environment. Have students make their own signs for an interpretive trail for other classes or groups. Discuss with students the significant aspects of the school yard. Interesting topics might be the kinds of materials used to make the school, fence, and sidewalk, the types of trees and shrubbery, the distances between certain items, and special aspects of outdoor equipment, such as swings or slides. Each student or a small group of students could select one item to interpret and then construct and place a sign in the appropriate place. Signs could be made of wood or heavy cardboard covered with *Contact paper,* polyester resin, or outdoor varnish. Magic markers, the typewriter, and press-on letters can be used for the written messages. Illustrations such as simple maps, pictures, or actual specimens protected by preservative spray, can add to the appeal of a sign. Directional signs can have arrows. These signs can be left up indefinitely or used only when interested groups wish to take an interpretive walk around the school yard. This type of activity will help students to take more pride in their schoolyard and also cause them to be more aware of such signs when they are visiting natural parks.

examples:

WHITE PINE

How do you identify a white pine?
It has five needles, one for each letter of the word *white*.
It is the only pine with five needles.
This tree is often called "The King of the Eastern Forest."

APPRECIATING NATURE

Nature's beauty is all around us. Watch and listen!
Open your eyes and ears to experience the different types of life on the
   playground.
Listen to the birds singing, the crickets chirping, and the wind blowing
   through the trees.
Watch for movement.
Look for differences in shapes and sizes.
As you walk in the outdoors, describe and count the different kinds of living
   things that you can see, hear, feel, and even smell.

9. Explaining Our World

Have students write out the dialogue of a first meeting with a being from
outer space who is visiting this planet. The visitor asks questions about the
natural things outside while the students answer the questions.
examples:
   What is soil?
   What is it used for?
   Is it important? If so, why?
   Do humans value and take care of it? If so, how?

10. Topsy-Turvy World

Take students outside and have them imagine and speculate about what
the world would be like if normal objects were of different sizes, shapes, or
textures—if, for example, grasshoppers were as big as horses, trees were
only two feet tall, grass was hard, and stones were soft. Students could
write their speculations down or discuss them orally.

11. Outdoor Personifications

Have students pretend that *they* are outdoor items and write stories about their experiences as fireplugs, tin cans rolling down the street, or icicles hanging from the school roof.

12. Drama in the Outdoors

Ask small groups of students to make up an original play or perform an existing one that prominently features the outdoor environment. They could even tape the sounds they hear, such as car noises, voices, and birds, and use them for sound effects. They could use library books, such as *The Lorax* (Dr. Seuss 1971) or *Blueberries for Sal* (McCloskey 1948), for ideas for their plays.

13. Choral Reading

Many choral readings can be enhanced by doing them outdoors where the children can feel free to be expressive without danger of disturbing others within the school building. Choral readings with an outdoor theme are often more effective when done outdoors. Students could also write their own choral readings and suggest ways for them to be performed.

POETRY IN THE OUTDOORS

The use of poetry is a natural and interesting way of improving reading and language arts skills. Reading and writing poems about outdoor subjects and themes can also help students make connections between the sciences, the arts, and reading.

Students will often feel more enthusiastic about writing poetry when they are outdoors in a different environment where a different mood can be created. Although they sometimes feel inhibited about writing poetry, students will better understand and appreciate it after they have written some poetry themselves. Their creations should be about things they have experienced directly in a natural environment. An excellent collection of poems about the outdoors to use for inspiration is *Poetry of Earth* by Adrienne Adams, which contains poetry by Frost, Dickinson, Sandburg, McCord, Millay, Austin, and others. Several collections of poetry books containing poems about the outdoors should be available so students can browse through them and select poems of their choice.

Encourage students to express themselves poetically as they take a brief walk in the rain, look at their reflections in a puddle, or lie in the sweet-smelling grass following the movement of a cloud. Read poems to the students and have them read poetry to others so that they will better appreciate this form of writing. Let students go outside for a ten or fifteen minute period to read and reflect on outdoor poems written by either well-known poets or by the students themselves. Students' poems could be illustrated, duplicated, and shared by all, and perhaps written with beautiful penmanship and compiled into a class outdoor poetry book.

The following activities can be used to stimulate interest in poetry:

1. Finding and Sharing a Favorite Poem

Let students browse through the classroom poetry collection and each find a favorite outdoor poem. Have them practice reading their poems orally with expression and have a poetry-sharing time outdoors.

2. Illustrating a Poem

Have students select a favorite verse from a poem about the outdoors, write or print it very carefully with India ink or a felt pen, and then illustrate it while outdoors.

3. Poets in the Field

Many poets were very interested in nature; it is said, for example, that Robert Frost was an ecologist at heart. Take the students on a short poetry walk during which poems are read to them. Tell them that there is to be no talking on the trip, either to each other or to the instructor; they are simply to enjoy seeing the outdoors and thinking about the poems they hear. When back in a central location, discuss the experience. After students have been on a teacher-led poetry walk, let small groups select the path to take and prepare and present appropriate poems.

4. Listing Descriptive Words

Ask students to look carefully at an object, such as a tree or fence, and then come up with a list of nouns, adjectives, verbs, and adverbs that are either associated with it or can be used to describe it.
examples:

Tree

Nouns: leaf, branch, stem, bark
Adjectives: green, tall, graceful, pretty, slender, leafy
Verbs: stands, sways, shakes, shadows, sheds
Adverbs: gracefully, violently

These words can then be arranged into different types of poetry.

5. Group Poetry

Have one student write one line of a poem and hand it to the next student. This second person writes a line that goes with the preceding one and then passes it on to the next person, and so on. This type of poetry does not have to rhyme. If necessary, at the conclusion of the activity, the poem may be revised.

6. Triplets

This type of poetry has three lines that rhyme. It can be written in a triangular form.

example:

It gives shade on sunny days to me.

Our Tree

7. Haiku

Explain to the students that for hundreds of years the Japanese have been expressing their feelings about nature with a form of poetry called *Haiku* (pronounced hä-e-kü by Japanese, hi-kü by Americans). Haiku is un-rhymed poetry about natural things. Its form is based on syllabication: The first line contains five syllables, the second seven and the third five. It is very easy to write and students will usually be proud of their results. Read some representative poems to the students and then have them create their own Haiku while they are outdoors. These poems are fun to illustrate with water colors or simple sketches. Tell the students that when the Japanese read Haiku aloud, they repeat the poem slowly three times. This gives the listener time to absorb the meaning of the poem.

examples:

Flowers drip raindrops	(5 syllables)
Robins sing, the sun glistens	(7 syllables)
The rain is over	(5 syllables)

Haiku Worksheet

_____	(5 syllables)
_____	(7 syllables)
_____	(5 syllables)

8. Cinquains

Tell students that the word *cinquain* is derived from the French and Spanish words for five and that this type of poem contains five lines, each with a set number of syllables. But in addition to these specifications, each line also has a particular purpose. Give students an example and a format with which to work.

examples:

      Our Sun   title, two syllables

    Shining, glowing   description of title, four syllables

Seen between the white clouds

Brilliantly making the sunset

Our life

description of action,
six syllables
description of feeling,
eight syllables
feeling about title,
two syllables

Cinquain Worksheet

_____ (title, 2 syllables)
_____ (description of title, 4 syllables)
_____ (description of action, 6 syllables)
_____ (description of feeling, 8 syllables)
_____ (feeling about title, 2 syllables)

9. Diamente

Explain to the students that a diamente is a poem shaped like a diamond. This type of poetry does not stress rhyming words but uses words that are related through shades of meaning from one extreme to the other, like growing and dying, rain and drought, forest and ashes, use and misuse, tree and log, habitated and deserted, caterpillar and butterfly. The words chosen should match the following pattern:

polliwog
(noun)

small   brown
(adjective)   (adjective)

scurrying   darting   swimming
(participle)   (participle)   (participle)

water   food   protection   warmth
(noun)   (noun)   (noun)   (noun)

eating   growing   aging
(participle)   (participle)   (participle)

grown   mature
(adjective)   (adjective)

frog
(noun)

Give students an example and a form on which to work.

_____
noun

_____   _____
adjective   adjective

_____   _____   _____
participle   participle   participle

_____   _____   _____   _____
noun   noun   noun   noun

<u>   </u>   <u>   </u>   <u>   </u>

   participle   participle   participle

<u>   </u>   <u>   </u>

     adjective   adjective

<u>   </u>

       noun

Suggested pairs of words with opposite or near opposite meanings might be:

city-country	raindrop-flood
caterpillar-butterfly	snowflake-blizzard
plant-harvest	summer-winter

Using the Outdoors to Excite Students About Reading

*Nature pleases, attracts, delights, merely because it
is nature.*[1]

One of the major goals of the reading program is to help turn students into avid readers who will read throughout their whole lives. Children who know how to read but never read are denying themselves the opportunity to enrich their lives. No one can become a truly competent reader without spending time practicing reading skills outside of the instructional setting. Many activities in the outdoors or related to the outdoors can help students to see that reading is a pleasurable, enjoyable experience directly related to their lives and interests.

1. Listening in the Outdoors

The outdoors is often a perfect setting for reading aloud to students. The types of materials can be varied but should have an outdoor theme.

[1]Alexander Von Humboldt, *source unknown.*

2. Silent Reading Under the Clouds

On a warm sunny day, have students each select a book to take outdoors, find a quiet, comfortable place, and just read for sheer pleasure for ten or fifteen minutes. Students could be allowed to select any book or they could be directed to select something to read that deals with the outdoors. (It might also be a good idea to spend a few minutes discussing how to take care of a book when outdoors.)

3. Indoor-Outdoor Reading Center

Place outdoor-related pictures, posters, books, magazines, pamphlets, reference materials, and actual specimens of such things as plants, animals, seed packets, snakeskins, owl pellets, and skeletons in a special spot in the classroom. Encourage students to spend time there each week. Reading-related task cards could be given for them to research and fill out in relation to an item of their choice.
example:

Snake Skins

Look at the snake skin on the shelf. Gently touch it. Then read pages 3 and 4 in Munroe's *Second Book of Snakes.* Answer the following.

1. Describe the snake skin. What does it look like? How does it feel?

2. Why do snakes shed their skins?

3. How long does it take?

4. What would happen if snakes did not or could not shed their skins?

4. Bringing Wildlife Indoors

Many small reptiles, amphibians, and insects adapt well to captivity if kept in similar surroundings to their natural habitat. This includes providing the right plants, proper soil and right amounts of water, moisture, sunlight, temperature, and correct food supply. Duplicate the animals natural habitat in a glass terrarium or aquarium. The container must be escape-proof for both the animal and its food. Drafts should be avoided as well as loud noises and wide shifts of temperature. In the cases of insects or small animals students have captured, keep them only for a short period and then release them. If students do want to keep an animal in the classroom, many interesting reading/language arts activities can be developed, such as the following:

a. Keep a log of what the animal is doing at the same time each day.
   example:

   Our Turtle at 9:15

   1. Monday _____

   2. Tuesday _____

b. Make a list of body parts.

example:

The Parts of Our Turtle

shell	toenails
feet	tail
toes	face

c. Keep a chart of its food intake.
   example:

What Our Turtle Eats

Monday: Two flies, lettuce
Tuesday: Piece of hamburger, lettuce

d. Write factual and fictional stories about the animal.

e. Read or listen to stories and poems about the animal.

f. Gather factual information about the animal from reference materials.

5. Outdoor Reading Unit

The outdoors can be brought into the school classroom by having a reading unit devoted to some aspect of nature. Students could do relevant reading on a selected topic in a variety of materials and different reading levels, including textbooks and reference materials such as encyclopedias, dictionaries, field guides, newspapers, and nature magazines. Topics might include:

Insects in Our Schoolyard
Pollution
The Outdoor Environment of _____ School
The Outdoors in Song

6. Outdoor Current Events

Ask students to search newspapers and news magazines for items concerning the outdoors. Students could bring the items to class each week and present their findings. The most interesting items could be posted on a bulletin board.

7. Dr. Seuss and the Outdoors

Read to the students or have them read any of the Dr. Seuss books that present the author's very creative picture of the outdoor world, such as *The Lorax* (1971), *Horton Hatches the Egg* (1940), *Yurtle the Turtle* (1958), and *McElligot's Pool* (1947). Have the students compare his stories with real life, act them out, write sequels to them, and even make up a dictionary of "Dr. Seuss words."

8. Reading Nature Myths

Explain to students that people of long ago did not know many of the scientific facts about things in nature, so they made up stories about them.

These stories or myths are usually short, contain action, suspense, sometimes a touch of humor, and show how people stretched their imaginations to try to explain phenomena in their world. Students will appreciate myths more if they are introduced to ones that relate to things they have already experienced in their environment. After listening to and reading myths, the students could write their own.

9. Having Fun with Fables

Most fables tell stories about animals and then state a moral at the end. Students usually enjoy fables in small doses only, as continued moralizing can become very tedious. Have students listen to and/or read and then discuss fables that deal with animals they have encountered in their environment, such as the hare and tortoise, or the ant and the grasshopper. Discuss commonly used expressions that have emerged from fables, such as "sour grapes," "don't count your chickens," "slow but sure," "haste makes waste," or "cry wolf." Encourage them to create their own fables containing the following elements:

a. one or two animal characters that represent certain personality characteristics

b. some action that illustrates the point

c. statements of the moral in one line at the end

The outdoors is indeed a natural resource for stimulating student interest in many school subjects, including reading. As a special learning environment of genuine interest to most young people, the outdoors can be easily and successfully utilized to promote growth in reading and language arts skills, often without students' even being aware of the purpose of the activity. Moreover, while improving reading skills, outdoor activity can also help to stimulate a lifelong interest in reading.

Readings and References

ADAMS, ADRIENNE. *Poetry of Earth.* New York: Scribner's, 1972.

FUNK, CHARLES E. *Horsefeathers.* New York: Harper & Row, Pub., 1958.

GUSTAFSON, JOHN. "Field Trips for Feelings." *The Communicator* (Spring 1972), pp. 19–21.

HICK, THOMAS L. "Responses of Migrant Children to Outdoor Education." State University of New York: Geneseo Center for Migrant Studies, 1970.

JAEGER, EDMUND C. *Source Book of Biological Names and Terms.* Springfield, Illinois: C.C. Thomas, 1978.

Life Camps Inc. *Extending Education through Camping.* New York: Life Camps. 1948.

McCLOSKEY, ROBERT. *Blueberries for Sal.* New York: Viking, 1948.

Malcombe County Intermediate School District. "Discovery through Outdoor Education." EGEA Title III Evaluation Report. Mt. Clemens, Michigan, July 1974.

ROWELL, ELIZABETH and THOMAS GOODKIND. "Making Reading More Enjoyable." *Developmental Reading Handbook.* New York: McGraw Hill (publication pending)

SAXON, GLADY R. *Secrets in Animal Names.* New York: Prentice-Hall, 1964.

Science Research Associates. *SRA Reading Laboratories Teacher Manuals.* Chicago: Science Research Associates, 1974.

SEUSS, DR. (Theodor Geisel). *Horton Hatches the Egg.* New York: Random House, 1940.

SEUSS, DR. *The Lorax.* New York: Random House, 1971.

SEUSS, DR. *Yurtle the Turtle and Other Stories.* New York: Random House, 1958.

SHOWERS, PAUL. *The Listening Walk.* New York: Thomas Y. Crowell, 1961.

SPYRI, JOHANNA. *Heidi.* New York: Macmillan, 1962.

Thames Science Center. "The Mystery of Animal Tracking." *The Communicator,* Fall-Winter, 1975, pp. 45–48.

INDEX

C

Carlyle, Thomas, 145
Chamfort, Sebastian R.N., 6
Characterization:
    accuracy, 62
    dialog, making of, 28
    costuming, 63
    emotions, 63
    empathy, 28
    and human character, 28
    likenesses and differences, 62
    and parts of speech, 61
    personal characteristics, 28
    speech patterns, 62–63
    TV personalities, 62
Choate, Rufus, 36
Cicero, 30
Compound words, 100–01, 205–06
Comprehension skills:
    and art, 110–120
    characterization, 114–15
    classifying, 31
    comparing, 64–65, 165–67, 222–23
    drawing conclusions, 167–68, 223–24
    determining main idea, 23–24, 59, 111–12, 161
    deciphering symbols, 116–17
    following directions, 111, 160–61, 217–18
    inferring, 119
    and music, 160–71
    and the outdoors, 216–24
    predicting, 116, 168–69
    recognizing details, 59–60, 112–13, 218–21
    sequencing, 113, 162–64, 221
    and TV, 59–60
Comprehension builders, 22–23
Confucius, 137
Context-clue usage:
    cloze, 16, 153
    missing plurals, 17
    and meaning, 101–02
    and music, 152–53
    and nature, 207
    and pictures, 101
    scrambled context, 17
    and TV, 53–54
Cornificius, Quintus, 103
Critical/creative thinking, 65–66, 117–18, 169

D

Dewey, John, 44
Dictation, 9

Dictionary practice, 17–18, 102–03, 116, 207–08
    alphabetical order mural, 102
    alphabetizing, 17
    and art, 103
    fun with, 17–18
    humorous definitions, 18
    in illustration, 102
    personal, 102
    pictures in, 103
    slang, 18
    unusual words in, 18
    word lists, 102
D'Israeli, Isaac, 120

E

Eliot, George, 160
Etymology, in nature words, 212–16
    animal characteristics, 213–14
    common names, 212, 214–15
    hypothesizing by students, 215
    Indian names, 213
    making up names, 215
    scientific names, 212

G

Gluck, Christoph Willibald, 208
Goethe, Johann Wolfgang von, 30, 175
Goldsmith, Oliver, 227
Greenfield, Jeff, 54, 74

H

Holland, Josiah Gilbert, 96
Horace, 3
Humboldt, Alexander von, 238
Humor:
    discussion of, 3–5
    materials, sources, 5
    studies about, 3ff.

I

Idioms, 24–27
    acting out, 26
    in comics, 25–26
    example, 24
    about humor, 26–27
    intended meaning, 24
    in riddles, 26
    table, 24–25

J

Juvenal, Decimus Junius, 216

L

Lamartine, Alphonse M.L., 180
Language arts, and humor:
    cartoon writing, 36
    context-clue usage, 16–17
    discussion, 35
    drama, 37
    letter writing, 36
    limericks, 36
    poetry, 36
    punctuation, 37–38
    rhyming words, 36–37
    and riddles, 37
    tall tales, 36
Language arts and TV:
    context-clue usage, 53–54
        missing word, 53
        pronouns, 53–54
        replacing incorrect word, 53
    creative writing, 76
    dictionary practice:
        alphabetical order, 54
        keys, 54
        multiple meanings, 54
    phonics review:
        advanced skills, 52
        beginning sounds, 51
        key words, 51
        name game, 52
        sound hunt, 52
        tongue twisters, 51–52
    sight-word recognition:
        commercials, 52–53
        review, 53
        TV treasure hunt, 52
        and word search in *TV Guide*, 53
    structural analysis:
        contractions, 55
        syllabication, 54
        syllables, 54
        takeoffs, 76
Language experience, and humor:
    class funny book, 10
    jokes, 9
    stories, 9
Lavater, Johann, 9
Longfellow, Henry Wadsworth, 154
Lowell, Amy, 121
Lubbock, Sir John, 87

M

Main idea, determining, 23, 24, 111–12, 161
Music, appropriate selection of:
    discussion, 140–41
    questionnaire, 141

244

245